The Arresting Eye

Cultural Frames, Framing Culture

Robert Newman, *Editor*

The Arresting Eye

Race and the Anxiety of Detection

JINNY HUH

University of Virginia Press
CHARLOTTESVILLE AND LONDON

University of Virginia Press

Printed in the United States of America on acid-free paper
First published 2015
9 8 7 6 5 4 3 2 1

LIBRARY OF CONGRESS CATALOGING-IN-PUBLICATION DATA

Huh, Jinny, 1968–
The arresting eye : race and the anxiety of detection / Jinny Huh.
pages cm. (Cultural frames, framing culture)
Includes bibliographical references and index.
ISBN 978-0-8139-3701-4 (cloth : acid-free paper)
ISBN 978-0-8139-3702-1 (pbk. : acid-free paper)
ISBN 978-0-8139-3703-8 (e-book)
1. Passing (Identity) in literature. 2. Race awareness—United States. 3. Detective and mystery stories, American. 4. African Americans—Race identity. 5. Asian Americans—Race identity. I. Title.
PS169.P35H84 2015
810.9'355—dc23

2014035707

THE AMERICAN LITERATURES INITIATIVE

A book in the American Literatures Initiative (ALI), a collaborative publishing project of NYU Press, Fordham University Press, Rutgers University Press, Temple University Press, and the University of Virginia Press. The Initiative is supported by The Andrew W. Mellon Foundation. For more information, please visit www.americanliteratures.org.

To
David,
our miracle girls, Amara and Naima,
and Matthew

Contents

Illustrations

Acknowledgments

As most authors are aware, writing is a very isolating endeavor. But it is also a very rewarding learning process. This book has taken too many years to complete. Without the support of friends, family, and colleagues, it would not exist. I have many people to thank who supported, inspired, and guided me along the way. They have nourished me with food, encouragement, love, companionship, wisdom, and laughter. I am truly grateful.

First, I would not be a literature professor today if it weren't for Lindon Barrett. When I first began my undergraduate studies at University of California Irvine, I was a biology major hoping to become a pediatrician. Lindon's "African American Slave Narratives" course caused me not only to change my major but to pursue a completely different life path. I will always be thankful to Lindon for helping a naïve undergraduate see the promise of literature and social justice work.

The Department of English at USC was an ideal place for me for many reasons. My unusually large dissertation committee of Teresa McKenna, Carla Kaplan, Tania Modleski, Viet Nguyen, Judith Jackson Fossett, and Jane Iwamura offered valuable advice and scholarly and intellectual stimulation and rigor. More importantly, they were a continuous source of support and inspiration throughout and beyond my graduate school years. I would like to give a special thanks to Jane, who has been a friend in good times and bad. Heather James, Joseph Boone, Alice Gambrell, Vince Cheng, and David Roman were inspirational teachers. Flora Ruiz always provided a smiling face and helpful hand in the department. I would not have been able to survive graduate school without comrades-in-arms Beth Binggeli, Karen Bowdre, Theresa Gregor, Belinda Lum, and Annemarie Perez. And, of course, my thanks to the Binggeli clan (especially Carol), who welcomed me into their home and hearts.

The Irvine Summer Dissertation Workshop spearheaded by George Sanchez and the Program in American Studies and Ethnicity (PASE) marked a turning point in my academic career. I will always remember and value that moment of intellectual, emotional, and political growth. Thank you, George, for including me in the American Studies cohort. I also thank the USC's Department of English for generously funding my graduate studies through dissertation fellowships and a three-year predoctoral merit fellowship. Finally, I thank UCLA's Institute of American Cultures for awarding me a much-needed and -appreciated postdoctoral fellowship in 2005.

Graduate students hear all kinds of horror stories about tenure-track jobs and department politics. I could not have asked for a more supportive and collegial home than University of Vermont's English department. I particularly would like to thank Sarah Alexander, Emily Bernard, Elizabeth Fenton, John Gennari, Mary Lou Kete, Loka Losambe, Tony Magistrale, Hilary Neroni, Sarah Nilsen, Val Rohy, Jennifer Sisk, and Sarah Turner. A special thanks to the department staff (Katherine Layton, Tilza Buschner, Justin Griffing, and previously Kathy Fitzgerald, Holly Brevent, and Peter Frechette), who have made the daily tasks much more manageable. A special thanks to UVM's Department of English and Dean Antonio Cepeda-Benito at the College of Arts and Science for providing funding for the images in this book and to Pat Mardeusz for helping me untangle the mystery of copyrights. In many ways, Vermont is a challenging place to teach and research on race and ethnicity. But there are many people here, in particular the ALANA community (including Wanda Heading-Grant and Bev Colston), who have paved the way and continue to strive for an inclusive and just community. The CRES (Critical Race and Ethnicity Studies) Committee including Emily Bernard, Rashad Shabazz, John Gennari, Nikki Khanna, and Jonah Steinberg have been especially inspirational the past couple of years. With their continued dedication and compassion, they have shown that certain struggles are beyond "committee work." I couldn't and wouldn't be here without you. Finally, warm thanks to Liz Fenton, Elizabeth Smith, and Todne Thomas, lifelong friends and colleagues near and far who have made the personal challenges during my tenure-track journey much more enjoyable and surmountable.

The East of California (EOC) and the Association of Asian American Studies have been especially inspirational and supportive the past several years. I have had the privilege of working with several members through the 2013 Junior Faculty Retreat organized by Sue Kim and Mark Chiang. Senior faculty volunteered their time and commitment to mentor, support, and inspire their junior colleagues. Thank you to Tina Chen, Camilla Fojas, Anna Guevarra, Nitasha Sharma, and Judy Tzu-Chun Wu for reading our works but also for guiding us through the tenure process.

Janice Murakami was a life-saver during the past several years and kept me grounded during my personal struggles as well as pretenure insecurities. I did it, Janice!

A heartfelt thanks to Cathie Brettschneider and the staff at the University of Virginia Press for their patience and continued support throughout my first book-publishing journey. The two anonymous readers provided smart comments that made the manuscript better. Thank you also to Oxford University Press and Johns Hopkins University Press for granting permission to republish chapters 1 and 3.

Finally, my family has given endless and tireless support throughout my academic career. My sister, Jennifer, and the Jung family were behind me all the way, even when they had no idea what I did. To my partner in life and love, David Bond, who continues to sustain me emotionally and spiritually, and our children, Amara, Naima, and Matthew, who keep us on our toes each and every day with their energy and their unconditional love—I love you. As I wrap up this book's journey, I can't help but think of my girls, Amara and Naima, who drive me crazy but also fill my heart with endless joy. This book began because I was interested in the topic; it ended with my life intimately living it through them. The beginning is mine, but the ending is theirs.

The Arresting Eye

Introduction

On July 22, 2005, police shot and killed Jean Charles de Menezes, a twenty-seven-year-old electrician living in London, in Stockwell Station in South London because they incorrectly identified him as the suspected terrorist Hussain Osman. The police shot Menezes repeatedly in the head in front of horrified passengers aboard a subway train. The shooting occurred on the day following a failed terrorist attempt in London and two weeks after the bombings (known as the 7/7 bombings) that resulted in fifty-two civilian deaths; London was on high alert. A statement by London's Metropolitan Police revealed that "the man who was shot was under police observation because he had emerged from a house that was itself under observation because it was linked to the investigation of yesterday's incidents. . . . He was then followed by surveillance officers to the station. His clothing[1] and his behaviour at the station added to their suspicions" (Cowell). Shortly after the shooting, it was revealed that Charles de Menezes was an innocent victim. Misidentified as Osman, a British citizen of Ethiopian birth, Menezes was later identified as a Brazilian citizen with no ties to the terrorists. Soon after discovering the mistake, Alex Pereira Alves, Menezes's cousin, asked, "How could they have confused and killed a light-skinned person who had no resemblance at all to an Asian?" (Cowell and Van Natta Jr.).[2]

Race Detective Anxiety Today

The Arresting Eye is a study of racial anxiety, particularly when race is not so easily discernible. That Menezes's racial identity could shift between Caucasian, black (i.e., Osman), and Asian reflects our current state of race detective paranoia.[3] That Menezes was tragically and mistakenly killed in a case of racial profiling gone wrong further demonstrates the interconnectedness of race and surveillance in our post-9/11 historical moment. But our current state of race detective anxiety is not only about terrorism, racial profiling, or, for that matter, the containment of criminal behavior. *The Arresting Eye* examines racial unease when discerning or acknowledging race (or the failure to do so) is an awkward and discomforting process. Alongside numerous recent cases of racial profiling (including, for example, that of George Zimmerman, acquitted, in a highly controversial ruling, of charges of murder and manslaughter in the death of seventeen-year-old Trayvon Martin), there is the recent insurgence of "miracle" births, sometimes facilitated by new reproductive technologies, resulting in new family formations. New reproductive practices as well as increased media focus on transracial adoptions reveal how race still conjures detective anxiety in our current not-so-color-blind moment.

One of the first highly publicized "miracle" birth stories occurred in 1993, when a Dutch couple, Wilma and Willem Stuart (pseudonyms), had heteropaternal (different fathers, multiple babies) twin boys, one white and one black. The Stuarts used IVF (in vitro fertilization) technology whereby the egg is fertilized with sperm outside the womb. Due to a lab technician's careless mistake, Wilma Stuart was impregnated with sperm from both her husband and a black Caribbean man. The hospital directors labeled this a "deeply regrettable mistake," and the Stuarts underwent psychotherapy sessions to deal with their "bewilderment and pain" (Simons). Much of their pain resulted from the accusations leveled by fellow villagers and neighbors in their small, isolated community. As Wilma reveals in a recent *Dateline NBC* interview, people would stare often and offer unsolicited comments: "They would say to me, 'Are these your children?' and I would say 'Yes.' 'Is this a twin?' 'Yes, it's a twin.' 'You must have gotten the scare of your life when he was born'" (Curry). The "scare of [Wilma's] life" is, essentially, the birthing of blackness and the stigma associated with her suspected cross-racial sexual transgression. Originally planning on keeping their IVF conception silent due to its social shame, the Stuarts finally revealed their story in order to ward off continued accusations of Wilma's cross-racial infidelity.[4]

The Stuarts are not alone in experiencing an IVF mix-up. In the United States, Donna Fasano underwent IVF treatment in 1998 and became pregnant with twins, one white and one black, due to another fertility clinic mistake. After a protracted legal battle, the biological parents of the black twin, Robert Rogers and Deborah Perry-Rogers, were awarded custody of their child. This outcome sparked a heated debate in medical and legal circles because, while the majority of the states (except for California) consider the birth mother (i.e., the gestational carrier, in this case, Donna Fasano) to be the legal mother, the visible racial difference in the Fasano twins necessitates, as Karla Holloway writes, that ethical and legal judgments should move away from a basis in precedent in order to "establish a new set of practices particular to identity" (58). In other words, racial difference and its very visibility (it is important to clarify the distinction here) demand a different set of questions and assumptions about parenting and kinship. Would a black child be better off with black parents? Who (or what) would this placement most benefit? Would keeping the twins together harm either twin's best interest? In short, the anxiety produced by such IVF "mistakes," heightened by media spectacle and subsequent public paranoia, occurs mainly because the error is evidenced by a racial visibility and the impossibility of racial passing.[5]

In addition to IVF "mistakes," several non-IVF but equally "miraculous" births have recently made headlines. Many focus on the Ebony-Ivory twin phenomenon (see Hodgson-Horder, Durant-Spooner, Kerry Richardson, and Gerth-Addo-Gerth stories) as well as the recent story of a black Nigerian couple, Ben and Angela Ihegboro, who gave birth to a blond, blue-eyed baby girl. In addition to these "miracle" births, Mark Riding's situation offers a different perspective on twenty-first-century visions of the "new family" via transracial adoption. As a black adoptive father of a young white girl, Riding's transracial adoption is counter to the popular image of today's transracial adoption: white parents adopting children of color (predominantly of African or Asian descent). Riding is outspoken about the resulting challenges he has encountered, including navigating through the adoption process itself as an African American couple trying to adopt a white child and accusations of kidnapping from bystanders (Dokoupil). I bring these stories to light to reveal the range of ways in which race provokes detective anxieties today. Whether a case involves racial profiling, "miracle" births (with or without the use of new reproductive technologies), or transracial adoptions, race is the central litmus test affecting how we negotiate our responses and sanction our behavior. The "miracle" birth examples or the fertility "mistakes" are significant because they illustrate how anxieties occur when race *cannot* easily pass. In other words, these "miraculous" stories are just that because race is the hypervisible proof of something not quite right, an *error* (involving IVF, potential infidelity, genetic mutation, potential kidnapping) that would not necessarily be discerned if the racial difference were not so easily evident. What is left unasked with these stories is: How often does this error occur when a "mistake" is not discovered because the baby can pass? If the Dutch black twin's biological father is white, would the "mistake" have ever been discovered? Would his mother get the suspicious looks from friends and strangers alike who accuse her of infidelity? Would people question the brothers' twin status? The Stuart story is international news due to the failure of racial passing. As the *Dateline* story states, the Stuart twins are dubbed "The Least Alike Twins," emphasizing that racial difference is *the* biggest confirmation of any difference (Curry). The above examples illustrate that the anxiety resulting from race detection occurs both at moments of racial passing as well as when race encounters an im(pass)e. Simply put, race, visible or invisible, provokes unease.

Implicit throughout this study is the role of family and family formations. Although this study does not centrally focus on the racial dynamics of family formation, it needs stating that each chapter's study of detective anxiety is in some ways simply about the fears of how families are formed (i.e., who can and is allowed to form a family unit, the subsequent products of those unions and their physical racial "evidence," and the continued "browning" of white America as a result of these mixings). The mystery of each chapter stems from familial racial secrets (chapters 1 and 2), the threat and allure of cross-racial romances and the subsequent offspring of these unions (chapter 3), the fear and subsequent erasure of racialized hypermasculinity (chapter 4), and speculations about racial mixings and the future "look" of race (chapter 5). In short, race detective anxiety is really about whom we mate with and whom we reproduce.

Historical Context

The Arresting Eye is a study of the intersection of race, detection, and passing and the subsequent anxieties produced by its various adaptations. This study examines the anxiety of detection when race is both visible and invisible throughout the twentieth century into the early decades of a color-blind twenty-first century. Offering case studies of detective anxiety, I show how moments of detection are differentiated by historical and cultural specificities and racial communities (namely, African American and Asian American). A central premise of this book is that we constantly experience anxieties over detecting, distinguishing, and deciphering race. For if the twentieth century was marked by the color line as famously delineated by W. E. B. Du Bois, then the entrance into the twenty-first century is characterized by the deterioration of those very boundaries. One has only to peruse recent covers of news magazines to realize that color lines are getting harder to differentiate due to increased rates of immigration and cross-racial mixing.[6] During the last decades of the twentieth century, racial fluidity stimulated discussions of "postethnicity" and "color-blindness." If markers of race are no longer reliable or evident, how is race to be determined? How will racial difference be understood when identities are constantly shifting and transforming themselves, transgressing into other boundaries and challenging our understanding of certain "racial knowledges"? In other words, how will "race" be defined and detected if no longer phenotypically visible? Finally, what are the consequences of race undetection and/or *mis*detection? For Menezes, the consequence was tragic and fatal. But moments of misdetection or, more specifically, the *unease* resulting from undetection, occur on a daily basis from cross-racial adoptions to terrorist paranoia to Affirmative Action. This study is an exploration of that unease and our negotiations (sometimes successful, but most often not) with it.

The Arresting Eye explores the above questions through a literary framework, specifically the intersection between detective fiction and passing narratives. The mid-nineteenth century was a historical moment that witnessed the simultaneous rise of both the detective and passing genres. The very idea of "detection" via detective fiction commenced with the popularity of Edgar Allan Poe's detective trilogy ("Murders in the Rue Morgue," "The Mystery of Marie Rogêt," and "The Purloined Letter").[7] While Poe's "tales of ratiocination" displayed the systematic and didactic methods of detection (including the recourse to and reliance upon certain types of knowledges and epistemologies), the passing narrative emerged to counter these very definitions for the mid-nineteenth century was also marked by significant advancements in human biology, including racial classification. With the publication of Johann Blumenbach's racial classification system in *On the Natural Variety of Mankind* in 1775, Charles Darwin's *The Origin of Species* in 1859, and *The Descent of Man* in 1871, exploration into racial difference (and, in turn, the legitimization of slavery and the hierarchy of races) culminated with works by Sir Francis Galton (who pioneered the field of eugenics), Paul Broca (who developed cranial anthropometry), Louis Agassiz (from whose work the term "scientific racism" arose), and Cesare Lombroso (father of criminal atavism) throughout the nineteenth century. Within this ideological climate where racial difference was defined, calculated, measured, and put on display,[8] the passing narrative began to emerge in popularity and illustrated the fallibility of racial epistemologies. Werner Sollors writes that the very first American instance of "passing" to signify "crossing the color line" occurs in notices regarding runaway slaves. As described in Richard Hildreth's *The Slave: or, Memoirs of Archy Moore* (1836), the notice reads, "FIVE HUNDRED DOLLARS REWARD . . . Run away from the subscriber . . . Archy and Cassy . . . are both very light colored . . . No doubt they will attempt to pass for white people" (qtd. in Sollors 255). It is telling that the first instance of passing occurs within the realm of criminal behavior. For a slave to escape is a crime demanding capture; for a slave to pass as white is a crime that is too unmentionable beyond the concluding warning here. The implied fear is deafening in its silence: if a slave can pass as white, how is s/he all that different from whites?[9]

The majority of this study explores the anxiety of race detection at the intersection of detection and passing narratives that includes both crime and non-crime-related plots. But, not all anxiety regarding race undetection centers on crime per se. Of course, the events of September 11, 2001, changed our understanding and potential expectations of race detection as the opening of this introduction illustrates. Although chapter 5 examines race detection in a post 9/11, color-blind context, *The Arresting Eye* is not merely a study of racial profiling as a result of the terrorist attacks (although the implications of this study are wide-ranging with direct relations to post-9/11 hysteria). Rather, I explore how the anxiety of detecting race has been a cultural phenomenon since the mid-nineteenth century. In this light, race detection angst goes beyond criminal behavior and acts of terrorism in that racial anxieties occur daily and most without much publication or notoriety. Thus, this investigation also highlights these daily occurrences. As such, I hope to show that we cannot understand the larger practice of race detection (such as racial profiling and national security measures) without also coming to terms with the little nuances that we (and, for some, daily) experience.

Undetective Anxieties

But, what *is* race undetection and why do we need to study it? To fully understand the responses to these questions is to also see the imperative need *now* to understand how anxieties of race and race detection affect us today in our contradictory post-9/11, color-blind moment in which we are both hyperaware of race yet must disavow it in the name of political correctness. Perhaps this is best illustrated with a culmination of "mental notes" that I have gathered over the past few years. Some derive from personal experiences, several from friends' experiences, and others are well-publicized accounts. I list them here in no particular order to offer the depth and scope of the study: my confusion and sometimes annoyance at constantly being mistaken for Japanese (I am of Korean descent) by both Koreans and Japanese alike; the rudeness or outright dismissal by mostly elderly Koreans during these moments; on a similar note, a Korean American friend who, while visiting Korea, is mistaken for Japanese and thrown out of a cab; a dark-skinned African American mentor/professor who, while holding her biracial baby, is asked by a white neighbor, "Whose baby you got there?"; similarly, an Asian American friend with another biracial baby is told by an Asian American that the baby looks quite *white* while a Caucasian friend tells her he looks *Asian*; Adrian Piper, a light-skinned African American scholar and performance artist, is often *seen* as white and, thus, is witness to many racist jokes and comments;[10] *www.alllooksame.com*, a website that offers a "race quiz" to test one's ability to identify the differences between Asian ethnicities (in this case, Chinese, Japanese, and Koreans); a Native American friend who although visibly Native (dark hair, dark eyes, and dark skin) does not meet the blood quantum level in order to be legally enrolled by her tribe and is subsequently restricted from gaining certain benefits such as land ownership; the same friend who is married to someone who looks white but has more Native blood than herself; again, the same friend who constantly gets comments about her blond son; Koreans and Chinese wearing buttons during World War II declaring "I am Korean" or "I am Chinese" to avoid internment; a blond and blue-eyed Caucasian friend mistakenly identified as *black* by an African American man because of her "kinky hair and ample buttocks"; the same Caucasian friend, having recently adopted a mixed-race baby who looks predominantly Latino, is constantly told, "Your son must look like his father!," or, in another instance, being stopped by the police while driving cross-country because someone at a rest stop thought she and her white husband were kidnapping a "brown boy"; a biracial Chicana who is not visibly raced overhears conversations around issues of illegal immigration and deportation from white colleagues; when asked how she can tell the differences between Asian ethnicities, the Korean

American student responds with, "Koreans are prettier, the Chinese have flatter faces, and the Japanese have bigger eyes"; on a similar note, a white man declares that the "Japanese are more docile while Koreans have a temper!"; a mixed-race couple from Ohio who had fraternal twins, one black with dark hair and brown eyes and the other white with blond hair and blue eyes, who are constantly asked if they are adopted or siblings at all; likewise, the continued controversy surrounding the discovery of black blood in Thomas Jefferson's "white" descendants; a young African American boy who refuses to believe Michael Jackson is, like him, African American; former U.S. secretary of state Madeleine Albright discovers, at the age of sixty, that she is of Jewish (not Catholic) descent; the rise of Asian women who undergo plastic surgery (such as double eyelid surgery, nose jobs, and skin bleaching) in order to look more "western";[11] this study's author continuously receiving comments about how her adopted daughter and biological daughter look *so much alike*. The list is endless.

Passing, Detection, Undetection

These instances all have one theme in common: the anxiety experienced at the moment of failed detection, including but not limited to the discomfort and threat of detective failure as well as the fear of being discovered and/or the discomfort and sometimes irritation of being misdetected. While most of the above examples may be somewhat harmless, others are not quite so innocent. The goal of this project is not to be comprehensive, but to offer a spectrum of differing ways race undetection can cause discomfort at the least and, at worst, death and war. Here, I differentiate between passing and undetection in that the former does not necessarily involve the threat of detection. In other words, one can pass without the knowledge that s/he is passing, thus making the threat of detection moot.[12] By examining the rapid rise of and desperate need for the detection of race since the nineteenth century, we can look through the eyes of both the detector and the (un)detected to investigate the relationship between detective fiction and passing narratives in the (re)construction and (re)negotiation of racial knowledges. The critic Amy Robinson's reading of passing as a "triangular theater of identity" is a helpful tool here. Distinguishing between the passer, the duped, and the in-group clairvoyant, Robinson clarifies that it is the in-group clairvoyant, the witness to the passing act who maintains the secrecy, who "establishes the conditions for the successful pass" because it is through his/her participation that the "perverse pleasure of duping the dupe . . . transforms a painful scenario of collaboration into an occasion to make and remake community" (736). The anxiety of race undetection, then, is not only about the inability to discern racial difference (i.e., being failed race readers) but also about the exclusion this failure subsequently entails. For the passer and the in-group, however, the anxiety also offers the potential for empowerment and uplift.

The relationship between detection and passing, then, is mutually constitutive; neither can be divorced from the other. *The Arresting Eye* examines the close intersection between passing and detection for several reasons. First, the *OED* defines "to detect" as "to uncover, lay bare, expose, display; to display (a person) by divulging his secrets or making known his guilt or crime; to inform against; to discover, find out, ascertain the presence, existence, or fact of (something apt to elude observation)." "To pass for," on the other hand, is "to be taken for, to be accepted, received, or held in repute as. Often with the implication of being something else." Here, the "implication of being something else" assumes that the act of passing is somewhat deceitful, manipulative, and untruthful. Thus, to pass for something else (whether on the axis of race, gender, or sexuality) always implies an act of deception or covering up. If detective fiction teaches us how to find/discover/uncover something or someone (i.e., the solution to the mystery and/or the suspect/criminal), then by its very definition the passing story reveals how the passer has avoided detection and most likely continues to do so. Simply put, passing and detection are sibling rivals whose participation in a game of racialized musical chairs reveals the ongoing trauma of the American family plot.

On another level, I also read passing narratives intersecting with the detective story through their mutual allusion to criminality, both legal and cultural. The detective story is most often a narrative about crime (usually murder) and the discovery of the killer. Similarly, I read passing itself as a type of criminal act or cultural criminality, if you will. As a response to racial hysteria in the wake of Reconstruction, passing is an act often described by both passers and the duped as one of betrayal and disloyalty to either the passer's community or the larger legal system. In a metaphorical and symbolic sense, there is also a "murdered" body in the passing narrative—that of the passer's former identity. In this sense, it is a type of what the cultural sociologist Orlando Patterson calls "social death." Passing, then, has a double meaning: (1) the act of crossing over and (2) the death of. One has only to remember *Plessy v. Ferguson* to understand the (white) cultural and legal insistence on the connection between passing and crime. This correlation is also evident in American literature with such examples as William Craft's *Running a Thousand Miles for Freedom* (1848), Harriet Beecher Stowe's *Uncle Tom's Cabin* (1852), and Mark Twain's *Pudd'nhead Wilson* (1894), among many others. In Craft and Stowe, light-skinned slaves escape slavery by passing as white (in Craft's narrative, the passing involves both a racial and gender crossover). While Twain's *Pudd'nhead Wilson* satirizes cultural and legal definitions of racial categories, the narrative ultimately connects the black-passing-for-white Chambers as a criminal when he kills Judge Driscoll and is sent to jail. Furthermore, Twain's problematic characterization of black criminal and immoral behavior as inescapable due to a black taint (via blood) is emphasized when Chambers cruelly mistreats his black birth mother, Roxy, throughout the tale. But even before these writers, Edgar Allan Poe, the father of detective fiction with his C. Auguste Dupin stories, also connects blackness with murderous criminality. In "The Murders in the Rue Morgue" (1841), the first story in his detective trilogy, Poe tells of a murderous orangutan that savagely kills two white women in their bedchamber. As the critics Lindon Barrett and Elise Lemire contend, here the act of passing is a metaphorical one in which the orangutan is a stand-in for the African, revealing the growing cultural anxiety and belief prevalent at the time that blackness was defined as "savage" and "primitive."

Twentieth-century passing tales, such as James Weldon Johnson's *Autobiography of an Ex-Colored Man* (1912), also equate passing with fraudulence and dishonesty (against the duped, against one's own community, and against one's own self) for selfish gain, one that is often achieved with remorse. As the narrator in Johnson's novel reveals, "I cannot repress the thought that, after all, I have chosen the lesser part, that I have sold my birthright for a mess of pottage" (154). In this sense, then, passing is "criminal" in that it breaks certain cultural, legal, and social codes, codes that may prove to be unstable by the very act of passing but are, nevertheless, often followed and relied upon by both passer and duped. Clare and Irene in Nella Larsen's *Passing* (1929) are also seen to adhere to hegemonic codes due to their very guilt and sense of betrayal. Additionally, because the insinuation at the novel's conclusion indicates that Irene kills Clare, Larsen's tragic tale again illustrates that passing is ultimately a criminal act. If read as a detective story, Larsen's story shows that (like *Pudd'nhead*) passing *produces* criminal behavior rather than merely *being* criminal. Some examples of detective fiction that center on passers as criminals include Ellery Queen's *The Roman Hat Mystery:*

A Problem in Deduction (1930), John Burdett's *Bangkok 8* (2003), and Pamela Thomas-Graham's *A Darker Shade of Crimson* (1998).[13] While recent passing narratives complicate the politics of passing at the turn into the twenty-first century, they still maintain a sense of passing as "bad behavior" or an act of betrayal. Examples include Danzy Senna's *Caucasia* (1999) and *Symptomatic* (2004), Philip Roth's *The Human Stain* (2000), and Colson Whitehead's *The Intuitionist* (1998). While the passers do not commit a legal crime, they are forever imprisoned within their psychological and emotional sense of illicit and immoral behavior for passing as white. The author Chang Rae Lee complicates the passing scenario within an Asian American context in *A Gesture Life* (1999), a novel featuring Franklin Hata, who is born to Korean parents but adopted by a Japanese family. The difficulties arise for "Doc Hata" when he is a paramedic serving in the Japanese army in Burma. While passing as Japanese, Hata's loyalty and ethics are questioned when he is confronted by Korean comfort women. Here, although Lee reveals how a demonstration of *intraracial* passing problematizes our understanding of the passing dynamic, he again shows that passing incites a sense of disloyalty and betrayal.

In the introduction to *Contesting Genres in Contemporary Asian American Fiction*, Betsy Huang writes that genre is a "site for developing a transformative Asian American politics of form" (4). Focusing on three popular genre fictions—immigrant narrative, crime fiction, and science fiction—Huang argues that generic form is a site of social, political, and literary struggle and possibility in Asian American literature. Huang writes that "the political impact of a work—whether resistant, accommodationist, or ambivalent—is ultimately located in the author's negotiations with the convention he or she is expected to execute" (5). Thus, authors writing genre fiction offer the potential not just by "contravening genre conventions, but by using them to rewrite the rules of the genre" (101) and, in turn, challenge regulatory norms of Asian American identity. Building upon Huang's insightful and groundbreaking study, *The Arresting Eye* argues that genre fiction (in this case, detective fiction and passing narratives) has the potential to reject and rewrite conventional rules. Throughout the chapters, I argue that foundational terms central to the detective plot—"crime," "criminal," and "justice"—are redefined and redirected from the previously detected onto the detectors. In addition to challenging conventional norms, however, the case studies examined here also reveal how conventions of genre are redeployed to reestablish boundaries and reconfine marginal subjects. One of genre's possibilities is its capability to conduct cross-generic dialogue (or, as Huang calls it, "genre mixing"). In the case of detective fiction and passing narratives, detection and passing are inevitable partners in a racialized game of hunter and hunted. This study examines the point of contact between passing and detection to illustrate that these two genres are intimately connected in their evolution and transformation in American literary history as well as their potential for political possibilities by marginalized communities.

Toni Morrison's short story "Recitatif" (1983) is a telling example of how genre mixing creates conversation across multiple literary forms for Morrison utilizes conventions of detective fiction and the passing narrative to ultimately reflect, question, and ideally transform the reader's literary and racial expectations and assumptions. Further, the story's aim of race detection also demands the reader's acknowledgment of race-specific nuances and clues across multiple racial formations, namely African American, Caucasian, and Asian American racialized bodies. In *Race for Citizenship*, Helen Jun writes that the "institution of citizenship compels racialized subjects to produce developmental narratives of inclusion in the effort to achieve political, economic and social incorporation" (4). Focusing on African Americans and Asian Americans, Jun argues that the "production of racial meanings is a relational process in which differential inclusions and exclusions are endemic to the institution of citizenship itself" (4). The desire for incorporation as a relational process is the underlying motivation for Morrison's main characters in "Recitatif," but with a slight twist: the reader is unaware of the main characters' racial identity. Morrison's only published short story reads like a detective tale where the passing act occurs as an experience for the reader rather than a narrative tool enacted by the characters. In this light, the story demonstrates how we see, categorize, and define certain racial groups, but it also highlights the reader's own anxieties of race detection and the failure thereof. We are forced to play race detective, deciphering between Twyla's and Roberta's characterizations, associations, and preferences as well as decoding narrative clues that may or may not be evidence of race. Because Morrison never divulges the racial identities of Twyla and Roberta, the reader is left in detective limbo, ultimately realizing that the real revelation to the mystery is that we are all acculturated to read and recognize racial markers. The story's mastery is forcing that recognition and leaving us to deal with the discomforts of such decodings. Thus, I examine Morrison's literary masterpiece as a pedagogical tool to highlight and dissect some of the theoretical questions outlining this project.

"Recitatif" as Paradigmatic Tale and Pedagogical Tool

In *Playing in the Dark: Whiteness and the Literary Imagination*, Toni Morrison reveals that her only published short story, "Recitatif" (1983), "was an experiment in the removal of all racial codes from a narrative about two characters of different races for whom racial identity is crucial" (xi). As such, "Recitatif" is a passing narrative in reverse where the reader (not the characters themselves) must decipher the characters' racial identity. At worst, the story brings to the surface our cultural stereotypes and assumptions regarding blackness, Asianness, and whiteness (specifically in relation to gender and class). At best, the story also exposes our own interpretive and epistemological preoccupations with detecting race by constantly making us question our beliefs in and reliance upon such stereotypes. In other words, while it is not a detective story per se, "Recitatif" forces its readers to *play detective* while concurrently making us uncomfortable with our detective abilities, emphasizing the often subjective (and, in this case, racist) nature of our declarations of intuitive and/or objective deductions. Morrison's story is, in one sense, a constantly shifting passing tale via the reader, one whose mission is to enlighten and irritate us, leading us to continuously waver between the racial identification of the two protagonists. But the goal of the story is *not* to conclude with a racial identification (i.e., to be a successful detective), but to force us to examine our own preconceived notions of racial difference. In this light, I read "Recitatif" as a story that crosses genres, incorporating the generic forms of both the passing narrative and the detective story in order to reveal the anxieties of race detection and undetection for the reader. Furthermore, and perhaps more importantly, I also read "Recitatif" as a type of racial and symbolic parable, foreshadowing much of the growing concern surrounding the erasure of racial borders, cross-racial mixing, and undetection that welcomes us into the twenty-first century.

"Recitatif" is told in five "scenes" throughout the lives of Twyla and Roberta, two young girls who meet at St. Bonaventure's orphanage around 1960 and form a conflicted friendship for the next thirty years. We see their development from St. Bonny's to Howard Johnson's years later, where Twyla, the narrator, is a waitress, and Roberta is a customer traveling to see Jimi Hendrix. Next, while living in Upstate New York, Twyla and Roberta encounter each other at the gourmet Food Emporium, where Roberta is clad in diamonds and accompanied by a limousine with a Chinese driver. The fourth scene shows Twyla and Roberta on opposite sides of the school busing crisis. Finally, Twyla meets Roberta in a café, where they reach a catharsis over the question of the racial identity of Maggie (the kitchen help at St. Bonny's). While this is a story about two girls from different races, or, as Twyla describes it, "salt and pepper" (244), Morrison never discloses who is white and who is black. Instead, she offers strategic clues throughout her story to reveal the large outlets of our racist stereotyping (hygiene, food, religion, activities, political choices, music, hair, fashion). Further, "Recitatif" also confirms that we define ourselves in opposition to each other via race as well as gender, class, sexuality, religion, and disability. Thus, the story demands that the readers be complicit in the detection process, slowly revealing racial "clues" and euphemisms in one section only to be teased with the opposite reading in the next, denying us the very possibility of knowing. Some of the questions readers may ask include: Is Twyla a white name or a black name? Does it *sound* black, or is Morrison referencing Twyla Tharp, a famous white dancer and choreographer (perhaps suggested by Twyla's mother, who "danced all night" [243])? On a similar note, is Roberta Fisk a black name with connotations to the black singer Roberta Flack and (previously all-black) Fisk University? Does Twyla's mother dancing all night mean she is a stripper? If so, is stripping generally a black or white profession? Does Twyla's observation of "they never washed their hair and they smelled funny" (243) refer to black or white hygiene? Does Roberta's Bible-carrying and cross-wearing mother (she was "bigger than any man" [247]) immediately conjure up the image of a big, black Baptist woman we imagine seeing in a Tyler Perry film? Is this implication solidified by the fact that Roberta's mother brings her chicken legs[14] and ham sandwiches? The list of stereotypes and reflections upon the stereotypes seems endless.

Of course, the interesting observation here is that readers generally recognize the racial stereotypes throughout the story, emphasizing how these stereotypes function as common, well-recognized clues or "knowledges" much like Sherlock Holmes's vast knowledge of cigar ashes (he, in fact, wrote a monograph on the subject, *Upon the Distinction between the Ashes of the Various Tobaccos*). But, unlike the typical detective story, Morrison's story is a detective plot whose purpose is *not* to find the solution per se, although that is the driving force behind it. Rather, the central mission is to deprive the reader of racial shortcuts in order that she/he may experience a much more proactive reading immersion. It is one thing to read about racial strife and the contradictions inherent in racial formation; it is another to *experience* them. As the readers, we have to remind ourselves that Twyla and Roberta know each other's race. It is the reader who is trapped in a racial blindness. That is why, as some critics have observed, Twyla's and Roberta's undetection of Maggie is significant and why the very last line of the story—"What the hell happened to Maggie?"—is key to understanding the story.

Maggie, the disabled kitchen help at St. Bonny's, is described "sandy-colored" (245). As such, Maggie is just as racially ambiguous to Twyla and Roberta as the latter are to the readers. But because they *believed* she was black, and because of her muteness and physical disability, Twyla and Roberta feel superior to her. Trudier Harris argues that "Maggie is the site on which Twyla and Roberta can exercise their mob psychology" (113). Although in the final scene of the story Roberta admits her uncertainty about Maggie's race, Harris contends the real crisis is that Twyla and Roberta are "busily *reinscribing* the very racial differences and prejudices the existence of which the story seeks to deny. . . . [In this light,] black and white human beings on American soil seem incapable of peaceful coexistence without tension based on race. *It is the norm*" (115, emphasis in original). Sandra Kumamoto Stanley offers a different reading of Maggie: "Maggie, whose primary marker of difference is her disability, is the one character for whom the novel's 'ideological construction of otherness' remains fixed" (72) for she embodies the shame and trauma of Twyla's and Roberta's past. Without agency, Maggie "becomes a repository for both Twyla's and Roberta's anxieties about their mothers and their identities" (82).

I would like to offer a different reading of Maggie's role in the story, one that may help us better understand how anxieties of detecting race can have long-standing and powerful consequences. In a story centering on race detection angst, the struggle over Maggie's racial identity is the final dilemma Twyla and Roberta attempt to overcome. When Twyla and Roberta meet at the Food Emporium, Roberta reminds Twyla about the incident in the orchard where Maggie was attacked by the "gar girls" (a mishearing of "gargoyle" and a reference to the big girls at the orphanage). Twyla does not remember the attack. In the following scene, when Twyla and Roberta are arguing over the school busing crisis, Roberta accuses Twyla of kicking Maggie (which Twyla denies): "You kicked a black lady and you have the nerve to call me a bigot." This accusation is supposed to clarify Twyla's and Roberta's own racial identities. Who is the bigot here? A black Twyla who kicks black Maggie? Or a white Twyla who kicks black Maggie? As Trudier Harris ponders: "If Roberta thought Maggie was black and still wanted to kick her, then what does that suggest about *intra*racial prejudice, if Roberta is the black character? And if Twyla is the black character, what does her desire to kick Maggie suggest about her conscious denial of her own blackness? If Twyla is the white character, what does it suggest about her willingness to deny the humanity of kindred?" (114). In this decoding, race matters in that one's racial identity determines the interpretation of behavior. Black Roberta kicking black Maggie is about black-on-black prejudice, but white Twyla kicking Maggie denotes an absence of humanity. This sounds eerily too similar to racial science's argument for race-based behavior (i.e., Lombroso's theory of criminal anthropology). The irony here is that Maggie's racial identity is unknown. We don't know whether or not she is black; they just *believed* her to be. Thus, the behavior (the attack) occurs due to a racial guessing game.

In addition to Maggie, however, there is another character in the story the identification of whose race does not require a guessing game yet who functions to reveal the limits of racial anxiety: the Chinaman. In a story that teases us with a game of race detection, the Chinaman is the only known raced figure in the entire story. Except for a brief mention by Ann Rayson (see below), he is the one character who is completely ignored by critics.[15] But what is the significance of the Chinaman's known racial identity? How does the Chinaman help us configure the racialization of the unknown raced characters? Echoing Michael Omi and Howard Winant's groundbreaking theory of racial formation, Helen Jun argues that within the racialized history of America, where identity is defined in relation to others, certain racial groups work in opposition to others in the racial formation process. Morrison herself discusses how racialized identity is relational in *Playing in the Dark: Whiteness and the Literary Imagination* when she declares that the white concepts of individualism, freedom, manhood, and innocence exist only in relation to the unfree black slave. Thus, if Morrison's goal in her story is *not* to detect racial identity but, rather, to highlight our own preconceived notions and stereotypes of race and ultimately to negotiate the unease with which we come to these conclusions, I argue that the inclusion of the "Chinaman" reveals another layer to our unease with race detection. Like Maggie, the Chinaman appears but does not have any narrative agency; in fact, he is not even a character as much a visual and narrative reference. Twyla sees him outside of the Food Emporium when Roberta offers her limousine. Her jest of "You married a Chinaman?" is received with giggles and more giggles. This is the only reference to the Chinaman, but his function as the object of laughter is unsettling here on multiple levels. First, the use of the racial epithet "Chinaman" linked to marriage implies an absurdity to this type of union, reflecting the century-old stereotype of Asian men as effeminate and asexual. Second, "Chinaman" rather than "Chinese man" also suggests a certain unknowability of Asian ethnicities (he could have been from any Asian background because "they are all the same"); the inability to distinguish between Asian ethnicities, in other words, is degraded to mere racial insult. Conversely, however, the potential threat of that very unknowability is alleviated by the fact that he *is* the only known raced subject in the story. The contradiction of the Asian body, then, is that s/he is always already passing (all look the same), but can never pass (forever foreigner). This was tragically displayed the year prior to the story's publication with the murder of Vincent Chin, a Chinese American mistaken for Japanese and beaten to death by a Chrysler plant supervisor and his stepson.[16]

In addition to the critics' complete disregard of the Chinaman, another possible racial reading is also ignored: the role of amalgamation and mixed-race identity in general. The significance of this is perhaps best illustrated with Roberta and her husband. An initial decoding of Roberta in the Food Emporium scene is that her newfound class identity and her IBM executive husband make her seem white. Twyla's reaction to Roberta's new wealth—"Everything is so easy for them. They think they own the world" (252)—seems to support this conclusion. But Elizabeth Abel's reading of the story includes a footnote in which she reveals Morrison's revelation that IBM was recruiting black executives at the time. Thus, she reads Roberta as black, completely disregarding the possibility of a mixed marriage. The critic Ann Rayson also offers a suggestive decoding of race based on amalgamation. Based on her interpretation of the "Chinaman" scene, Rayson concludes that Twyla must be white: "The black woman would probably not immediately assume that the white woman dripping diamonds is married to the Chinese driver, but Roberta, being black, could be easily be married to another man of color in Twyla's eyes" (43). This deduction is telling in several ways. First, it presumes that a wealthy white woman would be unlikely to marry a Chinese man, but a wealthy black woman could "easily" be imagined doing so. This reading reiterates the troubling stereotypes of Asian masculinity already mentioned, but it also assumes a distinct white racial purity that is not as characteristic of other marginalized groups. Second, this suggestion is simultaneously shielded with the disclaimer, "the black woman would probably not immediately assume." In a story that reflects the readers' own biases and presumptions of race, Rayson's speculation of what a black woman would and would not assume is telling in its own regard. My reading here is not to point fingers, but to uncover the anxieties we all experience in the race detection struggle.[17]

* * *

The Arresting Eye offers a wide range of perspectives to illustrate the intersection of detection and passing and its subsequent production of racial anxieties. The five chapters comprise three historical periods of various racial formations: (1) the late nineteenth century and the emergence of legalized segregation (chapter 1); (2) the interwar years of Jim Crow segregation and Japanese internment (chapters 2-4), and (3); the post–civil rights era of multiculturalism, color-blind ideology, and 9/11 paranoia (chapter 5). These three historical periods and their subsequent racial formations respond to the anxiety of race detection in varied ways. The chapters highlight not only the differences of historical context to the collision between detection and passing but also emphasize the pervasive and consistent anxieties of detecting race throughout the past century and beyond.

Chapter 1, "Whispers of Norbury: Sir Arthur Conan Doyle and the Modernist Crisis of Racial (Un)Detection," begins with an alternative rereading of the *Plessy v. Ferguson* landmark racial segregation case where the premise of the "separate but equal" doctrine is founded upon a racial distinction that cannot be deciphered (Plessy's passing body). The year following Plessy's arrest, Arthur Conan Doyle published "The Yellow Face," one of the few Sherlock Holmes stories in which the genius detective fails due to an encounter with American racial passing. This chapter also highlights Doyle's interactions with blackness (both Africans and African Americans) prior to his creation of Sherlock Holmes. What is generally unknown about Doyle and his creation of Sherlock Holmes is the pivotal impact of a racial discomfort that Doyle experienced in his early twenties. As both a scientist and the product of Enlightenment rationality, Doyle heavily relied upon the rhetoric of racial science predominant during his time as an objective and factual schema determining racial difference and hierarchy. However, when Doyle encountered Henry Highland Garnet, a famous African American abolitionist of the 1840s who promoted black resistance, his previous dependence and reliance upon racial knowledges were shattered. This chapter argues that in response to this racial crisis (as well as his subsequent encounters with African "natives" revealed in his ethnographic writings), Doyle creates an oeuvre of detective tales as a desperate attempt to assuage fears and anxieties resulting from both the chaos of modernity as well as, in some part, the rise of racial indeterminacy. The chapter concludes with an analysis of "The Yellow Face" (1893), a rare story of Holmesian failure in which the "Superman" of detective prowess encounters and is duped by a racially passing figure. Unlike his other cases in which Holmes displays an "exact science" of detection, "The Yellow Face" reveals the failure of science in detecting race during this historical moment.

Chapters 2 and 3 offer perspectives on race and detective anxieties through two pioneering female authors emerging from two very different racial backgrounds: Pauline Hopkins, a prominent African American novelist, journalist, editor, and playwright, and Winnifred Eaton, the first recognized Asian American novelist known for her Japanese romances. I introduce the partnership of these two chapters with the dramatic race passing case of *Rhinelander v. Rhinelander* (1925) to illustrate the Afro-Asian specificities and the thorny terrain of racial indecipherability (in this case, the racial ambiguity of George Jones, Alice's father, shifting between blackness and Asianness). With the *Rhinelander* case as background, chapters 2 and 3 focus on African American and Asian American case studies, respectively. Chapter 2 "Intuitive Faculties and Racial Clairvoyance: Pauline Hopkins and the Emergence of Multiethnic Detective Fiction," illustrates how the detection of race is revised and reformulated by the emergence of ethnic detectives in the twentieth century, particularly Pauline Hopkins's *Hagar's Daughter* and her detective heroine, Venus Johnson. Like Doyle's "The Yellow Face," which was published less than a decade before *Hagar's Daughter*, Hopkins's story illustrates the intersection of passing and detection. However, Hopkins comments upon detection and passing from the eyes of the previously undetected object-turned-subject. For if Doyle's story reveals an outsider's failed perspective of race detection (Holmes's failure in detecting blackness), Hopkins's tale shows an intimate insider's view into the politics of detection from a community previously fractured by slavery. A passing tale turned detective plot, *Hagar's Daughter* not only reconfigures the limited boundaries of classic detective fiction by redefining "crime," "justice," and "guilt" from an African American perspective, but it also reclaims and reunifies the black family once devastated by slavery by redefining the tropes of detection and passing.

In chapter 3, "Detecting Winnifred Eaton," I expand upon the black/white paradigm of race detection by introducing how detection and passing is complicated and renegotiated via a different racial lens—the

Asian American body. While detecting race is shown to be an almost obsessive fixation during the early part of the twentieth century, Winnifred Eaton, the first Asian American novelist, creates a counternarrative by promoting a rhetoric of *undetection* through her Japanese romances. What is significant about Winnifred Eaton is her own performance of ethnic passing. Because she passed as Japanese (Eaton was half-English and half-Chinese) during a historical moment that witnessed the superiority of Japan as a nation, Eaton was criticized as a race traitor by early Asian American critics. This chapter, however, reveals how Eaton critiques fixed racial boundaries but also displays a literary interference into the obsessions with race detection by illustrating how *undetection* could be used in what critic Amy Ling calls "guerilla tactics" (*Between Worlds* 26) for marginalized writers.

Soon after Eaton and her tales of undetection emerged, America experienced the political and cultural imperative to ascertain Asian ethnic differences. The detection of Asian America, particularly the nuances between various Asian ethnicities, was crucial during wartime hysteria. Chapter 4, "Jaundiced Eyes: Charlie Chan and the Mysterious Disappearance of a Detective Hero," begins with several educational "guides" offered to soldiers and citizens alike to aid in discerning between Japanese and Chinese, friend and foe. These "guides" function as detective tools, deciphering and transmitting racial and ethnic knowledges to a nation otherwise unfamiliar with the Asian and Asian American communities. But the persistent and desperate need to detect Asian and Asian American bodies occurred much earlier with, ironically, an Asian American detective hero, Charlie Chan. Created by Earl Derr Biggers in the 1920s, Charlie Chan is one of the leading stereotypes of Asian American male identity in the twentieth century. As a direct opposition to Sax Rohmer's Fu Manchu villain, who was created at approximately the same historical moment, Biggers's Charlie Chan is a complicated figure who is generally dismissed within the Asian American community as mere stereotype. However, this chapter argues that the legacy of Charlie Chan cannot be so easily dismissed, asking how we can reconcile Charlie Chan's status as detective hero with the concurrent rise of Yellow Peril paranoia? While many would argue that Charlie Chan's popularity is a direct result of racism and anti-Asian sentiments, we cannot ignore Biggers's (and Chan's) critique of Western culture and hegemony within the numerous literary and filmic tales. Thus, this chapter is a much-needed investigation into the legacy of Charlie Chan as both myth and stereotype. By examining both the novels and the films, I explore how Charlie Chan's heroism is countered and repressed via what I term "containment strategies" of race passing. In the novels, Charlie Chan's detective prowess is overshadowed and contained by a white amateur detective who not only overtakes the detective plot but also becomes the hero of a romance plot, completely marginalizing Charlie to that of sidekick figure. In the film representations, the struggle over white hegemony occurs via Charlie's yellowface performance as well as the introduction of racialized sidekick characters who erupt conventional (white) definitions of knowledge formation.

Finally, the last chapter focuses on racial anxieties during a color-blind, post 9/11 historical moment. Chapter 5, "Race Detection in a Color-Blind Era: Musings on the New Millennium," offers a different approach from previous chapters by providing a selection of "musings" from the past two decades. Using examples (some highly publicized, some generally unknown) ranging from print media to art installations to speculative narratives to reproductive technologies, this chapter concludes with an analysis of our current state of detective anxiety. As this discussion illustrates, our need to detect remains very much alive today. At a time when the general credo is to *not* see racial differences, detection takes on a whole new meaning.

* * *

In a project that is as fruitful as this one, it is impossible to cover all the bases. I have tried to focus here on some of the key moments where anxieties display themselves readily, unabashedly, anxieties that continue to reveal themselves today. This study focuses on three particular racial landscapes—whiteness, blackness, and Asianness—and is reflective of my background in critical race studies and comparative racializations. Some of the key scholars who have been instrumental in the development of my ideas include theorists of critical race studies (George Lipsitz, Toni Morrison, John L. Jackson, Ian Haney Lopez, and Dorothy Roberts), comparative racializations (Gary Okihiro, Claire Jean Kim, Vijay Prashad, and Frank Wu), passing and masquerade (Judith Butler, Valerie Smith, Michael Rogin, Amy Robinson, Tina Chen, and Leslie Bow), and genre studies (Betsy Huang, Megan Abbott, Sean McCann, and Maureen Reddy). There are, of course, specific anxieties around detection in both the Chicano/Latino and Native American communities (including but not limited to immigration and blood quantum controversies) that I have not addressed. While these issues are not discussed in this particular work, my hope is that the implications of this study will reach beyond the racial triangulation I have chosen here.

1 / Whispers of Norbury: Sir Arthur Conan Doyle and the Modernist Crisis of Racial (Un)Detection

One of this study's underlying premises is that we are all culturally, socially, and legally groomed to be race detectors. Notwithstanding the absence of the title "detective," everyday citizens are expected to know (and sometimes adamantly claim to know) the difference between white and nonwhite. This ability to discern racial difference is especially important in moments when knowing the difference determines access to white privilege. Before examining the literary examples of race detective anxiety, I offer a brief legal reexamination of the recourse to "common knowledge" detection by focusing on Jim Crow segregation laws as well as anti-Asian immigration practices that reflect the racial attitudes during the end of the nineteenth century into the early decades of the twentieth century. By its very premise, "common knowledge" detection is a consensual, cultural agreement on what race (and, as I show later, what gendered race) "looks" like. In that sense, the practice of detection assigns Everyman the authority to discern and categorize racial and gendered differences. In essence, we believe we know it when we see it. As evidenced below, this agreement and the claim to know provide evidentiary support for the regulation of racist, often legally sanctioned, practices.

Knowing It When You Don't See It

Plessy v. Ferguson (1896) is a telling example of the responsibility of Everyman detectives who are duty-bound to practice and uphold racist legal sanctions. In the *Plessy* case, the train conductor plays race detective, deciphering the clues that determine who is directed to the well-maintained white coach and who is relegated to the dilapidated black car.[1] But, as in numerous cases prior to and since *Plessy*, whether an individual should be granted admission at the racial gateways of trains, ships, buses, restaurants, public restrooms, park benches, and entrances was not always easily determined. The irony is that the *Plessy* case and its subsequent legal sanction of the "separate but equal" Jim Crow era were founded upon a racial ambiguity where the supposedly separate racial markers could not, in actuality, be differentiated. In essence, de jure segregation assumes clear racial distinctions and boundaries, yet de facto realities reveal that these borders are much less distinguishable and often misread or invisible to the discerning eye.

The possibility of racial misreading and its subsequent prevention is where the anxiety of detection enters in *Plessy v. Ferguson*. Let us consider the case in more detail. On June 7, 1892, Homer Adolph Plessy boarded an East Louisiana Railway train for a first-class passage from New Orleans to Covington, Louisiana. While onboard, Plessy was confronted by conductor J. J. Dowling regarding his racial background. Because Plessy was an "octoroon," or a person with one-eighth African blood, it was illegal for him to board a "whites only" coach. Upon declaring his blackness and his refusal to leave, Plessy was arrested by the private detective Chris C. Cain and taken to New Orleans's Fifth Precinct Station. Thus commenced one of the most important racial segregation cases in American civil rights history. *Plessy v. Ferguson* established the "separate but equal" doctrine that would form the basis of Jim Crow ideology until its repeal in *Brown v. Board of Education* in 1954. Ironically, Homer Plessy's blackness "was not discernible in him" (qtd. in Golub 564), rendering the mandate to separate difficult to enforce.

I include this landmark case because of the intersection between detection and passing at its core. I offer a rereading of the *Plessy* case here through the lens of detective fiction to illustrate how race detection failure is used as a foundation to sanction racial separation. As a detective story, the *Plessy v. Ferguson* case fails. Segregation assumes there is no mystery about race, that black and white are racial markers clearly read upon an individual's body, which is therefore easily placed in its rightfully raced corner. But, as Homer Plessy demonstrates, this does not account for mixed-race bodies in which racial borders are not so easily determined. In fact, one of the most interesting and somewhat disregarded facts of this case is that Plessy's racial identity was disclosed *prior to* his boarding of the East Louisiana Railroad train. Plessy's arrest was a well-strategized racial drama coordinated by the Citizens' Committee to Test the Constitutionality of the Separate Car Law. The goal of the Citizens' Committee, a group predominantly consisting of New Orleans Creoles, was to challenge the 1890 Louisiana statute that required all railways traveling within the state to provide separate black and white coaches. With the white lawyer, novelist, and pioneer civil rights activist Albion Winegar Tourgée serving as advisor, the committee strategized to "have someone of mixed blood violate the law, since to do so would allow him to question the arbitrariness by which people were classified 'colored'" (Thomas 4).

As an octoroon who could pass for white, Plessy proved to be an ideal participant in the committee's test case. In fact, the invisibility of Plessy's blackness required that full disclosure of his racial identity be made prior to his boarding, undermining the very premise behind the "separate but equal" doctrine. Thus, both conductor and private detective enacted their official parts as race detectors only because they were welcomed into the "in-group" (echoing Amy Robinson's triangular theater of passing) of Plessy's "real" racial identity prior to the incident. Not to have done so would have prevented the detection of Plessy's blackness and, thus, his disobedience of the law. The irony here needs to be emphasized: Plessy's unmarked blackness had to be divulged (as opposed to being recognized) in order for him to be denied access to whiteness and white privilege. Interestingly, in light of this study, Detective Cain's role as professional detector succeeded only because he was given the solution before the "mystery" was played out, illustrating that the "mystery" of Plessy's race required revelation rather than detection. Perhaps the real mystery of this racial plot is to ask how someone who is visibly "white" according to cultural definitions of whiteness can still be confined within the legal and cultural definitions of blackness? Tellingly, the U.S. Supreme Court ignored this conundrum when they upheld the constitutionality of state laws regarding racial segregation.[2]

If the *Plessy* case demonstrates the quandary of knowing invisible race, the racial prerequisite cases and their determination of citizenship established that some races (i.e., Asianness) are "commonly" recognized to always be known and separate from whiteness. Beginning with *In re Ah Yup* (1878) until the end of racial restrictions on naturalization in 1952, Ian Haney López states, the prerequisite cases and their determination of whiteness often entailed a series of contradictions, concessions, and departures from earlier precedents in the road to citizenship.

Decisions that involved a "mental tussle" (54) between scientific evidence and "common knowledge" rationale eventually illustrated the "falsity of natural notions of race, exposing race instead as a social product measurable only in terms of what people believe" (80). This is tellingly revealed in Haney-López's description of *Ozawa v. United States* (1922) and *United States v. Thind* (1923), two cases in which the U.S. Supreme Court ultimately based its decisions upon a "common knowledge" belief of racial difference. Whether an individual is white in skin tone (Ozawa) or falls within the anthropological category of "Caucasian" (Thind), "common knowledge" (the belief that any common person can clearly *see* that Ozawa and Thind are not white) trumps all other forms of evidence including scientific knowledge. As Haney-López emphasizes, "race is not a measured fact, but a preserved fiction" (102). As such, "race is nothing more than what society and law say it is" (103).

These cases illustrate a paradox between knowing and detecting: what one may know of racial knowledge (i.e., white skin equals whiteness) may not always determine the "truth" of that knowledge. In other words, Plessy's race, while visibly white, is not (legally, culturally) detected as white; conversely, while Bhagat Thind may be "scientifically" categorized as Caucasian, he does not pass the test of whiteness. These legal cases serve as brief background information to a discussion of the relationship between race, law, and detection. Because detective fiction is so centrally concerned with the maintenance and preservation of law, its partnership is a crucial one that reveals the intricacies of maintaining or abandoning certain strictures. Arthur Conan Doyle and his detective genius Sherlock Holmes not only question what it means to detect blackness and the boundaries of race itself, but they also interrogate the ethical relationship between crime and law.

The Encounter

Toward the end of his 1881–82 voyage to West Africa, twenty-two-year-old Arthur Conan Doyle met Henry Highland Garnet aboard the African Steam Navigation Company's *Mayumba*. Doyle's three-day encounter with Garnet occurred during the former's appointment as ship's surgeon on a four-month expedition. Garnet, a former slave who became one of the most famous black abolitionists in the 1840s, was the American consul at Monrovia. Doyle's biographer, Owen Dudley Edwards, calls this meeting "perhaps the most momentous encounter [Doyle] had yet sustained in the course of his life" (255). Edwards goes on to claim that Garnet "had done an extraordinary thing for Conan Doyle. He had given him his first authentic voice outside his own range of experience, *and the voice was black*" (269, emphasis mine). How could a three-day meeting have such tremendous impact? What transpired in the encounter in which Doyle experienced his "first authentic voice" of blackness? While we may never know exactly what was discussed between these two very diverse figures, we may discern the significance of the encounter from Doyle's own description. In his autobiography, *Memories and Adventures*, Doyle remembers, interestingly, an unnamed Garnet in a short yet revealing two-paragraph summary that I quote here in full:

> The most intelligent and well-read man whom I met on the Coast was a negro, the American Consul at Monrovia. He came on with us as a passenger. My starved literary side was eager for good talk, and it was wonderful to sit on deck discussing Bancroft and Motley,[3] and then suddenly realize that you were talking to one who had possibly been a slave himself, and was certainly the son of slaves. He had thought a good deal about African travel. "The only way to explore Africa is to go without arms and with few servants. You would not like it in England if a body of men came armed to the teeth and marched through your land. The Africans are quite as sensitive." It was the method of Livingstone as against the method of Stanley. The former takes the braver and better man.
>
> This negro gentleman did me good, for a man's brain is an organ for the formation of his own thoughts and also for the digestion of other people's, and it needs fresh fodder. We had, of course, books aboard the ship, but neither many nor good. I cannot trace that I made any mental or spiritual advancement during the voyage, but I added one more experience to my chaplet, and I suppose it all goes to some ultimate result in character or personality. I was a strong full-blooded young man, full of the joy of life, with nothing of what Oliver Wendell Holmes calls "pathological piety and tuberculous virtues." I was a man among men. I walked ever among pitfalls and I thank all ministering angels that I came through, while I have a softened heart for those who did not. (49–50)

Revealing in this short description is Doyle's rhetorical strategy, which comprises three distinct phases: (1) an epistemological crisis, (2) repression and consumption of that crisis, and (3) a reinscription/revalorization of Doyle's potentially threatened masculinity and subjectivity. The epistemological crisis occurs when Doyle "suddenly realize[s]" that Garnet could have "possibly been a slave himself, and was certainly the son of slaves." How could this probable former slave possibly be "the most intelligent and well-read man" among fellow British men and women that Doyle encounters on this journey? How could a "negro" satiate his "starv[ing]" need for intellectual stimulation? Doyle's sudden realization of these two possibilities involves two contradictory revelations. First, the realization is based upon Doyle's presumption of Garnet's lack of intellectual capabilities as a black man. Second, it simultaneously disrupts that presumption. Hence, the epistemological dilemma. But what is significant about this sudden realization is Doyle's immediate response to it. He, in fact, seems to compliment Garnet's logic and rationality: "It was the method of Livingstone as against the method of Stanley. The former takes the braver and better man." But, could this praise be a shield for Doyle's own anxieties? For not only does Garnet's existence forcefully confront Doyle with an epistemological paradox, dismantling his own secured position as a white, patriarchal, aspiring upper-class British professional, but Doyle may have also been confronted with the potential dangers behind this realization. It would be safe to assume from the plot centering around black rebellion in "J. Habakuk Jephson's Statement," written two years after this meeting, that Doyle was aware of Garnet's radical and revolutionary ideologies on race. Famous for his abolitionist rhetoric decades prior to their meeting, Garnet called on slaves to fight for their own freedom including using such means as killing their white masters. In the conclusion to his 1843 address, Garnet declared: "Let your motto be *resistance! resistance! resistance!* No oppressed people have ever secured their liberty without resistance" (96). While this potential threat to white bodies in "J. Habakuk Jephson's Statement" is displaced via Doyle's white appropriation of the black voice, Doyle immediately dismisses the threat in the Garnet encounter with repeated references to consumption.[4] The brain is an organ for the "digestion" of other people's [thoughts], and it needs fresh fodder." The "fresh fodder" here (i.e., his realization of black intelligence and/or superiority) is too much for Doyle. Therefore, the threat of blackness must be relinquished by a metaphorical act of cannibalism. Because Garnet does not easily fit into the discourses of Manicheism prevalent during this time (a discourse that I would argue Doyle, as a scientist, at the least, is aware of and, at the most, practices), Doyle must turn to consumption to repress and oppress the threat. To consume and digest something, to chew on it until its former form and appearance is no longer recognizable, is to contain and master it, using its nutritious elements while disposing of its wastes. For Doyle (and for Owen Dudley Edwards), Garnet is nutritious in that he gives Doyle "one more experience to [his] chaplet." But, some foods are too dangerous for a complete and easy digestion. Perhaps this is why Doyle consciously excludes Garnet's name in his remembrance, a move that denies Garnet his very subjectivity. Furthermore, this castration of black subjecthood is again emphasized with Doyle's reinsertion of his own masculinity at the end of this encounter: "I was a strong full-blooded young man, full of the joy of life. . . . I was a man among men."

I introduce this study with the encounter between black and white because it illuminates the complex relationship between race and the anxiety of detection. The "fresh fodder" that Doyle desperately desires results in the *indecipherability* of blackness; in other words, Doyle's desire for intellectual stimulation ironically paralyzes his own intelligence and skills of racial cognition. Garnet is the embodiment of an epistemological paradox: he does not comfortably fit into the theories of biological determinism predominant during this time, including such theorists as Georges Cuvier, Charles Darwin, Louis Agassiz, and Cesar Lombroso, among countless others. Garnet, in fact, disrupts Doyle's prior conception of racial knowledges, or what David Theo Goldberg defines as a "sociologics and rational(izing) mode," a "dual movement" of racial science that "imparts authority and legitimation" based on the "assumption and paradigmatic establishment of difference" (148–50). It is telling, then, that shortly after this encounter, Doyle's anxiety of racial detection leads to (demands?) an entire genre known as detective fiction in which the most famous and never-failing genius detective of all time, Sherlock Holmes (whom the critic Julian Symons calls the "Superman" of all detective figures), is introduced to the literary world.[5] In many ways, the emergence of detective fiction, then, comes in direct response to the anxieties produced by a failed race detection or, I would argue, a sort of racial passing. For as Elaine K. Ginsberg argues: "Passing is about identities: their creation or imposition, their adoption or rejection, their accompanying rewards or penalties. Passing is also about the boundaries established between identity categories and about the individual and cultural anxieties induced by boundary crossing. Finally, passing is about specularity: the visible and the invisible, the seen and the unseen" (2). While Garnet is without question visibly black, he is nevertheless a passing figure for Doyle in that the former rejects the ideology that blacks are uncivilized and intellectually inferior consistently imposed upon him. Garnet, in fact, tres-passes outside of his culturally prescribed place, performing a "boundary crossing." Thus, for a split second, the black Garnet is a white man for Doyle; he is a white man in blackface. In other words, his blackness is *undetectable* in that he is Doyle's intellectual equal and perhaps even guide and mentor (at the time of their meeting, Garnet is sixty-seven years old) until Doyle *realizes* his blackness by a visual reminder. While gazing upon Garnet, what Doyle recognizes and quickly suppresses is that race is a cultural construction. Garnet's epidermal signifier of blackness does not correlate to culture's definition or signifieds. Therefore, nature does not automatically birth blacks as inferior; instead culture promotes them as such. Unfortunately, Doyle does not use this discovery to create a critical dialogue of nineteenth-century racial constructions. Instead, he represses it and within a decade produces Sherlock Holmes, a superhuman detective who reveals the "exact science" (*Sign* 108) of detection. If we read this creation in psychoanalytic terms, detective fiction may be read in some ways as the *fetish* of the passing narrative. As Freud explains in his 1927 publication of "Fetishism," the fetish is a penis substitute, a "token of triumph over the threat of castration and a safeguard against it" (216). For Doyle, then, the detective story assuages and defers the anxiety of loss (i.e., his loss of an epistemological security) that occurs in passing. If passing demonstrates the instability and fabricated nature of our epistemological foundations of race, detective fiction and Sherlock Holmes offer the potential to contain and master that anxiety.

Doyle revisits the conflict between passing and detection in the 1893 publication of "The Yellow Face," a story that combines racial passing with, again, the failure of detection. I argue that this seemingly innocuous short story symbolizes the height of the modernist anxiety of race detection because it depicts the intersection of both passing and detection where knowing/not knowing, seeing/mis-seeing, security/chaos collide to dismantle previous conceptions and expectations of racial knowledges. I am aware that earlier examples of both passing and detection exist prior to the Sherlock Holmes stories.[6] However, "The Yellow Face" is the first story I am aware of where both the genres of detective fiction and the passing narrative unite to introduce a self-proclaimed professional detector of crime with the passing "criminal."[7] Significantly, this meeting opens the literary debate about race and detection, foreshadowing much of the twentieth century's central concerns around issues of multiculturalism, hybridity, and identity politics. Some of the questions addressed in this story include: How do we see race? Why do we see race the way we do? What does this way of seeing race reveal about the constructions of our own subjectivity? What are the consequences of undetecting racial markers? As a result, "The Yellow Face" is the literary site to which future anxieties of passing and detection refer, respond, and diverge. If, for example, Sherlock Holmes and Lucy Hebron (the passer in "The Yellow Face") are the archetypal detector and passer, respectively, how do these two figures define and construct the dynamics of the detection of race? How do their twentieth-century offspring complicate and revise race detection? While this study may not address all of these concerns, I hope my examination will commence the debate. But before examining "The Yellow Face" and its influence in detail, I will first briefly summarize the role of racial science in an understanding of nineteenth-century racial politics as well as its impact upon Doyle as both scientist and author. Then I will explore how Doyle utilizes the authority of scientific discourse in some of his previously unexamined writings of blackness (i.e., his ethnographic essays). Finally, I will conclude with a close reading of "The Yellow Face," a little tale of mystery that ignites the complicated tensions between passing and detection into the twentieth century.

Race-ing the Visible

In order to better understand the constructions of racial difference in the nineteenth century, it is crucial to grasp the historical context of racial science prevalent during this time. Racial science became the scientific schema of seeing and categorizing race, focusing on the visual detection of differences. As Nancy Stepan argues, scientific inquiry and the categorization or detection of human "types" go hand in hand. During the late eighteenth and early part of the nineteenth centuries, the hierarchization of different human types into species justified arguments for colonialism and slavery. A racial science developed to "objectively" and "factually" explain the "natural" inferiority of blacks and Native Americans to Europeans, differentiating the moral, intellectual, and physical worth of each group. But, as both Stepan and Stephen Jay Gould contend, "objective" science was often produced by subjective, racist methodologies and tampered data.[8] In *The Mismeasure of Man*, a study of biological determinism, Gould reveals that "objective" science is a socially constructed reality: "Science must be understood as a social phenomenon, a gutsy human enterprise, not the work of robots programmed to collect pure information" (53). Furthermore, because science is a "socially embedded activity," it "progresses by hunch, vision, and intuition. . . . Facts are not pure and unsullied bits of information; culture also influences what we see and how we see it. Theories, moreover, are not inexorable inductions from facts. The most creative theories are often imaginative visions imposed upon facts; the source of imagination is also strongly cultural" (54). It is this imagination that produced the blackening of white races as well, specifically the Irish and the Jews. While epidermically white, both Irish and Jews were observed to have "negroid" characteristics that rendered them as biologically and, therefore, naturally inferior.[9] Thus, as a socially constructed phenomenon within a society promoting white supremacy, scientific racism quickly turned into a sort of "scavenger ideology" (Stepan xix), relying on visual markers to detect and confirm inferiority and degeneration. The scientific studies that were relied upon to elucidate the "innate" differences between the races included craniometry, criminal anthropology, and phrenology. As a result, the maintenance of hegemonic discourse prospered under the authority of scientific law. Now science was able to use the law of nature to justify the economic, legal, and moral disenfranchisement of nonwhites. As Stepan claims, "the history of racial science is a history of a series of accommodations of the sciences to the demands of deeply held convictions about the 'naturalness' of the inequalities between the human races" (xxi).

Arthur Conan Doyle was well aware of the discourse of scientific racism during this period. In fact, not only was Doyle a medical doctor, but critics and biographers alike (including Rosemary Jann, Martin Booth, and Owen Dudley Edwards) have revealed the impact of Dr. Joseph Bell during Doyle's early medical training. As Doyle reveals in his autobiography, Bell's expertise as a doctor, specifically his skills of diagnosing patients, was central to the birth and characterization of Sherlock Holmes: "I thought of my old teacher Joe Bell, of his eagle face, of his curious ways, of his eerie trick of spotting details. If he were a detective he would surely reduce this fascinating but unorganized business to something nearer to an exact science. I would try if I could get this effect" (*Memories and Adventures* 69). For Bell, the "exact science" of doctoring included not only a physical examination but a close scrutiny into the entire aura and existence of the patient as well. Doyle's biographer, Martin Booth, explains Bell's philosophy: "It was Bell's dictum that a doctor had to be not only learned but also immensely interpretive of all relevant features of a patient. Diagnosis, he taught, was not made just by visual observation but also by the employment of all the senses: do not just look at a patient, he advised, but feel him, probe him, listen to him, smell him. Only then could a diagnosis be attempted" (50). For Bell, finding the cure for a disease or malady heavily depends upon not only the physical symptoms but an examination into the whole environment surrounding the patient such as his/her occupation, living conditions, diet and habits, etc. Here, the doctor must play detective, searching into these possible causes in order to obtain the cure or solution. What is significant in Bell's method is that medical science, specifically the detection of the physical body that is central to this study, is a type of systematized knowledge. Clues are gathered from not only natural or biological signs but also cultural ones to explain the nature of the subject being studied. The danger here, of course, is the potential that stereotypical and biased "evidence" can be used to explain nature's "truths."

Holmes's reliance upon scientific authority in his deductive skills is displayed in stories such as "The Boscombe Valley Mystery," *The Sign of Four*, "The Adventure of the Blue Carbuncle," and *A Study in Scarlet*. The recourse to an "exact science" is, according to some critics, a specific response to the anxieties uprooted by modernity. As Rosemary Jann observes in *The Adventures of Sherlock Holmes: Detecting Social Order*, Holmes's recourse to science as "elementary" is an act that performs the *illusion* of rationalism and logic during his fin-de-siècle moment. Jann further explains that this was a "period overshadowed by fears of cultural decadence and increasing fragmentation" (6). Amid these fears, Holmes's use of the certainty of science, with the aid of Lombrosian theories of criminal pathology, reassured his readers that "dangers [could be] contained, order restored, and values reaffirmed" (6). As William Greenslade further explains, it is the intrinsic combination of fiction and science that quenched readers' anxieties about their ever-changing world. Safe narratives such as the detective story or the scientific "tale" of biological determinism restored stability, normalcy, and predictability. They "invited a wholehearted response to narratives of control, where the inspected deviant subject is appropriated by an equally confident display of diagnostic acumen" (102). Critics of detective fiction reiterate the societal need to reinsert control by placing that responsibility upon the detective figure. In fact, critics such as R. Gordon Kelly claim that the rise of detective fiction occurred specifically as a response to the anxieties produced by modernity, such as the distrust and alienation caused by increased urbanization, mass migration, and an influx of immigration. Because trusting and having confidence in others have become radically destabilized in the modern world, Kelly argues, the function of the detective is to restore stability by displaying skills of "know[ing] the other better than the other is allowed to know the detective" (29). This asymmetrical relationship of power "enables the detective to identify, unmask, and entrap the other [while] simultaneously permit[ting] the detective to survive in a tricky and dangerous world of predators" (29). But, as Kelly also states, while Holmes has heterogeneous stores of encyclopedic knowledge, "much of what Holmes knows has to do with the habitual, the customary, the typical, the usual, the probable, or the 'natural'" (41). Thus, Holmes's detective skills depend upon a knowledge of "norms" or stereotypes of group behavior. Doyle's focus, then, is to make stereotypes seem natural and logical, which, in turn, creates comfort. As Jann writes, we find Holmes's methods of detection so attractive because they "systematize[ ] our own often unconscious assumptions that people can be judged by appearances" (58).

What passing narratives such as "The Yellow Face" demonstrate, however, is that appearances, especially racial markers, can no longer be presumed or systematized, overturning the asymmetrical relationship of power between detector and detected. But, before analyzing this story, I would like to explore some of Doyle's surprisingly ignored ethnographic writings published prior to "The Yellow Face." These writings demonstrate how Doyle's racial anxieties upon meeting Garnet produced a set of essays sanctioned by the scientific authority of ethnography. Doyle wrote these representative portraits of Africa and Africans during the same time he met Garnet. As such, they may give us a better understanding not only of Garnet's impact upon Doyle but the sustained anxieties of race that later culminate in the publication of "The Yellow Face."

African Outings

While Doyle is generally known as the creator of Sherlock Holmes, it may be surprising to his fans as well as to scholars and critics of ethnic studies that Doyle, in fact, represented black bodies quite frequently during and after his encounter with Garnet. Black bodies hover over every aspect of Doyle's writings, including journalistic essays, novels, short stories, and, finally, the Sherlock Holmes tales. Surprisingly, however, little critical attention has been paid to Doyle's ethnographic essays. Doyle wrote these articles for the *British Journal of Photography* to accompany the photographs of his voyage to West Africa. Writing a total of approximately a dozen articles between 1881 and 1885, Doyle wrote three articles specifically about Africa and its natives. Under the new editorship of W. B. Bolton, the *British Journal of Photography* was beginning a new series entitled "Where to Go with the Camera," a sort of ethnographic photographic essay or, as the editor of *Anthony's Photographic Bulletin* in

America called it, "outings."[10] In his first article on Africa, entitled "On the Slave Coast with a Camera," Doyle reveals a different perspective to his epistemological crisis described earlier with Garnet. Here, what Doyle undergoes is a war of representation with Africa itself. Perhaps it is both this struggle as well as his crisis with Garnet that provoke him to begin the article with the following warning: "I do not suppose that there is any reader of THE BRITISH JOURNAL OF PHOTOGRAPHY who is meditating a journey to the West Coast of Africa. If such there be, and he has any option in the matter, let me impress upon him *Punch*'s time-honored advice before matrimony—'Don't'" (13). Although this journey turns out to be ultimately a negative experience for Doyle, he reveals that it did not begin that way. Immediately following the warning, Doyle reveals the expectations and hopes he had before embarking on his travels:

> It was with a light heart that I packed up my boxes about the middle of October, and set out for Liverpool to join my vessel. There was a charm about the great list of ports at which we were advertised to call. . . . I had a beatific vision of strange negatives. The luxuriant growth of the African forest; the haughty grace of the untamed savage as he trod his native wilderness, or yearned in his simple untutored way for a slice out of the calf of your leg; the mighty rivers and the cloud-capped mountains—all these should be transferred to the tell-tale paper and be a record among countless generations yet unborn of the adventurous spirit of their ancestors. Such were a few of my milder aspirations. (13)

What is surprising about this article is that while Doyle (as a combination ethnographer and travel guide) warns against making an "outing" to Africa, he spends very little time in the rest of the article explaining exactly why. It is presumably the heat, the hurricane, and the sickness aboard ship that Doyle, ironically, dismissively mentions. In his autobiography, Doyle does describe becoming overwhelmed at the "death-like impression of Africa": "One felt that the white man with his present diet and habits was an intruder who was never meant to be there, and that the great sullen brown continent killed him as one crushes nits" (*Memories and Adventures* 48). For Doyle, Africa is, in essence, geographical designations that foretell the outcome for the white visitor. Sierra Leone, he tells his readers, is "The White Man's Grave," while Cape Palmas is known as "The Cannibal Coast." It is not surprising, then, that what Doyle fights for within this spiritual grave of whiteness is the constant maintenance of white subjectivity within a Self/Other binary. Instead of describing the "luxuriant growth of the African forest" or even the "untamed[, cannibalistic] savage[s]" he thought he would see, Doyle's article meditates upon the struggle of representation between the West/Africa, civilized/uncivilized, colonizer/colonized, ethnographer/native. The struggle occurs between Africa as the site that contests representation by the outside eye/lens and the prospective historian/ethnographer—Doyle—who yearns for eternal infamy "among countless generations" as a result of his skills of representation. Or, if examined within a colonialist context, Doyle reveals his own "fascinating cannibalism" of blackness, or what Fatimah Tobing Rony defines as the "fascination and horror . . . of the consumers of the images of the bodies—as well as actual bodies on display—of native peoples offered up by popular media and science" (10). While Doyle may be adamant about the attractive qualities of Africa as a tourist destination, he displays his hunger and desire for black bodies through his continued obsession with the devouring of blackness via photography. Like his need for containment through consumption expressed in his account of his meeting with Garnet, photographic consumption is what enables Doyle to maintain his mastery and subjectivity within a world that constantly shifts and destabilizes that position.

Initially, it appears as if this first article somewhat exhaustively progresses from a bland description of the instruments of representation (the lens, the tripod, chemicals used for development, etc.) to Doyle's methods of representation itself. Upon closer examination, however, what Doyle articulates is the constant struggle between the photographer and his tools with the object of the photographic gaze. Even Africa itself seems to reject any attempts from the outside world to eternalize it and its inhabitants within the photographic image. From the beginning, Doyle explains how he must be very careful of what to pack for his voyage, keeping in mind how harsh weather and travel can easily destroy the camera as well as the impossibility of accessing certain "refinements as photographic necessities" (Gibson and Green 14) on African soil. As a result, Doyle uses this opportunity to give his advice as an experienced and expert traveler/photographer: "It may be of interest to some other unfortunate wanderer to know the conclusions at which I arrived, and how far they were justified by my subsequent experience" (14). His "subsequent experience," it turns out, is rejection from a native prince. It would not be far-fetched to claim that Doyle was proud of his skills and knowledge of photography. His pride and joy in his abilities linger throughout the article. What is disturbing is that this Western art is used to ridicule and shock the African natives. As Doyle reveals, "I had a great desire to 'astonish the natives' by representations of their own hideous faces" (16). Here, to "astonish the natives," to demonstrate to them their own cultural ignorance and lack of worldly sophistication through a mirrored image of their own "hideous[ness]," is to promote white superiority on multiple levels. For Doyle, photography is used to perpetuate the Manichean binary of civilized/uncivilized. That he had a "great desire" to do so perhaps hints at, within a psychoanalytic reading, some anxiety within his own psyche. Just what this anxiety stems from may be revealed through his simultaneous encounter with Garnet as well as other discomforting moments during the journey through Africa. We discover a clue when Doyle further elaborates upon his thoughts on the "hideous faces" later in the article: "A great deal has been said about the regeneration of our black brothers and the latent virtues of the swarthy races. My own experience is that you abhor them on first meeting them, and gradually learn to dislike them a very great deal more as you become better acquainted with them" (19). While it is not exactly clear to what experience Doyle is alluding here, he does describe a revealing instance when he takes a picture of a native prince: "I had the privilege, while at Duke Town, of taking the portrait of a native prince. His highness did me the honour of informing me that it was wonderfully unlike him. The delight of his retinue, however, at seeing the ugliness of their lord so faithfully represented more than assuaged my wounded photographic feelings. It was an excellent likeness; but the monarch probably missed the smell of premature putridity which was so characteristic of the original, and yet could not be transferred to paper" (21).

What occurs in this point of contact between African and British is the struggle over representation. The native prince rejects not only the picture that is "wonderfully unlike him" but also Doyle's authority of representability. In other words, the native prince's rejection of Doyle is a rejection of the colonizing gesture Doyle is attempting. As Rony explains in *The Third Eye: Race, Cinema, and Ethnographic Spectacle,* photography was crucial to the ethnographic project of the nineteenth century: "Photography was used in both anthropological and geographical learned societies, especially in constructing racial types, photographed in left and right profile and head-on" (33). Photography, Rony continues, is a sort of "taxidermy" (89) used to describe the "ethnographiable" Savage as a "people without history, without writing, without civilization, without technology, without archives" (7). Rony also describes Félix-Louis Regnault's use of chronophotographie, or time-motion studies, to decipher the movements of the black body, including such titles as "Jump by Three Negroes," "Negress Walks," and "Three Clothed Men Walk." According to Rony, Regnault "believed that those he called Savage had no language, and instead spoke through the body in what he called *le langage par gestes*" (57). Thus, the "Ethnographic Body [becomes] a hieroglyph to be made sense of by scientists able to find the key to the *langage par gestes*" (62). What the native prince rejects here is the hieroglyphic status imposed upon him by Doyle the ethnographer/scientist. By claiming that the photograph is very "unlike him," the native prince emphasizes the impossibility of knowing the "real" him through pictorial representation. He refuses representation and, thereby, refuses the position as the ethnographiable subject. In turn, Doyle's response is quite similar to his response to the epistemological crisis encountered with Garnet. In order to assuage his "wounded photographic feelings," Doyle, like a little schoolboy, dismisses the attack upon his authority by immediately ridiculing the native prince's "putrid" smell. This rhetorical move not only returns the prince to the status of uncivilized Savage, but it also reclaims Doyle's jeopardized status of authority. Here, Doyle implies that some elements of savagery are so vile and grotesque that even technology and the most skilled of photographers cannot capture it.

In "Up an African River with the Camera," Doyle's second essay about Africa, he continues the portrayals of his "outings" in a more direct and offensive manner. While the first article illustrates the somewhat subtle tensions within the dynamics of representation, this second article displays, literally and metaphorically, the more active and rigorous attack upon Africa and its natives. The article begins with a telling "Bang!" that foreshadows the tone of Africa-as-game for the rest of the article. During a moment of leisure (it is a holiday, and the Africans "won't do a stroke of work" [23]), Doyle and some of the crew decide to take a cruise up the river. With camera and guns in hand, Doyle and the crewmen, respectively, wait for "every prospect of game" (25). This parallel game of photography and wildlife hunting, it turns out, is a "shooting" competition of sorts:

> I am mildly chaffing my companions on having drawn first blood, when their artillery opens with a roar, and a couple of gorgeous kingfishers, light blue and green, come fluttering down the river. We pass a native woman drifting down in her canoe, with a basket of palm nuts for the traders at Old Calabar. I put up the rapid lens and shutter, focus for "distance," and resume the lead by

> transferring the swarthy dame to the tell-tale plate; but the Captain equalises matters by the death of a magnificent squirrel, and the purser knocks over a bird resembling a snipe with a very long shot, which became longer every subsequent occasion on which he narrated the anecdote. (25–26)

It may be helpful to remember Garnet's earlier observation here. As he declares to an admiring Doyle: "The only way to explore Africa is to go without arms and with few servants. You would not like it in England if a body of men came armed to the teeth and marched through your land. The Africans are quite as sensitive." Doyle seems to have forgotten or dismissed this advice for what is disturbing here is that both wildlife and African natives are "game" for Doyle and his crewmen. In fact, within this narrative of gaming conquests, there seems to be little distinction between shooting kingfishers, squirrels, and birds and "shooting" native women. The distinction between the shotgun and the camera is blurred; they are similar tools in this parallel expedition—both are used to aim at and shoot the object of the gaze.

In "With a Camera on an African River," Doyle's final article about Africa, even the crocodiles mistake the camera for a rifle: "We turn our camera on him [the crocodile] and are about to perpetuate his charms, but he looks up, sees what he no doubt considers to be the latest invention in fire-arms turned in his direction, and at once shuffles off into the yellow stream" (80). More significantly, both gun and camera also signify a sense of capture and/or death of the object of focus. As Roland Barthes writes in *Camera Lucida: Reflections on Photography*, photographs do not reveal the life of the subject but, instead, the death of the subject-turned-object:"Photography transformed subject into object, and even, one might say, into a museum object . . . but when I discover myself in the product of this operation, what I see is that I have become Total-Image, which is to say, Death in person. . . . Death is the *eidos* of that Photograph" (13–15). Or, as Christian Metz writes in "Photography and Fetish," photography has a deeply rooted kinship with death. The "snapshot, like death, is an instantaneous abduction of the object out of the world into another world, into another kind of time. . . . The photographic take is immediate and definitive, like death" (84). Whether it is "perpetrat[ing the crocodile's] charms or "shooting" the native woman and transferring her ghostly image upon the "tell-tale plate," photography acts as a colonizing and metaphorical death here, robbing Africa and Africans of their subjectivity, their history, and their individuality.

However, as in the earlier article, photography is also used as the site of struggle between the colonized African and the white colonizer. While Doyle dismisses the Africans' ignorant gaze as "untutored" and "undeveloped," what this article reveals is that the act of seeing is culturally constructed. As such, Africans reject the camera as the tool that "captures" reality as well as the European method of seeing:

> It is curious to see the effect which a photograph has upon the perfectly-untutored mind. I have frequently observed it on the coast when showing natives prints of places with which they were familiar from their infancy. A portrait would be hailed with roars of delight; but landscape was a dead letter among them, and I have never known a savage recognize a place from its representation. Appreciation of perspective seems to be entirely a matter of training and cultivation. The savage eye sees a large hut and a small one in the picture before it, but the undeveloped brain fails to draw the inference that the small one is small because it is further away. Children and artists in the early days of art always depicted every object as being on the same plane. I have frequently observed in Africa that the first thing a native does when you show him a landscape is to turn it round and look at the other side of it. What the exact object of this manoeuvre may be I do not pretend to know, but the action is so unvarying and universal—whether among Kroomen, Mandingoes, Houssars, Ashantees, or any other tribe—that there must be the same good reason for it. Oliver Wendell Holmes formulated the proposition that every equal brain with similar factors to work on will evolve the same product, and the remark seems to hold good among the wild tribes of the coast. (26–27)

What is important to note in this description is that within one big rhetorical move, Doyle reiterates the rhetoric of biological determinism to "prove" the undeveloped and atavistic qualities of Africans. They are like children in their ignorance, reacting with "roars of delight" as well as dumbstruck paralysis. Thus, Doyle again displays the African as the "ethnographiable" subject—they are without time or history, subjects still frozen within the evolutionary past.

The Little Girl Who Stumps Sherlock Holmes

While the previous sections illustrate how Garnet and Africa(ns) may have affected Doyle in his struggle with race politics, I now want to direct attention to a little story that in many ways revisits and illustrates Doyle's continuing anxiety with the epistemology of blackness. If the experience with Garnet confronts Doyle with the disruption between the signifier and signified on an intellectual level, then "The Yellow Face" shows how the epistemology of blackness is further complicated by the breakdown of race on a visual level. Doyle will probably always be remembered as the creator of the international father of detection. Sherlock Homes, perhaps the most famous of detectives ever created, has the reputation of never failing at his detective prowess and is labeled by many as the "Superman" of all detectives. But, is Holmes ever confronted by failure? At the height of his popularity, the self-proclaimed "last and highest court of appeal in detection" (*Sign* 108) experiences one of his few failures and does so, remarkably, due to a little girl named Lucy Hebron. What Holmes discovers in "The Yellow Face" (first published in the *Strand Magazine* in 1893) is the collapse of racial knowledges. Unlike earlier cases such as *The Sign of Four*, Holmes now discovers that race is not easily accessible through a scientific categorization (such as anthropology) and refuses systematization. While Holmes's earlier recourse to science almost always leads to successful detections, he discovers that in detecting race, he is introduced to a redefinition of racial knowledges at this fin-de-siècle moment, a historical period that witnessed the continuing rise of the indecipherability of racial distinctions. This story demonstrates that prior knowledges of "clear" and "normal" distinctions of race are no longer dependable. Due to increased rates of amalgamation and the rise of light-skinned blacks, the recognition and detection of race is no longer a rational, obvious occurrence; in other words, bodily markers do not necessarily result in expected racial identities. Holmes's skills of detection in this case prove to be quite limited and confined, closing off other possibilities and solutions. For him as well as the majority of his Victorian audience, race is clearly distinct and categorizable, labeled by visible markers such as hair texture, skin and eye color, and half moons on fingernails.[11] What "The Yellow Face" demonstrates, then, is that socially constructed definitions of race neither adhere to nor account for black/white indistinctions. As it turns out, the father of detection is a master detective only within a very narrow and limited framework. Here, what Holmes discovers and is forced to confront is that certain "clues" are not easily or instinctually classifiable.

In "Sherlock Holmes and the Case of Race," Henry Cuningham claims that while "The Yellow Face" "ranks among some of the poorer in the Sherlock Holmes canon when viewed strictly as a detective story," it nevertheless is "half-a-century ahead of its time" when "delivering a didactic message on racial attitudes" (113). Cuningham's praise of Doyle is, I believe, presumptuous and not carefully enough examined. It is true that when Lucy's blackness and Effie's miscegenation are discovered, Munro, after "a long ten minutes" (493), ultimately accepts them. As Munro declares to Effie, "I am not a very good man, Effie, but I think that I am a better one than you have given me credit for being" (493). Miscegenation, commonly thought of as "criminal" in American law, is rewritten here to be clearly not so within a more liberal British context. Holmes, here, questions definitions of "crime" as well as the legal versus ethical actions of the policers of law.[12] What may be a legal and ethical crime in America is, on British land, morally permissible. However, there is still a sense of uneasiness at the end of this story. Even Holmes senses this when he says to Watson, "if it should ever strike you that I am getting a little overconfident in my powers, or giving less pains to a case than it deserves, kindly whisper 'Norbury' [the site of the plot] in my ear, and I shall be infinitely obliged to you" (493). But what remains so disturbing even with the happy ending of interracial unity? Why does Doyle choose racial undetection as one of the few moments of Holmes's failure? While it is true that Doyle did demonstrate concern for racial justice (such as his campaign against the racism experienced by George Edalji, a Parsee who was wrongfully accused of slander and animal mutilation, as well as his condemnation of the Belgian exploitation of the Congo), I contend that "The Yellow Face" cannot be fully understood without acknowledging the complexities of the racial politics of this time. As such, Doyle's tale of racial undetection is not only a direct response to the rapid rise of passing incidents that were evident in both fiction and fact during this historical period, but it is also a "tribute" or a remembering of his experience with Garnet a decade earlier. My focus here is to examine how Doyle chooses to remember that moment, one that resulted in a breakdown of Doyle's epistemological foundations of race. As revealed in "The Yellow Face," Doyle's anxiety of racial knowledges is still haunting his psyche almost a decade after his initial collision.

Perhaps in "The Yellow Face," Doyle was responding to the phenomenon of passing that was becoming increasingly popular in postbellum and post-Reconstruction America, especially since he discussed American race politics with Garnet years earlier. Central to early slave narratives such as William Craft's *Running a Thousand Miles for Freedom or The Escape of William and Ellen Craft from Slavery* (1860), racial passing became not only an economic threat (due to the loss of slaves) but undermined the institution of slavery as a whole. How could blackness be used to justify enslavement, especially according to religious arguments, when the distinction between black and white could no longer be made? William Craft cunningly plays with the potential threat of passing and the instability of color distinctions in the beginning of his narrative when he reveals the multiple instances of *white* children kidnapped into slavery by "passing" as light-skinned blacks: "It may be remembered that slavery in America is not at all confined to persons of any particular complexion; there are a very large number of slaves as white as anyone; but as the evidence of a slave is not admitted in court against a free white person, it is almost impossible for a white child, after having been kidnapped and sold into or reduced to slavery, in a part of the country where it is not known (as often is the case), ever to recover its freedom" (271–72). In a smart use of the irrationality of the ideological apparatus governing slavery, Craft shows here the potential dangers of equating race with visibility for both blacks and whites. In addition to Craft's narrative, a canon of racial passing began to emerge upon the American literary landscape to further threaten the stability of racial knowledges. According to Werner Sollors, although acts of American racial passing generally emerged during slavery, the phenomenon was highly popular at the turn of the century and during Doyle's popularity. Some well-known examples published during the same time as "The Yellow Face" include: George Washington Cable's *The Grandissimes* (1879), William Dean Howells's *An Imperative Duty* (1891), Frances E. W. Harper's *Iola Leroy* (1892), Kate Chopin's "The Father of Désirée's Baby" (1893), and Mark Twain's *Pudd'nhead Wilson* (1894), among many others.

In light of such passing narratives like *Running a Thousand Miles for Freedom*, I read "The Yellow Face" as a literary response to the very real threat of the consequences of passing for white subjectivity. As Craft's narrative shows, the possibility that not only blacks but whites are suffering as a result of the Manichean division created by slavery is suggested. It is one thing to enslave blacks who *look* white, but quite another to enslave whites themselves. Furthermore, passing demonstrates not only the impossibility of detecting blackness but whiteness as well. As a result, "The Yellow Face" attempts to recuperate this anxiety by undermining the act of passing itself.

"The Yellow Face" is a story of a happily married man, Grant Munro, who suddenly finds himself estranged from his wife of three years, Effie. Munro tells Holmes that when he first met Effie, she was a widow whose husband and child had died of yellow fever in Atlanta.[13] The mystery begins when Effie makes an unusual request for a large sum of money. Soon afterward, new neighbors move into a cottage near the Munro residence, one of whom Munro describes as "unnatural and inhuman . . . [with a face] of livid chalky white" (483). Later, Munro discovers Effie sneaking off in the middle of the night, and subsequently he witnesses Effie making multiple visits to this cottage. When Munro follows Effie on one of her excursions, he discovers that the house is empty, but he sees a photograph of Effie on the mantelpiece. As a result, Munro turns to Holmes, believing that the detective is a "man of the world" (480). Upon hearing Munro's narrative, Holmes concludes that Effie is a bigamist who is being blackmailed by her deceiving former husband. Holmes, however, is proven quite wrong. In truth, we discover that the "livid" face at the window is not that of a blackmailing husband but, instead, that of Effie's young, black daughter, Lucy, who is in disguise. A product of miscegenation (Effie's former husband was black), the yellow face at the window is, in fact, a "coal-black negress" (491) passing for white.

Prior to the revelation, what is fascinating about Holmes's hypothesis is his elaborate and entirely imagined construction of what he *thinks* may have happened. In his imagination, Holmes has fabricated a scenario in which Effie's former husband is not only alive, but is a blackmailer: "Her husband developed some hateful qualities, or shall we say he contracted some loathsome disease and became a leper or an imbecile?" (489). Therefore, according to Holmes's imagination, Effie is fleeing from Hebron and her identity by taking the name of "some man whose name she has assumed" (489). (This relinquishing of her old identity for a new one can be read as a sort of passing, one that becomes racialized by one critic's theory that I will discuss below.) Effie's new whereabouts are discovered by Hebron or, as Holmes interestingly suspects, "some unscrupulous woman who has attached herself to the invalid" (489). After numerous attempts of pleading with her former husband, Effie fails and is then discovered by Munro. According to Holmes, this theory, though "all surmise" to Watson, "covers all the facts" (490). More importantly, after Munro decides to again "force [his] way in[to the cottage]" (490), Holmes declares that "any truth is better than indefinite doubt" (490). The fear of "indefinite doubt" is, not surprisingly, quickly quenched when we discover Effie's real past. But what is important to note about the disparity between Holmes's elaborate fantasy of Effie's past to the "real" story is that, in actuality, the distinction is not all that different. While Effie is not being literally blackmailed by her former husband, she is in many ways forever haunted by her association with him, a "black male." The blackmail of the black male is, then, a sort of "tainting" of Effie's blood. Because she is sexually associated with and contaminated by blackness, she is essentially held in custody as a result. That Holmes equates the "black male" with the "hateful qualities" of blackmail is also telling in light of the discourse of criminal anthropology mentioned earlier that claims criminality as an innate quality of blackness (see Lombroso). Hence, Holmes's fantasy that Hebron was "diseased" is, again, not too far off considering that as a black man Hebron was probably marginalized as the "abject," unfit for white society. Furthermore, Effie and John Hebron were not only a (seemingly) legalized couple of miscegenation (something that critics have noted was quite uncommon if at all possible), but they blatantly disrupted the gender and racial "norms" of miscegenation at this time. Unlike the numerous examples of white male/black female unions (most of which are disturbingly common in slave narratives), Effie is a white woman who marries a black man, breaking not only the "cult of true womanhood" but the sexual taboo against black men fornicating with white women. As such, it would not be surprising that the Hebron family itself was considered "lepers" in their community, a family that was hated, feared, and rejected due to their blatant nonconformity to societal expectations and demands. Therefore, Holmes's extravagant and fantastic theory is, in actuality, not all that far-fetched.

What is interesting, however, is how Doyle creates a narrative plot that superficially seems revolutionary (due to Munro's acceptance of Lucy, which results in a happy ending) but is actually a shield that veils and displaces white, patriarchal anxieties of racial detection. In many ways, then, "The Yellow Face" not only is the primal scene for the narratives of racial detection to follow, but it also introduces miscegenation and its potential passing offspring as the site of forbidden origins. In other words, miscegenation is the forbidden primal scene, one that threatens to castrate whiteness with the promise of potentially passing offspring. While Doyle nervously displays the threat, he also quickly relinquishes it by utilizing two safeguards. First, by configuring the passer as a little girl (perhaps as a metaphorical and literary castration of Garnet?), Doyle foreshadows much of the narrative plot of passing narratives in the twentieth century. Initially, detective fiction and the passing narrative seem to be on opposite sides of the issue. The central theme of detective fiction is the detection of truth while the passing narrative is the role of undetection or the constant evasion of truth. But what is ultimately revealed is their surprisingly similar and conservative configurations of racial knowledges or the discursive construction of race and the circulation of racial "truths." In detective fiction, the types of knowledges that are accessible or denied are highly dependent upon the detective's race, gender, class, sexuality, and nationality. Contrary to Holmes's claim, then, detection is *not* an "exact science." Similarly, narratives of passing also perpetuate and reinforce essentialist arguments. Because the majority of the passing narratives conclude with unhappy endings,[14] these narratives ultimately promote the inescapability of one's "real" and biological/natural identity; this is the narrative desire of the passing plot. In "The Yellow Face," for example, while Holmes fails in his detection, Lucy's blackness is still discovered at the end of the story. More significantly, the passing, it turns out, is only a "passing fancy"; unmasked, Lucy's hyperbolic blackness is safely revealed, returning her to her "rightful" identity (like Twain's Tom in *Pudd'nhead Wilson*). Thus, the passing genre reads like the detective genre without the detective. The crime of passing is self-solving, and nature wins out in the end, even without a successful detective figure. Like the detective story, the passing narrative utilizes its stories to place "criminals" or (tres)passers of society in their rightfully raced place. In Doyle's story, what is "safe" about Lucy's act of racial passing as well as Holmes's failure is that Lucy's race is ultimately detectable and visible. The hybrid body here is a nonthreat and, in essence, is not passing at all, resulting in a "safe ending."[15]

Secondly, the quenching of white anxiety is also revealed in the title "The *Yellow* Face." What is the significance of the title that focuses on a "yellow" face rather than the "livid white" one described in the story? This might just be an error on Doyle's part, but could it also refer to something else? For example, "yellow" could be a reference to the mulatto skin tone. As Doyle mentions in "J. Habakuk Jephson's Statement," Septimius Goring is the product of a white master/black slave union. As such, Goring is described as having a complexion of "sickly, unhealthy yellow" (88). Although Doyle describes Lucy as being "coal-black," this reference to yellowness suggests a struggle of racial representation, specifically race as visual code, throughout this story. "Yellow" could also refer to the yellow fever from which Lucy may have died (like her father). Or, in a linking of disease to miscegenation, "yellow" could also refer to the unnaturalness or the diseased consequence of black/white unions. Finally, "yellow," while referring specifically to a type of Orientalist taint, could also refer to colonization in general as a "dis-ease" resulting from England's colonization of America and Africa. This is a theme that Doyle often treats in his writings, such as Effie's tragic experience in America or the greed and corruption resulting from African trade displayed in *The Firm of Girdlesone: A Romance of the Unromantic* (1890). While we may never know the exact reference, I suggest that it could also be an allusion to Doyle's anxiety about Lucy's passing for white. For Lucy must not be associated with whiteness in any way. This is supported in the narrative via three methods: (1) she is described as "coal-black" even though she is a product of miscegenation; (2) the threat of her passing for white is ultimately discovered and quenched; and (3) the title refers to her "yellow" mask, not white. Here, the fear of passing for white is so great that whiteness becomes dismissed and/or replaced with yellowness, a signifier for taboo unions (miscegenation), disease (yellow fever), and colonization (as Orientalist taint).

Although Doyle buries his fears of racial detection, the safe ending is reached only after the tension between knowing and not knowing is displayed throughout "The Yellow Face." In fact, it is this anxiety that drives the plot from beginning to end. Watson's disclaimer in the preface illustrates that this anxiety of knowing is also what silently serves as the catalyst as well as censor for our introduction to the Holmes canon. As he reveals, Holmes fails in many more cases than we are able to witness: "It is only natural that I should dwell rather upon his successes than upon his failures. And this not so much for the sake of his reputation . . . but because where he failed it happened too often that no one else succeeded, and that the tale was left forever without a conclusion . . . even when he erred the truth was still discovered" (477). But why is it "only natural" to display the successes rather than the failures? In his explanation, Watson desperately yet unsuccessfully tries to evade the reason for this censoring ("And this not so much for the sake of his reputation") by emphasizing Holmes's skills of detection *even in* moments of failure. Although Holmes does fail, Watson claims, no one else succeeds over him. As such, Holmes's powers of detection are the ultimate and final recourse. Perhaps it is this anxiety of detective failure that necessitates that almost all the Holmes stories begin with displays of detective genius. For example, in "The Yellow Face," Holmes does not disappoint readers when, upon merely gazing at John Hebron's pipe, he is able to deduce (prior to even meeting Hebron) that he is a "muscular man, left-handed, with an excellent set of teeth, careless in his habits, and with no need to practice economy" (479). What these immediate displays of skill demonstrate is not Holmes's detective prowess per se but rather his nervous fear of maintaining his status as "Superman" detective. In a sense, it is the repetition of these awesome detective skills in the beginning of each story that results in the heightening of the Holmesian reputation. In some ways, then, these opening demonstrations of detection reveal that it doesn't matter if he fails in some cases; his powers are still unmatched. In the detection of race, however, while Holmes's failure of detection is somewhat displaced by the narrative desire of the passing plot ("truth was still discovered"), he is still left with a sense of nervousness and discomfort at the breakdown of his detective skills. In other words, while the plot device may attempt to shield the anxiety of racial detection with a satisfying ending, the shadows of racial anxiety still haunt Holmes and, as we will see, twentieth-century discourses of race and detection.

It is this very anxiety of not knowing that is the catalyst for Munro turning to Holmes. In fact, "The Yellow Face" is a story about multilayered secrets (namely domestic secrets), the public versus the private, and the forbidden and taboo. As Munro states before giving his narrative: "It seems dreadful to discuss the conduct of one's wife with two men whom I have never seen before. It's horrible to have to do it" (480). In response, Holmes comforts Munro by telling him that the uncovering of secrets, especially "strange secrets," is his expertise: "My friend and I have listened to a good many strange secrets in this room, and . . . we have had the good fortune to bring peace of many troubled souls" (480). It is the "strange secret" of Effie's past that creates the rift between husband and wife. As Munro declares, "there's this secret between us, and we can never be the same until it is cleared" (481). Unbeknownst to Munro, the "secret" is of a domestic nature and one that is forbidden and taboo, namely miscegenation. As the subject that is both (physically) visible yet (verbally) invisible, Effie is well aware of the cultural prohibition against miscegenation: "'Trust me, Jack!' she cried. 'Trust me only this once. You will never have cause to regret it. You know that I would not have a secret from you if it were not for your own sake. Our whole lives are at stake in this. If you come home with me all will be well. If you force your way into that cottage all is over between us'" (486). Although Munro initially allows Effie to "preserve her secret" (486), what is interesting is Munro's ultimate fear behind his anxiety about Effie's secret. As he reveals, "this secret influence . . . drew her away from her husband and her *duty*" (486, emphasis mine). To what does "duty" here refer? On the one hand, it could refer to the expectation of mutual trust and honesty between husband and wife. On the other hand, though, in a story that is full of secrets and the anxiety of knowing versus not knowing, it could also refer to Effie's potential empowerment over Munro as a result of a secret. By not having access to knowledge, by not being able to uncover (through threat and/or pleading) his wife's secret, Munro becomes paralyzed. As he reveals to Holmes, "I've got to the end of my tether" (480). If a wife's "duty" here means the maintenance of her intellectual equality or inferiority, then Effie is transgressing her wifely role. Perhaps this is why Munro welcomes Lucy at the end of the story. Because he is now on an equal level with Effie, because there are no secrets that empower one over the other, Munro has nothing more to fear. In fact, the discovery of Lucy places Effie in a somewhat precarious situation. For it is up to Munro to make the final decision as to her and her daughter's outcome. As she queries, "I ask you what is to become of us, my child and me?" (493). By accepting Lucy, Munro not only appears a moral champion but he returns Effie to the desired position of submissive and dutiful wife.[16]

Perhaps what is most fascinating about "The Yellow Face" are the critical responses to it for they are (like Holmes) obsessed with returning racialized bodies to their "rightful" place. In fact, the critics' reactions to Doyle's fictional story are to "correct" the untruthfulness of its racial knowledges by responding with "real" truths. For instance, in "Some Problems in *The Yellow Face*," Robert H. Schutz questions the reality of the interracial marriage between Effie (as a white woman) and John Hebron (as a black man) in 1880s Georgia. Furthermore, Schutz also questions whether Hebron could have possibly been a "negro lawyer." He ultimately validates Doyle's "truthfulness" by proposing that the Atlanta mentioned in the story is actually Atlanta, New York (Georgia is never mentioned in the story, just presumed by the readers). As such, New York State not only had "several negro lawyers" but it also "did not prohibit inter-racial marriages." Hence, in this instance anyway, "Watson's statements can, as usual, be accepted as factual" (31). The question of intermarriage is also central to Manly W. H. Wellman in "Two Southern Exposures of Sherlock Holmes." In this article, Wellman begins by revealing that this fictional intermarriage "has occasioned recent lively dispute, both verbally among Sherlockians and in the letter department of a Massachusetts periodical called . . . the *Atlantic Monthly*" (422). In order to get to its truthfulness, Wellman enacts a timeline of the story, concluding that Grant Munro came to Holmes in the spring of 1882 or 1883. Therefore, he concludes, Effie must have traveled to America circa 1872, when "Atlanta was under Reconstruction rule" (423). Therefore, because blacks were given "equal and even preferential treatment" during this time, it would not be impossible to believe that Hebron made a "professional success" (424). What is strange about Wellman's historical evidence is that he combines history with fictional *possibilities* to give Doyle's story more validity:

> But how about Hebron's death? It *might still have been* yellow fever, though not in an epidemic. Or it *might have been* something more deadly still: a bullet.
>
> They married some time before 1874, when Georgia's carpetbagger regime was in full control, but with the days of its existence numbered. In that year the native whites won political victory under the able leadership of John B. Gordon, and with it a return to laws operative for white supremacy. The Hebrons *would be well advised* to move a hundred miles or so into South Carolina, a state still snugly carpetbagged. It was two years more before history repeated itself there. In 1876 Wade Hampton, a distinguished cavalry officer under Robert E. Lee, and a notable Southern moderate in politics, headed a campaign for restoration of South Carolina home rule that, before it finally succeeded, was characterized by fierce riots and considerable bloodshed. Hebron, with his gift and reputation, was undoubtedly prominent on the side of the forces then in power; and *perhaps* at Cainhoy, Hamburg or some other scene of argument even to exchange of shots, he was killed.
>
> After the establishment of Hampton's government in 1877, Mrs. Hebron and her little girl *would* depart again. From up North *perhaps*, she conducted a campaign to secure her husband's property. *Very likely* Hampton himself, kind and wise conciliator that he was, helped to do her justice in the matter. And afterward, back to her native England and a new love—together with a new anxiety, that seemed to threaten a new tragedy.
>
> The rest of it we know. (424, emphasis mine)

What Wellman seems to forget here is that "The Yellow Face" is fiction. Yet, in a fictional discussion of racial knowledges that is already full of the anxiety of racial detection, the critic blurs the distinction between reality and fantasy. The racial anxiety in fiction is somewhat assuaged by a "historical" insertion of "perhaps," "very likelys," "mights," and "woulds." If Doyle can't or won't answer questions about racial confusions, then the critic will. Here, the obsession with race is to have concrete, explainable answers that dismiss any potential for racial instability and anxiety.

The critics' preoccupation with concretizing race is perhaps best illustrated in the case of Lucy Hebron, a product of miscegenation who is nevertheless "considerably darker than either of her parents" (Drazen 16). In

"Next Stop, Norbury: Reflections on *The Yellow Face,*" Patrick E. Drazen attempts to prove the very possibility of Doyle's story and, specifically, the possibility of Lucy's "coal-blackness." In addition to proposing the possibility that Watson's description of Lucy could have been incorrect due to dark lighting ("Is it not possible that Watson was in error as to the precise shade of Lucy Hebron?" [17]), Drazen also addresses scientific and genetic explanations for Lucy's complexion by giving, yet again, another fictional possibility in the case of *Effie*'s (not Lucy's) racial background. In his scenario, Effie is actually a product of a white master and a mulatto slave in Atlanta, Georgia: "It has been documented that children born of white masters and pale mulatto slaves sometimes exhibited *no* physical Negroid features such was the case with Effie" (18, emphasis in original). Hence, the real passer in "The Yellow Face" is not Lucy but her mother, Effie. Effie, Drazen continues, never realizes her true mixed ancestry, a secret that is kept from her by her biological father's family. Thus, the probability that Lucy is dark-skinned is not extraordinary when both parents have black blood. As Drazen explains, "the odds become better if both parents are able to contribute genetic Negroid traits, if even in limited degrees" (19). What is fascinating about this scenario is Drazen's justification at the end of his article:

> I realize that many Sherlockians will regard this hypothesis as over-sentimentalized, and others will call it absurd. It is, however, a theory that fits the available facts. Objections to this case's Canonicity have been based on the premise that someone—Grant or Effie or Watson—was lying. There is no internal evidence in Watson's account, however, that would allow us to challenge the truthfulness of the players in this drama. My hypothesis is all surmise, but I say with Holmes that "at least it covers all the facts. When new facts come to our knowledge which cannot be covered by it, it will be time enough to reconsider it" (Yell). In the absence of Effie's maiden name, we can do no other. (20)

Again, the obsessive reactions to Doyle's story are never-ending. Accessing racial truths, specifically the necessary discernment of blackness, is the inescapable core of this story. While Effie may have escaped detection from not only the readers but herself, Drazen proves his skills of detection to be superior to all others by pointing out Effie's "real" racial identity. In a strange mixture of reality and fiction, passing and detection, Drazen's theory (which is a direct repetition of Holmes's method) again reiterates anxieties of detection in narratives of racial indeterminacy.

It is important to note that these three responses all occurred within the same time period (1963, 1974, 1979), a historical moment that witnessed a revolutionary change in racial politics heightened by the civil rights movement. It is telling that that moment as well as the post-Reconstruction period in which Doyle met Garnet and witnessed the publication of "The Yellow Face" both called for an expansion and redefinition of racial knowledges while also witnessing a movement to *return* race to its "proper" place. Doyle's anxiety of racial detection, unfortunately, has come full circle. What these twentieth-century critics reveal is that racial anxieties or "whispers of Norbury" are still very much a menace, threatening to explode at the blink of an (unseeing) eye.

2 / Intuitive Faculties and Racial Clairvoyance: Pauline Hopkins and the Emergence of Multiethnic Detective Fiction

In Nella Larsen's 1929 novel *Passing*, Irene Redfield ponders the consequences of Clare Kendry's race passing and its potential discovery by her white husband: "What if Bellew should divorce Clare? Could he? There was the Rhinelander case" (228). This brief and mysterious reference to the Rhinelander trial, we quickly discover, embodies the stakes of race passing for Larsen's protagonists. Larsen's tale is a passing narrative–turned–crime drama in which light-skinned Clare Kendry dupes her white husband by passing for white and dies (is killed?) shortly after the discovery of her concealed racial identity. Similarly, the case of *Rhinelander v. Rhinelander* (1925) involves a much more complicated web of deceit (or not) in one of the most scandalous cases of American legal history. The story of Alice Jones Rhinelander is one that combines racial melodrama with detective intrigue and legal maneuverings. It begins as a love story between Alice Jones and Leonard Kip Rhinelander that quickly turns into a detective narrative of racial ambiguities, fraud, and betrayal. More importantly, it is the tragic love story of our nation's contentious and embattled relationship with race, racial mixings, and the cultural/legal demarcations of difference.

How Could He Not Know? Racial Knowings and the Rhinelander Case

On December 5, 1925, the jury in the annulment trial of *Rhinelander v. Rhinelander* found in favor of mixed-race Alice Jones Rhinelander, who was sued for marriage annulment by the New York socialite Leonard Kip Rhinelander. Alice Jones, a working-class woman of mixed-race parentage (mother was white British and father was mixed-race British) was accused of fraudulently misrepresenting her racial background in a "vamp and dupe" (Lewis and Ardizzone 58) relationship as represented by the plaintiff's attorney, Isaac Mills, during his opening statement. Mills and the rest of the courtroom were shocked when, after the trial's opening day, in which Mills targeted Jones as a "manipulative gold-digging vamp" (51) who hid her real racial identity, the defendant's attorney, Lee Parsons Davis, admitted to Alice's "colored" status rather than fight for her claim to whiteness.[1] With both sides agreeing to Alice's nonwhite racial identity, then, the case now hinged on the question, "Did Kip Rhinelander know of Alice's nonwhite identity prior to marriage?" The remainder of the trial, with each side attempting to prove what Rhinelander did or did not know about Alice's racial identity, entailed a race detection plot consisting of official records, genealogies, and visual observations culminating with the disrobing of Alice in court.

After the first day of opening statements, the case quickly turned from the defendant's burden to prove her whiteness to one of race detection and deception. In essence, how could Leonard *fail to see* Alice's and her family's nonwhiteness? But, as evidenced throughout the trial and beyond, the Jones family's racial identity was constantly in flux, wavering between whiteness, blackness, and Asianness via the contradictions of state, national, and transnational decodings of racial definitions. That Alice's mother was white was never questioned and speaks to one type of racial reading/seeing: the normalization of whiteness. "You can see it on her face," Davis claimed. She "comes from the purest kind of old English stock" (Smith-Pryor 73). However, Alice's father, George, was a different story; he confounded both sides of the legal debate as well as the journalists who reported on the early coverage of the trial. These revelations, as revealed by Earl Lewis and Heidi Ardizzone, enacted a sort of desperate detective plot in and of itself in which reporters played the careful game of racial outing without, due to liability concerns, the actual labeling of blackness as such. For instance, photos of Alice (by herself or alongside a white woman) were published with the caption, "Does she look like a Negro?" (Lewis and Ardizzone 24). The reports described Alice as "dark," "of light complexion," and "a pretty girl of the Spanish type" (24) without direct reference to blackness. Race decoding as a result of familial affiliations were also made with comments upon Alice's African American brother-in-law, Robert Brooks, who was described as "dark skinned" or, because his racial identity was not questioned, plainly as "black" (24). It was also speculated and widely disseminated that Alice's father, George, was of West Indian descent. "But did that leave," as Lewis and Ardizzone ask, "'no doubt' that George was 'colored'"? (25).

However, official documents (often officiated by white civil service employees) revealed quite a different racial narrative. As Elizabeth Smith-Pryor writes, the federal census enumerator listed the family as "white" in 1900, 1910, and 1920. But in 1930 (a few years after the trial), the census identified George as "negro" and Elizabeth as "white." Interestingly, Alice was initially designated as "white," but that designation was eventually replaced with "negro" on this census. Alice's sister, however, was deemed "white" (108). Attorney Mills also included evidence that George Jones's application for naturalization identified him as "colored" and that the three Jones daughters, Emily, Alice, and Grace, were identified as "mulatto," "black," and "black, negro, mixed," respectively, on their birth certificates. In contrast, Alice and Leonard's marriage license identified both parties as "white" (65).

But aside from both the official and unofficial racial speculations produced throughout the trial, George Jones's racial ambiguity highlights the very struggles at the core of unknowing and unknowing race at the heart of this case. As such, I offer an alternative reading of the Rhinelander trial that expands the matrix of knowing and not knowing beyond whether or not Kip Rhinelander knew of Alice's racial identity to the larger question of knowing and not knowing one's ancestry—as illustrated by *George* Jones—due to British imperialist rule and its continued aftereffects. The Rhinelander trial, then, is not just a story of race deception as much as the larger story of broken kinships and, subsequently, denied racial knowledges of one's own kind. For George Jones, who was a product of a white British woman and a racially unknown father who died when George was two years old, having access to one's ancestry and genealogy is a privilege very much prescribed by circumstances of race and class. In an affidavit filed in December 1924, George Jones revealed that he knew very little about his father's national or racial origins: "My mother was a Caucasian of pure English descent. The only information which I have about my father is that he was a native of one of the British colonies" (Lewis and Ardizzone 74).

Which British colony, it turns out, is the real mystery behind George Jones. Lewis and Ardizzone write that according to Davis, George's white mother told him that his father was *East* Indian rather than the West Indian often reported by newspapers (66). As a result, Alice's cocounsel,

Samuel Swinburne, argued that, as Indians, George and Alice Jones are "members of the Aryan race, which is collateral with the Caucasian" (qtd. in Lewis and Ardizzone 73). How does this change in ancestral genealogies and histories—from Asian to black—alter our reading of Alice Jones Rhinelander and the legal and cultural uncovering of her racial identity? First, this distinction may explain George Jones's confusion of his racial metamorphosis upon immigrating to the United States: "As a colored man in England, George Jones had been accepted as equals by whites. . . . He had never thought of a 'taint in his blood' (black ancestry) until they arrived in the United States and realized that he was considered black here" (Lewis and Ardizzone 66). In the United States' rigid demarcation between white and nonwhite, George's "obvious" nonwhiteness (i.e., his dark skin), while perhaps viewed as Asian in England, denoted blackness in his new homeland. Hence, this transnational racial conversion may also explain the nuances and complexities of the Jones family's self-racial designations as "white" rather than "black." It also highlights that race is very much a cultural and national construct.

Introducing the possibility of an Asian identity rather than a black one also had larger implications and repercussions for the trial. Swinburne and Davis must have been aware of the landmark Supreme Court decision in *United States v. Bhagat Singh Thind* (1923) that had been decided just two years prior to the Rhinelander case. As a recent soldier of the U.S. Army during World War I, Thind declared he was eligible for U.S. citizenship based on the anthropological definition of Asian Indians as "Caucasians." While the Court acknowledged his Caucasian status, it also declared that "the average man knows perfectly well" that he is not: "It is a matter of familiar observation and knowledge that the physical group characteristics of the Hindus render them readily distinguishable from the various groups of persons in this country commonly recognized as white" (Haney-López 89, 91). Physically, George Jones has been described as "long-faced" with a "trim and sporty mustache" and looked "like a picture of an old Spanish hidalgo" (qtd. in Smith-Pryor 62). Telling the jury to look directly at Jones, Plaintiff's Attorney Mills claimed that "every feature of his face is distinctly Caucasian except the color. I say if by some miracle you could change the color of his skin as he sits there he would pass anywhere for a white man" (qtd. in Smith-Pryor 225). These descriptions place George within the mixed-race conundrum of not quite white, not quite black. But, speculating on George's Indianness and, hence, possible whiteness suggested an issue too dangerous to contemplate. Like the Court's appeal to the "common knowledge" of the "average man" in *United States v. Thind*, there was no option but to see George Jones and subsequently Alice as obviously nonwhite.

When Attorney Davis was addressing the Court about George's ambiguous racial background, he made the following claim: "It is true of all of us that we get our lineage and our ancestors a great deal by what the law calls hearsay" (Smith-Pryor 73). As Elizabeth M. Smith-Pryor writes, "By equating knowledge about ancestry with hearsay (a form of secondhand evidence generally kept out of court due to its presumed unreliability), Davis raised the disconcerting possibility that no one really knew his or her racial background" (73). In other words, by opening up the possibility that, in some ways, we are all race passers, Davis positioned the Court on the same level with Alice herself. The artist and scholar Adrian Piper makes a similar claim about American racial ancestry when she states, "The longer a person's family has lived in this country, the higher the probable percentage of African ancestry that person's family is likely to have" (17). To declare to the almost entirely white courtroom that many there could also be tainted by blackness was to suggest an idea too explosive to contemplate. Thus, the subsequent disrobing of Alice Jones to test the jury's racial reading skills necessitated the ruling in favor of Alice. Of course, behind the ruling is the implication that Alice is nonwhite. To not see her as such highlights not her racial invisibility but rather the observer's unskilled and faulty skills of race detection.[2]

The question commencing the trial—did Rhinelander know of Alice's mixed-race status prior to marriage?—quickly turned into an accusation with, "How could Rhinelander not have known of Alice's race?" This was startlingly demonstrated when Alice, at the Court's behest, exposed her body to an all-white, all-male jury, baring her breasts, back, and legs:

> The Court, Mr. Mills, Mr. Davis, Mr. Swinburne [another attorney], the jury, the plaintiff, the defendant, her mother, Mrs. George Jones, and the stenographer left the courtroom and entered the jury room. The defendant and Mrs. Jones then withdrew to the lavatory adjoining the jury room and, after a short time, again entered the jury room. The defendant, who was weeping, had on her underwear and a long coat. At Mr. Davis['s] direction she let down the coat, so that the upper portion of her body, as far down as the breast, was exposed. She then, again at Mr. Davis'[s] direction, covered the upper part of her body and showed to the jury her bare legs, up as

> far as the knees. The Court, counsel, the jury and the plaintiff then re-entered the court room. (Onwuachi-Willig 14–15)

The most widely publicized imagined image of the disrobing was the composograph created by the tabloid the *New York Evening Graphic*. According to Angela Onwuachi-Willig, while photographers were not permitted, the editor of the *New York Evening Graphic* and his assistant art director "set up a mock courtroom scene with a chorus girl, instead of Alice; retouched the picture; and then placed the actual faces of those involved in the trial onto posed bodies. The *Evening Graphic* published the composite photograph with the headline 'Alice Disrobes in Court to Keep Her Husband,' on November 25, 1925" (14). What were the clues witnessed by the jury to prove Alice's nonwhiteness? Writing for the *New York Daily News*, Grace Robinson writes that "the breasts, indisputable evidence of negro origin, were obviously those of a colored woman" (qtd. in Smith-Pryor 203). After returning to the witness stand, Leonard Rhinelander was questioned by Davis:

> DAVID: You have just viewed portions of your wife's body?
> LEONARD: Yes.
> DAVIS: Is it the same shade it was when you saw her in the Marie Antoinette [a hotel where they would regularly meet]?
> LEONARD: Yes.
> DAVIS: That is all. (qtd. in Lewis and Ardizzone 159)

Davis's quick and simple questioning of Kip echoes back to the "common knowledge" rationale seen in the racial prerequisite case of *United States v. Thind* discussed above. He does not have to directly ask Rhinelander of Alice's coloring because the average intelligent and racially astute individual would clearly see it on her body; deliberately avoiding the question, in essence, explicitly makes obvious the only racial reading of Alice Jones. Shortly thereafter, the Court ruled in favor of Alice Jones Rhinelander. Although many see this as a victory for civil rights (a woman of color triumphed over a representative of the white elite), I argue that it is not so much a civil rights victory as a reprimand delivered to Kip Rhinelander—not for marrying across racial boundaries per se but for explicitly declaring to the world that nonwhiteness cannot be discerned from whiteness. By "seeing" race on Alice's body, the jury is rejecting Rhinelander's claims and asserting the ease of racial recognition. As such, the jury is proclaiming its superior detective acumen; while Rhinelander may be an easy dupe, they certainty would pass the test. In short,

Figure 1. Composograph of Alice Jones Rhinelander disrobing during her trial, published in the *New York Evening Graphic* on November 25, 1925.

there was no option but for Alice to win the case. To not win would have unleashed a racial pandemonium too volatile and caustic to imagine.

As Lewis and Ardizzone movingly remind us, Alice's disrobing thrust her into a "long history of race and color" (157):

> This excruciating image both demands and defies explanation. It reverberates through a violent racial history and flickers with the remembrances of a multitude of atrocious vignettes: enslaved men and women standing on auction blocks, stripped before the examination of potential purchasers; the icon of a half-dressed woman in chains on her knees pleading to her white abolitionist "sister" for help; the "Hottentot Venus," a southern African woman named Sara Baartman, brought to England and put on display, usually nude, for scientific and curiosity-seeking audiences; Sojourner Truth baring her breasts to prove to a hostile audience at the Akron, Ohio, Women's Rights Convention that she was a woman, reminding them that white men had seen her breasts before when she wet-nursed them as a slave—that the shame of her nudity was theirs, not hers. (156–57)

Although Lewis and Ardizzone write that Alice "had no ancestry that tied her to an African past, she was black in the eyes of most" (157). Thus, her disrobing reflects our long history of exhibiting and examining black female bodies in contexts ranging from auction blocks to scientific experiments. In light of Alice and George Jones's possible ancestral ties to India, I also want to include here that Alice's disrobing also highlights the legacy of Asian American immigration history and the traumas that Asian Americans have endured and continued to tolerate right through the Rhinelander trial. One has only to remember the Angel Island detention center in which hundreds of thousands of Asian immigrants were detained, examined, and interrogated from 1910 to 1940. Separated from family members and compartmentalized by gender, the immigrants underwent medical procedures that included being disrobed, measured, and tested for parasitic infections. They then endured grueling interrogations that tested their detailed knowledges of facts that a "genuine" applicant would know (family history and relations, crucial dates, locations of village and homes, personal belongings and daily routines, etc.). Interrogations could last for hours or even days. If they passed, immigrants waited for their release behind unsanitary, locked dormitories amid immense hardship and psychologically damaging conditions. Detention could last for weeks, months, or years. The longest was of a Chinese woman, Quok Shee, who was detained for six hundred nights from September 1916 to April 1918 (Barde and Bobonis 106; see Lai/Lim/Yung). I include this history here to remind us that the history of Alice Jones Rhinelander is not just one of black versus white but a triangulation (to echo Claire Jean Kim) of racial struggles for citizenship and national belonging. To see the Rhinelander case as a black-white struggle is to erase the parallel efforts of two very diverse but interconnected racial communities in U.S. history. While George Jones's real racial ancestry of either East Indian (i.e., of Indian descent) or West Indian (i.e., of Caribbean descent) lineage may never be known, both the United States and Britain share a history of slavery and racialization that resulted in thousands if not millions of people with broken kinship ties. In this regard, George's not knowing of his paternal ancestry is indicative of the legacy of imperialist forces that prospered by the very perpetuation of not knowing through the selling of familial relations. It is also telling that the Rhinelander family, as noted by Lewis and Ardizzone, made its fortune through trade via the West Indies (9). In this light, the Rhinelander trial symbolizes the larger fraught relationship between race and knowing via the racially triangulated matrix of whiteness, Asianness, and blackness.

This chapter and the next closely address the politics of knowing via detection through the works on two pioneering race women at the beginning of the twentieth century: Pauline Hopkins and Winnifred Eaton.

Searching for "My People"

The African American detective genre begins with a search for and reunion of family, highlighting the role of detection in African American lives. Forced familial separation and, subsequently, the potential threat of nonrecognition are movingly told in a scene from Toni Morrison's Pulitzer Prize–winning novel *Beloved* (1987) when Sethe's mother directs her to a scar under her breast. Pointing to a circle with a cross burned into her skin, Sethe's mother declares: "This is your ma'am. This . . . I am the only one got this mark now. The rest dead. If something happens to me and you can't tell me by my face, you can know me by this mark" (61). As this scene pointedly suggests, the African American narrative is, tragically, often about the intersection of passing and detection. Sethe's recognition of her mother is possible via the brand of slavery. The institution of slavery promotes the separation of parent from child and, as a consequence, propagated a social system in which the family unit was broken and its members were often unknown and unrecognizable from one another. When asked by Beloved whether her mother "never fix up [her] hair" (60), Sethe reveals that she was rarely in her mother's presence:

> If she did, I don't remember. I didn't see her but a few times out in the fields and once when she was working indigo. By the time I woke up in the morning, she was in line. If the moon was bright they worked by its light. Sunday she slept like a stick. She must of nursed me two or three weeks—that's the way the others did. Then she went back in rice and I sucked from another woman whose job it was. So to answer you, no. I reckon not. She never fixed my hair nor nothing. She didn't even sleep in the same cabin most nights I remember. Too far from the line-up, I guess. (60–61)

For Sethe, discerning her mother is only accomplished via the recognition of slavery's scar of ownership. As mere chattel, mother and child are denied the traditional comforts and bonding rituals between mother and daughter like fixing hair or nursing. As Frederick Douglass wrote in his famous autobiography, *Narrative of the Life of Frederick Douglass* (1845), slaves were often denied the legacies of their birth, including knowledge of birth date and place. In *Beloved*, Baby Suggs describes the source of this deprivation when she describes how "men and women were moved around like checkers. Anybody Baby Suggs knew, let alone loved, who hadn't run off or been hanged, got rented out, loaned out, bought up, brought back, stored up, mortgaged, won, stolen or seized" (23). As checker pieces, slaves were often bereft of the most common of inheritance rights from their birth date to property to even their own name. Slaves often lost the inheritance of kinship and family legacy, sometimes unaware that perhaps the person standing next to them was their child or parent, brother or sister, cousin or aunt/uncle. Unlike our common understanding of race passing, then, the loss of inheritance (including the various properties therein such as name, legacy, birthright, etc.) is the other ugly side of slavery in which "passing" is a type of nonrecognition of one's own family.[3]

A larger argument this study makes is that race detective anxiety is foundationally about the formation of (or the disruption in) the family unit. Historically, who is or is not allowed to form the family unit becomes a eugenics-inspired practice as determined by anti-immigration and antimiscegenation legislation. For African Americans enslaved within a "peculiar institution" that justified the separation of parent from child, husband from wife, and siblings from each other, the role of passing and detection takes on layered meanings. This chapter focuses on how the institution of slavery and the post-Emancipation years fostered and necessitated a climate of detection as a result of the forced disintegration of familial bonds. In some ways, I read slavery and the period after Emancipation as an era of detective urgency where a search for "my people," as Heather Andrea Williams has recently discussed, is a story about passing of a different sort where kinship, not just race, is the invisible marker to be detected, rediscovered, and reclaimed. For as children are taken from their mothers and siblings are separated on auction blocks, how is the slave family to recognize and reunite with its members? How does a mother recognize her baby who years ago was torn from her and sold to the highest bidder? Williams's *Help Me to Find My People: The African American Search for Family Lost in Slavery* details the heart-wrenching search that African American former slaves conducted after the Civil War through "information wanted" advertisements. According to Williams, many continued their persistent and stubborn search for decades, and it was rare for reunification to occur. Nevertheless, the longing for reunion with (or, at the very least, knowledge of) lost family was a great motivator, a legacy that still lives on today via a focus on genealogy with shows such as PBS's *African American Lives 1* and *2* (2006, 2008). Williams also notes that this desire for reunion took on a more possessive tone in the ads after 1890 by including the phrase, "my people." "Perhaps," she writes, "use of 'my people' revealed a desire to connect to anyone with a common ancestry. Perhaps it was an assertion of a claim of having had people, even if . . . you had never seen them" (193). I would add that the search for (or, detection of) common ancestry for the wider African American community enables a reclaiming and ownership of stolen legacies, relations, and inheritance rights previously dispossessed from them as slaves.

It is within this context of detecting one's "people" that Pauline Hopkins published *Hagar's Daughter: A Story of Southern Caste Prejudice* (1901–2), the first African American–authored detective story featuring a black detective figure. As a passing narrative–turned–detective plot, *Hagar's Daughter* not only responds to the white male authors who have constructed the detective genre before her, but she does so with a black, post-Emancipation, post-Reconstruction perspective where tropes of knowledge and detection are reimagined and reconfigured, revealing the foundations of the passing-detection matrix in the formation of the American family plot. Specifically, Hopkins's foundational novel is a story about the reclamation and reunion of family once devastated and torn apart by slavery and its aftermath. For the African American community that was simultaneously embodied with certain "knowledges" through scientific racism that justified enslavement while also denied other knowledges as property (birth date, birthplace, name, genealogy), the role of detection is particularly vexed and political. Thus, Hopkins's intervention into the detective genre reveals that detection is a strategic practice instrumental to the survival of the African American family and the community at large.

Family Secrets: Pauline Hopkins and the Emergence of African American Detection

Pauline Hopkins (1859–1930) was a prominent African American novelist, playwright, journalist, and editor. Hopkins is considered by many to be the most prolific African American writer during the first decade of the twentieth century. As the influential editor of *Colored American Magazine*, Hopkins was responsible for much of the magazine's political and social commentary, commencing what Hazel Carby describes as a black renaissance years before the renowned Harlem Renaissance of the 1920s and 1930s (xxxi): "The *Colored American Magazine* was a direct response to the political climate of the turn of the century—that is, to black disenfranchisement, Jim Crow laws, the widespread murder of black people in the South, and political apathy in the North. Hopkins viewed the journal as a vehicle for social intervention, as an attempt to replace the politics of compromise with political demands for changes in social relations" (xxxii). Hopkins's political mission is evident in her literary works, many of which were published in the *Colored American Magazine,* including "Talma Gordon" (1900). A "locked room" short story, "Talma Gordon" is considered the first mystery story written by an African American and precedes many of the themes and concerns of *Hagar's Daughter,* serialized the following year. As social commentary and intervention, "Talma Gordon" both decries white racism against blacks as well as cautions against the myth of white purity. Further, as a murder mystery that prioritizes the hidden racial intermixture of society's elite classes rather than the actual solution to the murder, "Talma Gordon" commences Hopkins's intervention into the detective genre wherein she questions a social order defined and confined by race prejudice and calls for a reflection upon traditional definitions of "justice" and "crime." According to the critic Frankie Bailey, early African American writers strategically moved from nonfiction to fiction, adapting and modifying genre conventions in order to reach a larger audience and to report the crimes enacted upon their community (*African American Mystery Writers* 22). Hopkins's adaptation of the detective genre to reveal the atrocities of slavery and its continued aftermath not only "names the crime," to use Bailey's words, but places responsibility of criminal behavior upon the judicial system at large and specifically upon the white ruling elite. In *The Blues Detective: A Study of African American Detective Fiction*, Stephen F. Soitos acknowledges Hopkins's contribution: "[Hopkins] was the first African American writer to utilize detective fiction for a social and political attack on racial discrimination in the United States. Interestingly, Hopkins regarded detective fiction as a powerful tool that could be used to celebrate African American cultural values and critique white racist ideology, and she does this by using the detective form to question the moral and cultural foundation that typical detective fiction supports through the reestablishment of the natural order" (60). In utilizing the form of the detective tale, Hopkins questions our assumptions and expectations of the genre (namely, the prioritizing of and discovering the solution to the "whodunit" question) and highlights, instead, how justice is defined and criminality is detected. In "Talma Gordon," the solving of Captain Gordon's murder becomes secondary to the larger mystery of Talma's hidden racial background and, as a result, the cautionary revelation of tainted bloodlines in the white ruling classes. As such, Hopkins's initiation into the mystery genre redirects the accusatory finger from the individual murder to the white community at large by illustrating how racism and sexism facilitate the demise of the family unit.

The ostensible mystery of "Talma Gordon" is the murder of Talma's father, Captain Gordon, his second wife, and their son. Jonathan Gordon's family is descended from old New England Puritans who arrived on the *Mayflower* and made their fortune in the East India trade. When Captain Gordon meets his first wife, Isabel Franklin, his financial and business security is threatened. With her own family fortune, Isabel brings Gordon the capital he desperately needs to regain and restore his place in society. Tragically, their union ends when Isabel dies soon after the birth of her third child (a son, who dies soon after birth), leaving Captain Gordon with two daughters, Talma and Jeannette. Captain Gordon soon remarries, and his second wife and Talma have a tumultuous relationship. Thus, when Captain Gordon, his wife, and child are found murdered and it is revealed that the Gordon daughters were almost entirely written out of his Will, Talma is accused of murdering her father in order to save her inheritance. Due to lack of evidence, she is released only to face the community's continued suspicions. The Gordon sisters travel abroad to Rome, where Jeannette soon dies and Talma disappears. One day, Talma returns to the States and visits Dr. Thornton, the narrator of Hopkins's tale and the Gordon family physician. During the visit, the identity of Captain Gordon's murderer is revealed, but this discovery quickly usurped by the larger mystery at hand: the exposure of Talma and Jeannette's black ancestry. Jeannette's deathbed letter exposes how the birth of their dark-skinned brother disclosed the secret history of their octoroon grandmother "abandoned by her white lover" (15). The sisters' mother, Isabel, had no physical trace of black blood (it is unclear, in fact, whether she was aware of her blackness). Isabel's adopted parents, the Franklins, raised her as their own blood relation, namely white. As a result of this discovery, Captain Gordon severs almost all familial ties with his daughters, fearing that revelation will bring a "dire disgrace" (15) to the Gordon family name. In fact, upon hearing of Talma's blood taint, her lover remarks: "God! Doctor, but this is too much. I could stand the stigma of murder, but add to that the pollution of Negro blood! No man is brave enough to face such as situation" (16). Being tainted with black blood, it turns out, is far worse than murder. Blackness is the ultimate mystery and "crime" to be hidden, shielded, and better left unsolved.

Thus, as a detective tale in search of the murderer, "Talma Gordon" is weak. In fact, after the trial, we are fleetingly told that although Talma hires the "shrewdest of detectives" (11) to uncover the mystery, he fails to solve the crime. The larger mystery—secret racial origins and the anxiety produced by its discovery—brackets the story as narrated by Dr. Thornton, the Gordon family physician. Making the detective plot secondary to the larger mystery (in this case of racial origins) is a narrative device that Hopkins emphasizes with her commencement of the African American detective genre. Doris Witt writes that African American detective authors are more concerned with "addressing the diversity of contemporary African American urban life" (168) than in the "whodunit" of the mystery. For Hopkins, the central mystery in "Talma Gordon" is the unknown and secretive nature of family relations and the lengths to which the characters will go to maintain and/or revenge these secrets. The primacy placed on domestic secrets and familial obligations over murder is emphasized when the killer's identity is finally revealed at the conclusion of the story. Filial piety, it turns out, is the very motivation behind the murder of Captain Gordon. Thus, while critics like Sigrid Anderson Cordell argue that the revelation of the killer's identity is "ancillary" and "cursory" (62) and is overshadowed by the revelation of Talma's blackness, I read the ending quite differently. The revelation of the killer's identity is, in fact, a crucial and necessary component to the narrative's final impact of race detective anxiety.

At the end of Hopkins's story, we learn that Simon Cameron, an East Indian, killed Captain Gordon as revenge for Cameron's father's death. I read this brief encounter between the medical professional and the racialized murderer to be quite revealing, especially in light of the story's larger mystery of undetectable racial bodies. Upon his first encounter with Cameron, Dr. Thornton is immediately suspicious. Operating as the story's respected interlocutor and, as Talma's husband, the model of progressive racial politics, Dr. Thornton acts as a sort of Watson figure to an absent Sherlock, guiding us through the central mystery as well as functioning as the story's moral arbiter. Thus, when he remarks that he "seemed fated to be involved in mysteries" (11), Dr. Thornton's minor moment of detection is significant beyond the initial observation. In attempting to decode Cameron, Dr. Thornton states, "He was an enigma to me; and his nationality puzzled me, for of course I did not believe his story of being English" (12). Interestingly here, while Cameron's foreignness is a puzzle not easily decipherable, what is certain is that nonwhiteness equates to non-Englishness. In other words, having an Anglo name with a non-Caucasian face evokes a "not quite right" racial reading. Further, as Dr. Thornton is a medical doctor with probable knowledge of racial science rhetoric, including the worldwide popularity of the eugenics movement in the 1890s as espoused by the British anthropologist Francis Galton, his initial description of Cameron is particularly telling in light of our subsequent discovery that Cameron is Captain Gordon's murderer: "Seldom have I seen so fascinating and wicked a face. The lines of the mouth were cruel, the eyes cold and sharp, the smile mocking and evil" (11–12). According to the Italian criminologist and physician Cesare Lombroso, whose theory of criminal atavism established that criminals were distinguishable from noncriminals through telling physical anomalies, Cameron's "cruel" and "evil" physical traits would reflect his criminal nature. But Hopkins intervenes in this predictable conclusion by showing that Dr. Thornton's racial reading of Cameron proves to be a complete miscalculation. For as he confesses later, Cameron's murderous act is one that avenges his father's death at the hands of a greedy and scheming Captain Gordon, who himself commits cold-blooded murder by killing his longtime friend, Cameron's father, for gold. "An East Indian never forgets," Cameron states, "and I swore by my mother's deathbed to hunt Captain Gordon down until I had avenged my father's murder" (17). Here Hopkins debunks the myth of racial science that asserts that an individual's character can be read from his/her physical body by reversing Cameron and Captain Gordon's moral nature. Ironically, the "cruel" and "evil" traits read on Cameron's body seem true in that he is the killer legally defined. But in a narrative that questions the relationship between social justice, crime, and race, Cameron is shown to be loyal to his family through his seeking a rightful justice, one that is neglected by the legal system. Conversely, Captain Gordon's exterior façade of wealth and nobility shields his internal qualities of greed, avarice, and homicidal tendencies. His death, as implied by the narrative, is the just end for a criminal who otherwise would have never been convicted.

Setting up Simon Cameron's background performs three important functions for the story's ultimate commentary of race detective anxiety: (1) it gives the reader not only the "who" but the "why" behind the criminal act, forcing us to question the relationship between justice and crime; (2) by revealing the fallacy of reading physical markers as evidence of character, Hopkins's story puts blame upon those previously unmarked for criminal behavior; and finally, and perhaps most importantly, (3) Cameron's racial "enigma," paralleling Talma's and Jeannette's racial invisibility, shows race detective anxiety operating in two very different albeit corresponding ways: simply, anxiety is produced both when race is "not quite right" and invisible. In other words, the full impact of

Talma's racial disclosure depends on Cameron's parallel story. If Cameron signifies loyalty and pride in family, then Captain Gordon's death represents the complete breakdown of family. It is important to mention here that shortly after Cameron kills Captain Gordon, Jeannette attempts patricide in revenge for her father's betrayal and abandonment of herself and Talma. It is no coincidence that Jeannette utilizes an East Indian dagger to kill her father; her choice of weapon conjoins her and Cameron's murderous motivation (the absence and complete disregard of family loyalty versus the very strict obligation to it, respectively). Further, the dagger also functions as a bloody murder weapon that works by the violent relinquishing of blood, the source of the very racial anxieties Gordon feared.

Blood, pure or tainted, and the racial anxieties it produces lead to the final unraveling of Hopkins's mystery. The concluding climactic revelation that Talma is Dr. Thornton's wife is what transforms this mystery story into a political manifesto. By divulging the secrecy of racial mixings within the bloodlines of our nation's elite classes as well as promoting continued racial mixings via Dr. Thornton's revelation that he married Talma, Hopkins outs America's racial mystery of amalgamation. By unmasking her blackness rather than shielding it, Talma disrupts the temptation (perhaps urgency) to pass for white as well as publicly acknowledges and reclaims her ties to the octoroon grandmother who was abandoned by her white lover (demonstrating, essentially, a refusal to participate in this family structure). Further, Talma's acknowledgment also retains the blackness that was racially and biologically erased when the Franklins adopted her mother as their own. Thus, Talma's refusal to pass at the end of the story as well as her and Dr. Thornton's disclosure (not detection) to Boston's elite necessitate a more nuanced reading of the passing-detection relationship than Hopkins's critics have previously given. As Dr. Thornton asks a roomful of Boston gentlemen in the beginning of this tale, "Did you ever think that in spite of our prejudices against amalgamation, some of our descendants, indeed many of them, will inevitably intermarry among those far-off tribes of dark-skinned peoples, if they become a part of this great Union?" (5). With his foreshadowing of amalgamation, Dr. Thornton then describes Talma's story, which, as Sigrid Anderson Cordell argues, calls into question the "hagiography of the American elite and instead celebrates the figure of a mixed-race woman who has been scorned by her white father, a scion of New England society" (52). As such, "Talma Gordon" is a cautionary tale of racial impurities and tainted bloodlines but also a tale of racial disclosure wherein Dr. Thornton's marital revelation serves as a speculative imagining of America's racial future. Hopkins's simultaneous disclosure of racial impurities in the American elite as well as her forewarnings of an impending "mulatto millennium" (as labeled by Danzy Senna) continues in her subsequent tale of detection, *Hagar's Daughter.*

Another Little Black Girl

When Cuthbert Sumner discovers the racial identity of Aurelia Madison, he is forewarned about the commonplace reality of black blood throughout white bloodlines: "But black blood is everywhere—in society and out, and in our families even; we cannot feel assured that it has not filtered into the most exclusive families. We try to stem the tide but I believe it is a hopeless task (160). The threat of black contamination is further cautioned in a newspaper article at the end of *Hagar's Daughter*: "This story, showing as it does, the ease with which beautiful half-breeds may enter our best society without detection, is a source of anxiety to the white citizens of our country. At this rate the effects of slavery can never be eradicated, and our most distinguished families are not immune from contact with this mongrel race. Mrs. Bowen has our sympathy, but we cannot, even for such a leader as she has been, unlock the gates of caste and bid her enter. Posterity forbids it" (266–67). Both of the above quotes, spoken by minor characters in the novel, Elsie Bradford and an anonymous editor, respectively, reveal the underlying anxiety of miscegenation and passing bodies that was rampant during this time. It is important to note that all the passing bodies (with the possible exception of another figure that I will discuss later) in this novel are eventually detected and re-placed in what some would argue is their recognized "place" of blackness. However, instead of arguing that passing ultimately reinstates the essentialist binary of black and white (a somewhat limited argument that inevitably gets us nowhere), what I want to focus on here are the following questions: How is passing detected? How does race help or hinder the act of detection? Why is Venus Johnson, an uneducated black maid, the most successful detective figure represented in Hopkins's novel? Finally, what is the role of intuition versus rationalism in a racialized mode of detection? Before investigating these questions, it is necessary to first give a brief synopsis of *Hagar's Daughter,* a story that foreshadows much of the twentieth century's anxieties of race (especially blackness), miscegenation, hybrid bodies, and detection.

The plot of *Hagar's Daughter* is in many ways a story of familial separation and reunion as dictated by the mandates of racial integration. A love story between two neighbors, Hagar Sargeant and Ellis Enson, the narrative begins in antebellum Maryland, where, after a quick courtship, Ellis and Hagar marry. While the birth of their only child (a daughter) is a happy occasion, it is also the catalyst that ignites the tragedy of the Enson family because this birth displaces Ellis's brother, St. Clair, as heir to the Enson estate. Upon learning of his loss, St. Clair returns home after an extended absence, bringing with him Walker, a notorious slave trader. Having sold Hagar as a young child, Walker quickly recognizes her and reveals that she is a black orphan who was adopted by the Sargeants and passed off as their own, unbeknownst to Hagar. Shocked, Ellis initially rejects Hagar, claiming that "the shame of public ostracism and condemnation seemed too much for inherited principles" (60). But Ellis soon declares he has "no hope, no life" (61) without Hagar and reveals a plan to escape abroad. However, their plan is tragically disrupted two weeks later, when the family physician reveals that the body of a man, believed to be Ellis, was found dead with a wound to his head. St. Clair claims his heritage and property and imprisons Hagar and her daughter. Hagar, refusing the fate of slavery and finding no other recourse, escapes and jumps off a bridge with her daughter in her arms.

The passing plot quickly turns into a detective plot when the story restarts twenty years later in postbellum Washington. Here, we are introduced to what seems like an entire new cast of characters. Senator Zenas Bowen, a millionaire from California, his wife, Estelle, and his daughter by a first marriage, Jewel, are new residents in the nation's capital and the center of the city's gossip. Cuthbert Sumner is Jewel's love interest and future husband and also the private secretary to General Benson. Due to financial difficulties, Benson is provoked to scheme a plan in which he would marry Jewel and acquire her family fortune. In order to accomplish this, Benson obtains the aid of his old friend Major Henry Clay Madison and Madison's daughter, Aurelia, a passing quadroon born to Madison's slave. Aurelia's goal is to lure Cuthbert away from Jewel in order to pave the way for Benson. Coincidentally, however, it turns out that Aurelia and Cuthbert were already once previously engaged, their engagement broken due to Cuthbert's discomfort with Aurelia's "siren charms" (104). After revealing her love to Cuthbert and reacquainting herself with Jewel (in another coincidence, it turns out Jewel and Aurelia were once classmates), Aurelia succeeds in her scheme and separates the engaged couple.

The narrative climaxes when Benson murders Elsie Bradford, his secretary as well as secret lover and mother of his illegitimate child, because of her threat to reveal his past indiscretions. Elsie's murder begins the exposure of all the underlying mysteries within *Hagar's Daughter.* Because he was the last known person to see Elsie, Cuthbert is accused of the crime and imprisoned. This ignites Jewel's reconciliation with him (which consequently leads to a secret wedding in jail) as well as her turn to professional help, leading her to the "celebrated detective" Henson (186), who is the head of the federal government's detective agency. In the meantime, Benson kidnaps Jewel and imprisons her in the old Enson estate. While there, Jewel discovers another prisoner, Aunt Henny, a longtime slave-turned-servant to the Enson family who witnesses Elsie's murder. What is significant at this juncture in the narrative is the revelation of *two* plots: the murder plot and the passing plot. For not only is Benson discovered to be the real murderer, but we also learn that the Washington cast is really the old Charleston cast reincarnated in masquerade: Estelle is really Hagar, who survives her drowning attempt and journeys to California, where she meets Senator Bowen; Benson and Madison are St. Clair and Walker, respectively, who flee to the North after being found guilty of conspiring to assassinate Abraham Lincoln; Detective Henson is the surviving Ellis Enson, who, believing himself stripped of family and fortune, joins the army "seeking death" (260) but survives to become the head of the government's detective agency; and, most incredibly, Jewel is the long-lost daughter of Hagar and Ellis, who is adopted by Senator Bowen and his wife after being rescued from the river. Most importantly, the discovery of both the murder and passing plots would not have been achieved without the detective skills of Venus Johnson, Aunt Henny's granddaughter and Jewel's maid, who, following her intuitive suspicions, passes as a black boy and discovers the whereabouts of both Jewel and Aunt Henny. While Detective Henson is ineffective in his profession, we see that it is the intuitive and ingenious skills of a little black maid that result in the capture of a murderer and the reunion of a wrongfully separated family.

But who is Venus Johnson, and why does Hopkins choose her to represent the first black detective figure? There are three main reasons behind her choice: (1) a literary reclamation, (2) making present an *un-presence*, and (3) redefining questions of justice and criminality. First of all, we can begin to answer who Venus is by referring back to little Lucy Hebron, the "coal-black negress" who stumps the all-knowing Sherlock Holmes in "The Yellow Face," published less than a decade prior to Hopkins's novel. As I indicated in chapter 1, Lucy Hebron's blackness is the source of Holmes's deductive failure; blackness and, in Lucy's case, masked blackness, are the site of irrational and failed deduction. But what we see in *Hagar's Daughter* is that that subject of undetection now becomes the source of detection. In many ways, then, Venus is the literary reincarnation of Doyle's Lucy; she is now the passer-turned-detective. Further, Venus is the passer-turned-detective who uses passing (in this case, gender passing) in order to detect. While it is true that we may not know whether or not Hopkins read any of the very popular Sherlock Holmes stories (or, for that matter, this specific one), I argue that this act of literary reclamation is, in a sense, an uncovering of the history of silenced black female subjectivity. While previously silenced in "The Yellow Face" and elsewhere (such as Topsy in Harriet Beecher Stowe's *Uncle Tom's Cabin*), the seemingly inconsequential little black girl reappears in Hopkins's narrative with her own voice and her own autonomy; she switches from being the object of scrutiny to being the active scrutinizer. In her creation of the black detective genre, Hopkins rescues Doyle's passive character and re-places her into the role of heroine while also reestablishing the detection/passing dynamic.

Secondly, rather than asserting an essentialist claim that Venus's blackness is what empowers her to detect, I argue that her racialized blackness is what allows and enables her to detect successfully. As the mediator between her upstairs white employers and her downstairs family, Venus is able to negotiate between both the white and black worlds as well as to put on a different mask accordingly. Furthermore, her invisible servant status allows Venus to see and hear clues that would be unavailable to white spectators. This is also evident in Jon Edward Bruce's *The Black Sleuth* and Barbara Neely's more recent Blanche White series, where blackness is seen to be the best tool in detection because of its very invisibility. Bruce writes:

> And we must not forget Randolph, the black, whose role in this little drama, about to be enacted, was, to say the least, as difficult as it was delicate and dangerous, yet for which he was admirably fitted in view of the fact that his black face disarmed all suspicions as to his true character. To this precious [white] quartette full of complacent conceit of their species, he was simply a black. So far as they knew he was simply a few removes from a benighted heathen, and, unlike the Anglo-Saxon, incapable of understanding the meaning of things said in his presence. He was quiet, unobtrusive, obsequious, a model servant. (67)

Like Randolph's, Venus's presence is an unpresence. As a result of her race and gender, Venus's subjectivity is taken away from her, rendering her a nonthreat. Similar to Ralph Ellison's unnamed narrator in *Invisible Man* who desperately tries to be seen and recognized in an unseeing world, Venus uses that unseen status to empower herself by accessing and trespassing across class, racial, and gendered borders. In fact, it is her status as the Bowen family servant that allows her to witness St. Clair/Benson threatening Hagar/Estelle. When a ransom note arrives soon afterward, Venus directly suspects Benson: "I just made up my mind it was Venus for General Benson, and that I'd got to cook his goose or he'd cook mine" (226). Furthermore, after some strategic questioning of her father's past history, Venus also suspects him of aiding Benson:

> "It's as sure as preaching that somebody who knows something must take hold of Miss Jewel's case or that son of Sodom will carry his point. The police are slower 'n death. Dad's up to his capers. He can fool ma, but he can't pull the wool over my eyes; I'm his daughter. Hump! well, we'll see about it. It's a burning shame for dad to go on this way after all Miss Jewel's kindness to us. But I'll balk him. I'll see him out on this case or my name ain't Venus Johnson. . . . I'll see if this one little black girl can't get the best of as mean a set of villains as ever was born." (221)

In order to detect successfully, however, this "one little black girl" must first transform into a little black boy. Interestingly, what may be perceived as an unpresence in white society is not necessarily so in a black one. Because Venus cannot wander unseen and unnoticed within a black environment (especially an environment in which her family is well known and in which her father is hiding), she disguises herself in drag in order to bypass the black gaze at the old Enson estate where Jewel is imprisoned. As "Billy," Venus is not only able to shield herself from the "prying eyes" (233) of her family's old friends and acquaintances, but she is also able to disguise herself from her own father, leading to the discovery of Jewel and Aunt Henny.

Finally, by showing detection via a black gaze, Hopkins is also commenting upon definitions of justice and criminality when she points to the white male characters—St. Clair and Walker—as the sole criminals in this novel of blackmail, conspiracy, and murder. For it is quite telling that the final status of Isaac Johnson, Venus's father and St. Clair's coconspirator, is unknown at the end of the novel. While St. Clair and Walker are both imprisoned for their behavior and eventually die, we are left ignorant of Isaac's fate after he attempts to rescue St. Clair from jail. Furthermore, Aurelia, another coconspirator, also escapes punishment and mysteriously disappears in a quick narrative closure: "Nothing criminal was charged against Aurelia; in fact, no one desired to inflict more punishment on the unfortunate woman, and when she left the court room that day she vanished forever from public view" (272). With these two exceptions, Hopkins makes a subtle yet significant statement about crime, justice, criminality, and guilt. As a novel of detection seen through a black and female perspective, *Hagar's Daughter* shows the tragic consequences of slavery, racism, and sexism. As victims possessed and ruled by white men (St. Clair and Walker, respectively), Isaac and Aurelia are shown to have little choice in their actions and moral upbringing. Hence, in a reversal of earlier tales where blackness is synonymous with crime, Hopkins chooses to legally, philosophically, and morally punish the owners rather than their "property" for murder, kidnapping, and fraud. In a tale full of gazing and surveillance, a theme that I will discuss below, this is one angle that Hopkins refuses to acknowledge.

In addition to "undetecting" Isaac and Aurelia, Hopkins also shows that other types of blackness cannot be detected as well. For instance, Amy Robinson's argument that racial clairvoyance is not about ontological truth claims is evident in *Hagar's Daughter* when we see that black eyes do not necessarily detect markers of hidden blackness. Upon hearing of Hagar's "real" racial identity, for example, Marthy asks her mother, Aunt Henny, "do you b'lieve Miss Hagar got nigger blud in her?" (65). Aunt Henny responds, "Course not, honey. Somebody roun' hyar done conjured her. Dat Debbil, St. Cla'r, I spec" (65). As in-group members, both Aunt Henny and Marthy cannot see blackness in Jewel. Furthermore, Hagar herself is the most shocked by her discovery of her racial identity. Soon after Walker's accusation, Hagar examines herself in the mirror where "even to her prejudiced eyes there was not a trace of the despised chattel" (57). To Hagar, blackness is synonymous with phenotypical features: "Hagar suddenly arose, caught her [Marthy] by the shoulders and turned her toward the light, minutely examining the black skin, crinkled hair, flat nose and protruding lips. So might her grandmother have looked" (56). As Ellis questions, "How were we to know? How could we tell? (61). Hopkins's underlying premise here is that passing cannot be visually detected. In fact, Hopkins shows that passing is detected only when the detector has prior knowledge of the passing or the passer reveals him/herself. For example, Walker knows of Hagar's passing only because he sold her to the Sargeants and thus knows her history. Similarly, St. Clair/Benson recognizes Estelle's passing when he meets her in Washington because he recognized her as Hagar, not necessarily as a black woman passing for white. Jewel's and Aurelia's passing is also discovered because their hidden histories are revealed by Senator Bowen's letter and Elsie Bradford, respectively. Finally, Hagar's passing is revealed at the conclusion of the novel because she admits to her blackness herself when in the courtroom she cries, *"Ellis! Ellis! I am Hagar!"* (261, emphasis in original). Thus, if passing is not detectable, why does Hopkins create the first novel of black detection centering on passing? More significantly, what is she saying about the relationship between detection, passing, and empowerment? Finally, what is the role of black detection in both the white and black communities?

Before answering these questions, I want to discuss the role of the gaze in this novel in which everyone is constantly and persistently watching everyone else throughout the narrative. In fact, in many ways this is a story of racialized voyeurism where characters are relentlessly glancing, studying, and scrutinizing themselves and each other. From the very beginning, Hopkins's tale is full of visual references from the act of seeing to the eyes themselves. These descriptions range from the merely descriptive ("dazzling eyes," "laughing eyes," "straining eyes") to the revelation of emotions ("piercing gaze," "down-cast eyes," "accusing eyes," "pitying glance," "covertly watched") to potential hints of racial affiliation ("long-lashed eyes of brilliant black," "dark eyes," "his eyes were a shrewd and steely gray"). From the prospective buyers who are inspecting the slaves "on view" to Ellis, who turns his "flaming eyes" (54) on Walker upon hearing his accusation of Hagar, to the "fast-glazing eyes" (198) of Senator Bowen on his deathbed, to St. Clair/Benson's "furtive glance" (114) at Hagar upon seeing her for the first time after twenty years, the act of gazing at or being gazed at persistently haunts almost every other page in the narrative. More significantly, Hopkins makes clear that everyone, not just blacks or whites, passers or nonpassers, is watching and studying. Therefore, I would like to describe four specific scenes that highlight the racially coded mechanics of the gaze. What these scenes reveal, however, is that in a story that depicts the visual undetectability of the passing body amid a maze of surveillance, Hopkins shows that racial and gender differences often equip marginalized detectors with intuitive skills unavailable to the Eurocentric white gaze. Furthermore, unlike Eurocentric detective narratives that emphasize the affirmation and uncovering of detection, the black detectors in *Hagar's Daughter* show that not all detections should be verbalized nor exposed.

While the first scene does not necessarily display skills of intuition, it does describe the schizophrenic obsession with the gaze that often occurs within the black passing psyche. As such, I would like to return to Hagar's observation of herself in the mirror after the discovery of her black identity in order to lay a foundation for how Foucault's panoptic model gets restructured within the dynamics of passing and detection:

> Once more Hagar crouched upon the floor. She felt like writhing and screaming, only her tongue seemed paralyzed. She thought and thought with agonizing intensity. Vaguely, as in a dream, she recalled her stay in Rose Valley and the terror of her childish heart caused by the rough slave-trader. Could it be true, or was it but a hideous nightmare from which she would soon awake? Her mother a slave! She wondered that the very thought did not strike her dead. With shrinking horror she contemplated the black abyss into which the day's events had hurled her, leaving her there to grovel and suffer the tortures of the damned. Her name gone, her pride of birth shattered at one blow! Was she, indeed, a descendant of naked black savages of the horrible African jungles? Could it be that the blood of generations of these unfortunate ones flowed through her veins? Her education, beauty, refinement, what did they profit her now if—horrible thought, Ellis, her husband, repudiated her? Her heart almost ceased beating with the thought, and she crouched still lower in the dust of utter humiliation.
>
> Then she rose and walked about the room; it was crowded with her wedding finery. . . . She examined her features in the mirror, but even to her prejudiced eyes there was not a trace of the despised chattel. One blow with her open hand shattered its shining surface and the pieces flew about in a thousand tiny particles; she did not notice in her frenzy that the hand was torn and bleeding. (57)

In this scene, Hagar experiences a *triple* vision of her self in her moment of discovery. With the knowledge of her black taint, Hagar becomes simultaneously the Foucauldian guard *and* inmate(s). She enacts axial visibility upon herself by gazing at her self through the eyes of a guard or policer of racial boundaries: "Was she, indeed . . . ?" "Could it be . . . ?" That she is defining herself within the binary oppositions of a hegemonically racist definition ("black savages" versus "education, beauty, refinement") shows that prior to the discovery, Hagar is positioned as the guard dwelling within the distant and elevated tower. However, this scene also displays the double conscious struggle of the two Hagars. When looking at her reflection, Hagar positions herself as neighboring inmates, placed side by side in a play of schizophrenic lateral visibility. In one cell, Hagar's white passing body is on display, self-scrutinizing that body for evidence of blackness. In the next cell, Hagar's blackness returns the gaze, reminding her that she will never escape the constant surveillance of her black taint. This multiply gazing moment resulting from Hagar's discovery initiates the struggle between passing and detection that occurs in the rest of the narrative. In Hopkins's story, black passing identity has now become a play of eye-dentity. As I argue above, invisible race is not detectable. However, what we see in the following scenes is that while race may not be visually perceived, race detection is often intuitively detected within the black community. Furthermore, these moments of in-group clairvoyance, whether conscious or not, take place specifically between black women.

The Oxford English Dictionary defines "intuition" as follows: "The immediate apprehension of an object by the mind without the intervention of any reasoning process; immediate apprehension by sense; direct or immediate insight; the action of mentally looking at; contemplation, consideration; perception, recognition; mental view." The ability to "immediately apprehend" something without any "reasoning process," at least a Eurocentric reasoning process, is what occurs in the next two scenes beginning with Jewel observing Aurelia during a night at the theater. Unlike Hagar, who wrestles with her gaze in the above scene, Jewel is mesmerized by Aurelia, unable to take her eyes off her:

> As the curtain went down on the second act she lifted her glass and slowly scanned the house. Suddenly she paused with a heart that *throbbed strangely*. Directly across from her sat a woman—young in years, but with a mature air of a woman of the world. *"Surely," thought Jewel, "I know that face."* The girl had a woman's voluptuous beauty with great dusky eyes and wonderful red-gold hair. Her dress of moss-green satin and gold fell away from snowy neck and arms on which diamonds gleamed. Just then Sumner uttered an exclamation of surprise. He had turned, almost at the same moment as Jewel, and swept a careless glance over the house. . . . Passing, as it were, a box on the left, his glance had rested on a face that instantly arrested it and caused him to exclaim. . . .
>
> The lady was watching their box intently, and seeing herself discovered smiled a brilliant smile of recognition as she inclined her head in Sumner's direction holding his glance. (90–91, emphasis mine)

While Jewel's recognition of Aurelia is later dismissively explained away by them being old school friends, the significance of this scene lies in its foreshadowing of Jewel's eventual discovery of her blackness at the end of *Hagar's Daughter.* For the "immediate apprehension" here is Jewel's intuitive albeit unconscious recognition that she and Aurelia are mirrored reflections of each other as two undetected passing women. Their unspoken racial bond is evidenced by the constant descriptions of them in unison. For example, both Jewel and Aurelia are objects of Cuthbert's affections. While Cuthbert views Jewel as a "fair fragrant lily . . . [who encapsulated] womanly goodness and truth" (103), he sees Aurelia as a "gorgeous tropical flower . . . [who] caused his blood to flow faster" (103). Although Jewel and Aurelia are described as opposites in Cuthbert's view, they are still often described singly when together. For instance, when seeing them together for the first time, Hagar declares, "No lovelier *vision* was ever seen than these two girls as they entered the Bowen drawing-room" (106), emphasis mine). Later, Senator Bowen also states, "What a *sight* for sore eyes the pair of them makes!" (108), emphasis mine). As a unified "vision" and "sight," Jewel and Aurelia have been conjoined in their multiplicity. Thus, Aurelia (like Hagar's reflection above) mirrors Jewel's future black self looking back at her, foretelling not only their mutual conspiracy of passing (although Jewel is unaware of it for the majority of the narrative) but the fate of black passing women in general for the ending of *Hagar's Daughter* portrays them both tragically; one dies, and the other is banished. Furthermore, Jewel's strangely throbbing heart and adamant recognition of Aurelia—"I know that face"—is, I argue, a result of Jewel's uncanny, intuitive recognition of Aurelia as this double. As Freud explains, the uncanny is that which is frightening not because it is unfamiliar and unknown but because it is a *reoccurrence* of the old and familiar. The uncanny "is in reality nothing new or alien, but something which is familiar and old-established in the mind and which has become alienated from it only through the process of repression. This reference to the factor of repression enables us, furthermore, to understand Schelling's definition of the uncanny as something which ought to have remained hidden but has come to light" (241). Thus, what eventually comes to light for Jewel as a result of this encounter is her repressed and hidden blackness. That Jewel may not yet recognize this reoccurrence is irrelevant. It merely supports my claim that intuitive knowledge—in this case, an intuitive knowledge not yet recognized as such but nevertheless is still in play—is silently but persistently at work within Jewel and, as I show below, within the African

American community of *Hagar's Daughter*. As a community that has been historically profiled and "scientifically" detected as criminalized figures (whether in literature, racial science, or criminal anthropology), it is not surprising that this community has fashioned an intuitive faculty that enables them to be highly sensitive and strategic detectors. In fact, *Hagar's Daughter* shows that detection is a necessary tool of survival for the black community, one that the white detectors in this novel do not possess. Thus, when Ellis/Detective Henson praises Jewel for her "woman[ly] intuition" (190) when she suspects St. Clair/Benson of wrongdoing, what he does not recognize is that Jewel's gender-based gift of intuition is racially influenced as well.

Jewel's intuitive skills are also evident in her yet undiscovered mother, Hagar/Estelle. The third scene occurs soon after the aforementioned scene when Aurelia visits the Bowens at home. While Hagar/Estelle is immediately drawn to Aurelia, she quickly becomes aware of a sense of unease at her presence:

> She [Hagar] conversed freely and pleasantly with the unexpected guest, although after the first feeling of wonder and satisfaction at so much loveliness, she was surprised and puzzled at the vague feeling of distrust and dislike that personal contact with her young guest brought her. It was intangible. She shook it off, however, the beautiful face and voice were so enchanting that she could not resist them, and felt ashamed of her distrust. (107)

Although ashamed of her doubts, Hagar's intangible feeling of "distrust and dislike" is very accurate because Aurelia is in a plot to separate Jewel and Cuthbert. What is interesting here is Hagar's immediate intuitive feeling of this distrust for her unease is not just due to Aurelia's plot against her daughter but also Hagar's intuitive recognition that Aurelia, like herself, is a passing black woman. But, unlike Jewel's uncanny attraction to Aurelia where she is completely ignorant of her racial identity, both Hagar and Aurelia are very much aware of their own secret passing. As such, Hagar shows distrust here because she intuitively understands that her deceit can be detected, much like Aurelia's passing is later on. Furthermore, unlike in the encounter between Clare and Irene in Larsen's *Passing* in which both women acknowledge the other's passing, Hagar's intuition is a result of her unconscious in-group clairvoyance. Whether she knows it or not, Hagar/Estelle's suspicions prove to be ultimately true.

Finally, another episode of black on black female gazing occurs in the encounter between Hagar/Estelle and Aunt Henny. This scene takes place soon after Venus recovers Jewel and Aunt Henny from Enson Hall and begins with Venus telling her tale of discovery. It is also the first time that Aunt Henny and Hagar/Estelle reunite, sparking some recognition on Aunt Henny's part: "Aunt Henny said nothing, but once in a while she would nod her turbaned head in seeming perplexity, as she furtively watched every movement made by Mrs. Bowen. For her part, Mrs. Bowen seemed uneasy under the old woman's persistent regard" (241). Aunt Henny is an interesting figure in *Hagar's Daughter* because next to Venus she self-admittedly possesses the most powerful skills of detection in this novel: "Yer Aunt Henny *was born wif a veil.* I knows a heap o' things by seein' 'em fo' dey happens. I don' tell all I sees, but I keeps up a steddyin' 'bout it" (43, emphasis in original). But, whether Aunty Henny's powers are hoodoo (as Stephen Soitos would describe them) or intuition, I want to emphasize here the significance of the relationship between silence and detection within the black community. In the above encounter, Aunt Henny recognizes Estelle as Hagar yet remains silent. Furthermore, in an earlier scene, Aunt Henny also recognizes Benson as St. Clair—"I'se seed a ghos'!" (178)—and remains silent. The significance of these two moments of silent recognition is *when* and *if* Aunt Henny decides to verbalize it for it is telling that she maintains her silence about Hagar/Estelle's real identity to the end, yet she announces not only St. Clair's murder of Elsie Bradford but also his true identity in a public courtroom:

> "He ain't Gin'ral Benson no more'n I'm a white 'ooman. His name's St. Clair Enson; he was born nex' do' to de Sargeant place on the Enson plantation. Ise one ob de fus' ones what held him when he was born. Ise got a scar on me, jedge, where dat imp ob de debbil hit me wid a block ob wood when he warn't but seven years ol'. Fus' time I seed him in dat 'partmen' I know'd him time I sot my eye on him, an' den I know'd thar'd be rucktions kicked up, fer ef eber der was a born lim' o' de debbil it's dat same St. Clair Enson." (256)

By accusing St. Clair under an authority of legal jurisdiction, Aunt Henny reverses the binary of guilty/black versus innocent/white that is evident in earlier narratives of crime and detection. Furthermore, by placing her on the witness stand, Hopkins also criticizes the illegality of allowing blacks to testify. Although the courtroom reacts hostilely to Aunt Henny's testimony and is pacified by Ellis/Detective Henson's own revelations shortly afterward, the significance of Aunt Henny's accusation strongly stands. By speaking out against St. Clair while remaining silent about Hagar, Aunt Henny displays a loyalty to her black community. Additionally, in keeping Hagar's secret, a secret that is unfairly imposed upon her as a result of a racist and sexist society, Aunt Henny demonstrates loyalty not only to her black community in general but to black female subjectivity in particular. As the first author of color to write a black novel of detection, Hopkins illustrates through Aunt Henny's lateral visibility of silent detection that telling (or not telling) is sometimes much more important than knowing.

I would like to conclude by referring back to the anxiety of miscegenation that began this section. On the one hand, Hopkins shows that passing bodies and the undetected intrusion of black blood are everywhere, perpetuating the anxiety of detection and blackness. On the other hand, though, she seems to quench these anxieties by re-placing all the passing bodies in their "rightful" place by the conclusion of the narrative. In some ways, Hopkins's narrative may be read as an antimiscegenation plot for all the offspring of interracial unions as well as the unions themselves end tragically and somewhat hopelessly: Jewel and Cuthbert's happy marriage is cut short due the discovery of her black blood and his subsequent rejection of her; Cuthbert's attraction for Aurelia is also quickly quenched by his realization of her blackness; and Ellis and Hagar's otherwise happy reunion is tainted by the death of their only child, Jewel. Although Cuthbert realizes at the end that his rejection is really the "sin [of] the nation's" (283), the ending seems to support the longevity of blood purity by showing St. Clair and Elsie's son, the "last representative of the Enson family" (284), playing joyfully on the Enson estate. As a result, *Hagar's Daughter* seems to end rather conservatively and problematically. However, I want to propose another possibility to this somewhat ambiguous ending by claiming that there is another implied albeit invisible passing figure in *Hagar's Daughter*—Senator Bowen. From his very first appearance, Senator Bowen's racial background is somewhat suspicious. Physically, he is described as a "dark man" of "dark complexion" (76) with "the hair and skin of an Indian" (80). Furthermore, his personal background, rather than giving us a satisfactory appraisal of his history, stimulates more questions about his origins:

> The Honorable Zenas was an example of the possibilities of individual expansion under the rule of popular government. Every characteristic of his was of the self-made pattern. In familiar conversation with intimate friends, it was his habit to fall into the use of ungrammatical phrases, and, in this, one might easily trace the

> rugged windings of a life of hardship among the great unwashed before success had crowned his labors and steered his bark into its present smooth harbor. He possessed a rare nature: one of those genial men whom the West is constantly sending out to enrich society. He had begun life as a mate on a Mississippi steamboat. When the Civil War broke out, he joined the Federal forces and at its close was mustered out as "Major Bowen." His wife dying about this time, he took his child, Jewel, and journeyed to California, invested his small savings in mining property in the Black Hills. His profits were fabulous; he counted his pile way up in the millions. (80)

Couldn't it be possible that Senator Bowen's "self-made pattern" here is that of a poor, struggling, uneducated ("it was his habit to fall into the use of ungrammatical phrases") light-skinned black man who passes into the white world and succeeds, both racially and financially? Couldn't it be possible that his own identity of blackness is the real reason behind Senator Bowen's quick and easy acceptance of Hagar's racial passing? While we may never know the answer to Senator Bowen's racial identity, we do know that Hopkins releases Aurelia, a known passing figure, into society again. Furthermore, we can safely assume that she will continue to pass. Therefore, by letting Aurelia go free as well as casting doubts on Bowen's racial affiliation and thus representing him as an undetected passing figure, Hopkins's narrative, while seemingly conservative, again reconfirms the anxiety of race detection to a potential white audience. As such, *Hagar's Daughter* concludes not only with a rebuke against racism, but it also maintains the instability of the detection of blackness, foreshadowing much of the twentieth century's anxieties about passing, hybridity, and race detection.

3 / Detecting Winnifred Eaton

The story of Winnifred Eaton is full of detective anxieties. By now, students and critics familiar with Asian American literary history are also well acquainted with the debate surrounding Edith and Winnifred Eaton's status as pioneers of the Asian American literary canon. Rediscovered in the 1970s and remaining a focal point in academic studies, Edith and Winnifred are generally acknowledged as foremothers of Asian American literary history. I do not wish to revive the controversy over the Eaton sisters' standing within Asian American studies; many scholars, including Viet Nguyen, Tomo Hattori, Dominika Ferens, and Karen Skinazi, among others, have recently dismantled the good versus bad sister paradigm. Instead, this essay offers a rereading of Winnifred Eaton's legacy via the lens of detection and the anxieties produced by its failures, especially the threat of race passing. That Eaton[1] was publishing at the height of both classic detective fiction and African American passing tales is not mere coincidence; that she has not previously been viewed against this historical and literary context is a surprising omission.[2] This analysis is a response to this oversight. I argue that Eaton's reliance on a racial/ethnic passing trope (both in her choice of pseudonym as well as within her Japanese romances) cannot be fully appreciated without situating her within the context of the detection-passing panic that swept America during the first quarter of the twentieth century. This interpretive framework enables us to reconceptualize Eaton as a foremother of Asian American fiction. It also highlights her familiarity with rules of genre (especially detective fiction and African American passing narratives) and her participation in the construction of racial epistemologies then being codified by law and perpetuated by racial science.

Further, my reading reenvisions Eaton's legacy to Asian American studies via Zhou Xiaojing's call for a resistance to and transformation of traditional hegemonic European American literary genres. As Xiaojing states in the introduction to *Form and Transformation in Asian American Literature*, this critical approach "demonstrate[s] a much more dynamic and complex relationship between Asian American and traditional European American literature" (4). Eaton responded to European white America's increasing racial anxieties and demands for detection—the central practice in detective fiction—with narratives of *un*detection. As a genre then predominantly authored by white males, detective fiction promoted and relied upon conventional racial knowledges and boundaries under the guise of rationalism and critical reasoning. As a biracial woman performing ethnic passing, Eaton questioned these very strict racial borders while simultaneously highlighting the constant insecurities and anxieties fostered by undetection. At the same time, Eaton not only responded to but added to the growing breadth of passing narratives—a traditionally African American genre—by providing an Asian American perspective. Through her use of three popular genres (romance, detective fiction, and passing narratives), Eaton addresses both European America *and* Black America, arguing for an inclusion of Asian Americans as participants and not just objects of study.

Eaton's rise to fame through her Japanese romances occurred during the heyday of the passing narrative. Popularized in the second half of the nineteenth century into the Harlem Renaissance by writers such as Pauline Hopkins, Kate Chopin, Mark Twain, Nella Larsen, and Charles Chesnutt, among others, the passing narrative has been a well-established genre of academic study in recent years.[3] Much of Eaton scholarship focuses on passing, especially on Eaton's own passing for Japanese, but little has been published that offers a comparative race perspective on passing.[4] Eaton's authorial and fictional passing took place within the larger discussions of racial passing evident during the first quarter of the twentieth century and, therefore, must be contextualized within this literary and cultural milieu. While traditional African American passing tales focus on light-skinned characters passing for white in order to escape racist restrictions and injustices, Eaton's "passing" stories predominantly center on mixed-race Japanese heroines who reject racial passing and maintain their Japaneseness. But why does Eaton simultaneously perform ethnic passing while concurrently rejecting passing in her fiction? Perhaps we need to examine Eaton and her romances from a different angle that does not highlight passing per se but, rather, the anxiety of detection, an often overlooked partner to the passing plot. As I illustrate below, Eaton's novels are tales of undetection where the heroines *refuse* to pass for white although each published novel portrays them becoming increasingly white. The passing act, in fact, is imposed upon Eaton's heroines by the outside observer who struggles with the disjuncture between what s/he sees versus the "passer's" self-identification. These stories do not adhere to the generic conventions of the passing narrative where the central plot is driven by the passer's fear and avoidance of detection; instead, Eaton's Japanese romances epitomize an antipassing plot where the fear of detection (or, more specifically, the fear of *failed* detection) is a destabilizing threat encountered by the detective figure him/herself.

For Eaton, the passing act does not merely display the insecurities or the desperation of the passing figure but also reveals the anxieties of the detector. The interdependent relationship between passer and detector is not an arbitrary one. It is not a coincidence, for instance, that the rise of the passing tale in American literary history and culture occurs simultaneously with the emergence and popularity of the detective narrative. The parallel here is not too surprising since the underlying fear in the passing narrative is the explicit or implicit threat of detection. Concurrently, one of the central concerns of the detective story is the stabilization and alleviation of (racial) chaos. The point at which passing and detection intersect is the focus of this study.

Many critics have written about detective fiction's appeal to a society overwhelmed by the ever-changing demands and chaos of urbanization, industrialization, and modernity. As R. Gordon Kelly argues, it is within this modern state that the fundamental stance of the detective involves an "asymmetrical relationship of knowledge, and hence of power" (29). In other words, the detective must "know the other better than the other is allowed to know the detective" (29). This asymmetrical relationship, however, became reversed when fears of immigration and amalgamation and their combined subsequent threat of racial erasure entered the scene. As one of the most sensitive and precarious moments in the formation of the American nation-state, the commencement of the twentieth century is clouded by the quandary of how one detects race when it is no longer phenotypically visible? The inability to detect race has not only disabled the detective from "knowing the other," but it has enabled the other to strategically utilize the detective's knowledge for his/her gain. This long-standing cultural dilemma stretching from the end of the nineteenth century until today presents racial ambiguity and the subsequent need to identify and contain uncertainty as the ultimate driving force of the passing-detection matrix. Recent scholarship on law, immigration, and citizenship (Ian Haney Lopez's *White by Law* and Ariela Gross's *What Blood Won't Tell*), miscegenation (Peggy Pascoe's *What Comes Naturally,* Elizabeth Smith-Pryor's *Property Rites*, and Heidi Ardizzone and Earl Lewis's *Love on Trial*), and racial science (Stephen Jay Gould's *The Mismeasure of Man* and Nancy Stepan's *The Idea of Race in Science*) reflects the historical urgency of the passing-detection relationship.

In literary history, it is telling that several of the early detective authors—Edgar Allan Poe, Arthur Conan Doyle, and Mark Twain—all include the anxiety of detecting race via passing in their tales ("Murders in the Rue Morgue," "The Yellow Face," and *Pudd'nhead Wilson*, respectively), undermining the ratiocinative and deductive reasoning skills of superhero detectives like C. Auguste Dupin and Sherlock Holmes and their abilities to detect race. It is important to note here that all three of these early narratives display the intimate connection between anxieties of race detection to fears around black-white sexual mixing. As argued by Lindon Barrett and Elise Lemire, the not-so-subtle hidden message in Poe's "Murders," in which two white women are viciously murdered by a knife-yielding orangutan, is one that displays the fear of black male bodies and the threat of miscegenation.[5] Further, Lemire argues that the detective genre, while keeping the sexual violence center stage, ensures that the reader and the detective "will never have to confront their own involvement in the violent and erotic spectacle from which they cannot avert their eyes" (199).

In addition to Poe, Doyle and Twain also reveal the destabilization of undetectable black bodies and its relation to law, crime, and detection in "The Yellow Face" (1893) and *Pudd'nhead Wilson* (1894), respectively. Published less than a year apart, both "The Yellow Face" and *Pudd'nhead* explicitly illustrate the fears and results of cross-racial mixing and the subsequent destabilization to the detection of racial borders. In Doyle's short story, the superhuman Sherlock Holmes fails in his detection due to little Lucy Hebron, a passing girl who is the product of a white British woman and an American free man of color (FMC). While Doyle simultaneously critiques and scandalizes American race relations by creating a tale that sexually unites white femininity with black masculinity as well as empowering the black male (he is free *and* a lawyer by trade),

Twain's tale illustrates the ultimate unmentionable threat to race passing: race switching. In the end, both Doyle's and Twain's tales result in failed detections: Holmes completely miscalculates in his solution, and although the race switching is discovered at the end of *Pudd'nhead* by Pudd'nhead Wilson's fingerprinting technique, white Tom is forever tainted in his blackness.[6]

The mutual connection between the detection and passing tropes is further illustrated in the passing tale in which the threat of detection is almost always the implied subtext (hence the hidden nature of passing).[7] As such, the narrative desire (à la Peter Brooks) in the passing narrative is the need to detect the passing figure(s). As Brooks argues in *Reading for the Plot*, we are driven to read in order to create meaningful order out of chaos. In the passing narrative, I would add that this narrative desire for closure may or may not be realized by detection due to the difference between the act of passing and the act of undetection. Here, James Weldon Johnson's *Autobiography of an Ex-Colored Man* is a telling example. *Autobiography* may be an example of unrealized narrative closure or one that maintains the threat of passing because the unnamed narrator continues to pass undetected at the conclusion of the story. Hence, for the conservative race reader, the desired closure is not achieved because the unnamed narrator maintains the threat of racial indecipherability and an intrusion into whiteness. However, Johnson's tale of successful passing also assuages some of the threat of detective failure by the narrator's admission that his passing was like "selling his soul for a mess of pottage" (207). This admission as well as his self-identification as an "unfound-out criminal" in the very first paragraph of his narrative place Johnson's passer into the role of wrongdoer and identify passing as a criminal act. The narrative, in fact, reads like a criminal's confession, and while he may still wander the streets in his passing identity, this confession of guilt, I argue, negates some of the subversive gain of the passing act. Hence, I differentiate between the act of passing and undetection in that passing may not always be acknowledged or discovered (i.e., the successful pass), thus the absence of detection.[8] It is in the moment of discovery and, I would even argue, self-chastisement (such as that of the unnamed narrator in Johnson's *Autobiography*) that detection and undetection come into play.[9]

While the anxieties of detective fiction may be eased by what John Cawelti defines as formula stories (such as the western, mystery, and romance) that give "satisfaction and a basic emotional security in a familiar form" (9), the potential threat of racial indecipherability in stories like the above may or may not be ultimately mastered and contained within the detective formula: the mystery may be solved, but assurance may not be attained. Eaton's antipassing tales play into and counter the satisfaction and security achieved through formula because, unlike the traditional formula of the African American passing tale where the plot of the story centers on the passer's success and/or failure at passing, Eaton's antipassing romances refute the passing story formula in order to counter the rules and regulations of racial formations. Although Eaton's heroines *can* pass, they choose not to, disrupting the detector's expectations and assumed competence in deciphering racial codes. Eaton utilizes the formulas of detective fiction, passing narratives, and the romance in order to debunk the formulas of race predominant during her time.[10] While detective fiction relies upon rational thinking and intuition (such as the ratiocinative methods used by Poe and Doyle) to solve the crime, Eaton shows that racial knowledge is not rational or intuitive for, as her heroines reveal, looking white does not necessarily make you white, a direct opposition to the racial science and legal discourse of her day, which relied on visual markers of racial difference or, as Ian Haney-López describes, "common knowledge" rather than scientific categorization.

Thus, for Eaton, race passing fosters an anxiety of detection for both the passer (who simultaneously fears detection and must avoid it) and the duped (who, in response to the threat of being duped, must consistently practice the game of detection). As a biracial woman who was often the subject of racial (un)detection, Eaton was highly attuned to the possibilities and limitations of what Amy Robinson refers to as the passing triad of passer, duped, and in-group. In "It Takes One to Know One," Robinson describes the cultural performance of passing as a "politics of optics" (716) in which the triangular theater of the pass is a "complex system of cultural literacy" (720) rather than an intuitive clairvoyance. Thus, the game of detection and undetection is acted out between the in-group and the duped, with the former recognizing the apparatus of passing of which the latter is unaware. The passing theater, then, operates on multiple levels of seeing and reading rather than epistemological certainty. For Robinson, the value of the passing act is in the *telling* over the knowing: "To read the apparatus of passing . . . is to value telling over knowing because the availability of codes of deception does not predict access to the authenticity of the subject of deception. If 'it takes one to know one' articulates a spectatorial position rather than an ontological truth claim, then identity politics is indeed a skill of reading and not merely a feeble reproduction of dominant ideologies" (723 emphasis in original). If the value of passing lies in *telling* rather than *knowing*, Eaton's romances claim the authority of telling via the passer who refuses to pass. In other words, because each of Eaton's Japanese and Eurasian heroines (from full-blooded Japanese Lady Wistaria in *Wooing of Wistaria* to the blond and blue-eyed mixed-raced Sunny in *Sunny-San*) maintains control over *how* they wish to be seen, they become subjects who tell rather than objects to be told upon. By empowering these heroines to control the telling, Eaton also proclaims that the detection of race is not based on epistemological truth (as maintained by legal or scientific discourse) but a "cultural literacy" that depends upon specific contexts and perspectives.

The Japanese Romances

Between 1899 and 1933, Eaton published numerous short stories and nonfiction essays as well as more than a dozen novels under the pseudonym Onoto Watanna. Ten of these novels, known as her Japanese romances, take place primarily in Japan and focus on a Japanese or Eurasian heroine and her white lover. With the publication of her first two critically acclaimed novels, *Miss Numè of Japan* (1899) and *A Japanese Nightingale* (1901) (which was made into a Broadway play and a silent movie), Eaton entered into the New York literary scene. There she garnered praise from such authors as William Dean Howells and, as Amy Ling reveals, "moved in a distinguished circle including such luminaries as Edith Wharton, Anita Loos, Jean Webster, David Belasco, Mark Twain, and Lew Wallace" (*Between Worlds* 29). Surprisingly, while there has been some analysis of Eaton's individual novels,[11] little critical attention has been paid to Eaton's oeuvre of Japanese romances as a whole.[12] Although space limitations here prevent an analysis of all ten romances, this study adds to the scholarship of Jean Lee Cole, Dominika Ferens, and Diana Birchall by reading Eaton's Japanese romances schematically and strategically. In short, Eaton's romances read as a progressive literary response to anxieties of race detection and antimiscegenation sentiment prevalent during the first quarter of the twentieth century.

Although Eaton's heroines become progressively whiter toward the end of her oeuvre, they also stridently maintain their Japaneseness despite their whitened exteriors. Since Eaton, the "bad" sister, is often condemned for passing as Japanese, it seems necessary to examine how she employs racial/ethnic indecipherability (i.e., the source of her "badness") not only in her literary persona but in her novels as well. Therefore, I focus on Eaton's three most radical works, *The Wooing of Wistaria*, *Tama*, and *Sunny-San*, concentrating on her explicit use of the passing trope (whether narrative or visual) to comment on passing not only from an Asian American perspective but also on the anxiety of detection and undetection occurring within the Asian American racialized landscape. In this reading of Eaton's Japanese novels, the author consistently promotes a rhetoric and alternative value system of *undetection* throughout each story. Eaton's Japanese romances endorse and celebrate racial/ethnic erasure or indecipherability. This does not constitute a denial of race or ethnicity (as some critics may claim), but rather calls into question her contemporary culture's obsessive reliance upon the categorization of racial difference. Further, the fact that Eaton operates within the romance genre is not a coincidence, for what is race passing if not a result of the taboo on racial mixing? At the most basic level, then, the threat of passing *begins with* the anxious union between white and other.[13]

I read Eaton's romances as divided between two thematic strands: (1) the all-Japanese story line that incorporates acts of passing (gender, switched identities) as catalysts to the plot, and (2) the interracial plot (which often is a passing plot). When read as a whole, both types—the intraracial and interracial narratives—present a telling and revisionary critique of detection and the anxiety of passing. For while the detection and acquisition of certain racial "truths" was the ultimate goal at the time, Eaton instead advertises a sort of empowerment via the perpetuation of undetections in her Japanese romances. The following analysis focuses on one example from the intraracial story line (*The Wooing of Wistaria*) and two examples from the interracial plots (*Tama* and *Sunny-San*) to illustrate how Eaton imagines the possibilities of the passing trope in a spectrum of both racially homogenous and racially mixed landscapes.

STRAND ONE: INTRARACIAL PLOTS AND THE UNDETECTION OF GENDER PASSING

The all-Japanese story line occurs within only three of the ten Japanese novels: *The Wooing of Wistaria* (1902), *Daughters of Nijo: A Romance of Japan* (1904), and *The Honorable Miss Moonlight* (1912). The all-Japanese tales are centered on lovers who are socially separated by caste and/or clan rivalries. Each of these three story lines incorporates acts of passing (namely gender passing and switched identities) that become essential to the happy conclusion of each tale. Thus, while the all-Japanese narratives do not necessarily comment upon the erasure of racial difference per se, I read them as a critique against the restrictive rules that confine and oppress the fluidities and flexibilities of identity formation. Similar to Deborah McDowell's reading of Nella Larsen's *Passing* in which race passing is the "safe" plot that shields the more dangerous secrets of sexuality, Eaton plays with hints of homoeroticism hidden behind an act of gender passing. However, any discomfort with oblique homosexuality is, unlike Larsen's "double burial" of both race and sexuality in *Passing*, negated by the heroines of Eaton's later novels and their refusal to pass. Here, I turn to one of the all-Japanese narratives to reveal how Eaton not only lauds passing and undetection as a strategic tool but also how she uses this tool to shield and provide room for other potentially transgressive acts.

The Wooing of Wistaria

The Wooing of Wistaria (1902), the first of Eaton's all-Japanese narratives, is, like all of her Japanese romances, a rendition of the *Romeo and Juliet* tragic love plot but with a *Twelfth Night* twist. More importantly, however, *Wooing* is also a story of detection and undetection, visibility and invisibility. Like Shakespeare's plays, it is a story of two opposing factions—the Shogun and the Mikado—ultimately coming together through the reunited marriage of Lady Wistaria and Prince Mori. While large portions of the novel are dedicated to battle scenes and military maneuvers (so much so that some critics believe the novel was cowritten by Eaton's husband, Bertrand Babcock), the book's general message is to emphasize the transgression of socially sanctioned borders (in this case, clan rivalries as well as caste divisions). Here, the unions of Wistaria and Mori are culturally and socially forbidden not only because they belong to opposing factions but also because Wistaria's mother was an "Eta," or "untouchable," woman. The opening of *Wooing* begins with the simultaneous staging of visibility while being denied vision. Lady Wistaria undergoes the "education of a Japanese maid" (8), which involves the "moulding of her whole character" (8), including looking, acting, and believing in the part. The narrator reveals that while the average girl "succumbs to the hereditary instinct of implicit obedience" (8), Wistaria is not an average girl. Operating against a backdrop that presumes such "instincts" to be hereditary, Wistaria shows instead that such "instincts" are not genetically predetermined but that belief in such hereditary instinct exists to implement a strict, gendered behavior. Hence, *Wooing* begins with the explicit transgression of normal, "hereditary" behavior.

This is demonstrated early on when Wistaria, having seemingly completed her education, is displayed in court. Although she is warned that "while all eyes might gaze upon her, she must see no one" (9), Wistaria steals not one but two glances, which are met with astonishment and scorn from The Lady Evening Glory, her aunt and educator. Wistaria's purposeful gaze is seen as an act of rebellion and lack of humility, and it results in a quick departure from court. Not surprisingly, her departure is hastened under a covered veil, again denying her vision.

This seemingly simple act of rebellious gazing may seem inconsequential in itself, but it is significant in light of its relation to a pivotal moment of gender passing that occurs later in the plot. After Wistaria is denied and punished for her gaze, she in turn subverts the seeing/unseeing dynamic when she secretly disguises herself as a young boy in order to help her disgruntled lover in battle. As "Jiro," Wistaria not only helps turn the direction of the battle, but she does so as a brave, talented, and cunning soldier who later, at the end of the novel, saves Mori from performing seppuku, or ritual suicide. As "Jiro," Wistaria switches from one who is denied active viewing to one who sees everything (she is often described as secretly watching Mori's every move as well as having access to the "enemy's" secrets). Ironically, in her passing garb, her true self remains unseen. Wistaria's passing not only critiques the limitations of socially constructed caste divisions but also calls into question the gender restrictions of a culture deeply steeped in traditional male and female roles.

Eaton takes Wistaria's passing beyond boundaries of caste and traditional gender by introducing a subtle yet significant moment of homoeroticism between Mori and Jiro. Due to Jiro's continued loyal and dedicated service, Mori becomes "strangely drawn" (329) to "him." This relationship culminates in a curious scene toward the end of the novel shortly before Jiro's passing is revealed. Here Mori is reunited with Jiro after a long absence. At this reunion, Mori realizes that he is drawn to Jiro and a "longing, throbbing into wistfulness, pervade[s] him" (377). It may be that Mori is experiencing homosocial rather than homoerotic feelings toward Jiro. But it is telling that this moment of "longing [and] throbbing" immediately leads into a jealous lovers' reunion.

While we may never know whether Eaton meant this to be a homoerotic moment and, therefore, another moment of transgression in a novel full of transgressions, we cannot help but suspect Eaton's motives when we step back and remember that, after all, this story is a romance. Not surprisingly, the potential dangers of such a reading are dismissed and interrupted when, at their next encounter, Jiro reveals her true identity. Thus, Mori and Wistaria are reunited, and the homoerotic subtext is safely and forever silenced. The point here is that if *Wooing* uses the passing trope as both a challenge to essentialist strictures as well as to create anxiety at failed detection, then it is not too far-fetched to suggest that Eaton may be playing with other possible undetections, including those of sexuality. That Jiro's passing goes undetected (except by her servant and personal samurai guard, Genji) until she chooses to reveal herself is also significant. The success of Wistaria's gender passing demonstrates the potential limitations and failures of boundaries and socially constructed "truths." No one could discern Jiro's true identity because no one could decipher his/her disguise, thus diminishing the power of such boundaries. However, given the time it was written, the homoerotic play between Mori and Jiro makes it *necessary* that revelation (not detection) occurs. While Eaton flirts with gender subversions, she is not willing to completely entertain or explicitly disclose the possibility of a homoerotic relationship and, therefore, returns Mori and Jiro/Wistaria back to a heterosexually normative coupling. Nevertheless, this subversion of gender is emphasized via a schizophrenic moment when Mori is confronted with the discovery in the novel's final scene. Here, although he *hears* Jiro's voice, he *sees* Wistaria.

> "If it please thee, my lord, I am Jiro."
> "Lady Wistaria!" he gasped.
> "I am Wistaria," she said. (388)

At this moment, Wistaria embodies both Jiro and herself ("I am Jiro. . . . I am Wistaria"), simultaneously blurring the distinction while safely melting together the homoerotic into the heteronormative. Wistaria must be the one to self-disclose her passing because it is only through this revelation (and, therefore, her return to her female-ness) that Mori regains his heterosexual status.

More importantly, I want to emphasize the function of self-revelation (or the telling) *in opposition to* detection. To be detected is to be caught in the act of deception, necessitating punishment. This is the formula by which classic detective fiction functions. Wistaria, in an act of self-control and agency, chooses to reveal herself, maintaining her power and control over this masquerade. In other words, while Eaton may hesitate before a suggestion at homoeroticism, she still maintains the heroine's complete agency. Here, the detective figure (namely, Mori) fails in his detective skills; passing is a game in which Wistaria has full control. In a somewhat comedic conclusion, the novel closes with Mori collapsing to the floor while Wistaria soothes his aching head, perhaps the result of an unconscious denial of homoerotic desires. While the revelation provides a safe return to normative behavior, Eaton suggests that there are potential dangers and secrets behind undetection that may afflict the duped, like Mori, with a debilitating headache and that often hide a deeper layer of hidden desires potentially leading to transgressions too unmentionable to be explicitly discussed. Eaton clearly understands the significance of a passer's self-revelation. If detection is the passer's worst nightmare, then self-revelation takes away any fears of being caught.

STRAND TWO: INTERRACIAL LOVE AND THE ANTI-PASSING PLOT

If *Wooing* demonstrates how undetection is used on multiple levels within an intraracial paradigm, to fully understand Eaton's vision and re-vision of undetection, we must also examine how Eaton addresses passing within an interracial model. The second and most prolific strand of Eaton's Japanese romances includes the interracial plot. On a basic level, cross-racial admixture or amalgamation may by its very definition be read as a symbol of literal and metaphorical erasure or undetection. Through amalgamation, boundaries are crossed and integrated, erasing the borders present at the initial mixing. Eaton slowly yet consistently reveals this throughout her seven interracial story lines through two separate but closely connected themes: (*a*) the interracial love story involving an Asian woman and a Caucasian protagonist, and (*b*) the interracial love story involving a biracial/multiracial heroine and her white lover.[14] This distinction is significant because I read these interracial tales somewhat progressively, each leading into a more nuanced and prophetic imaginary of Eaton's views on race, racial epistemologies, and detection. In fact, one way of reading the two subplots within these interracial narratives is to think of the first subplot (the love story between the Asian and the Caucasian) as the precursor to the second subplot (romances between the hybrid, undetectable Asian women or offspring of the former full-blooded Asian heroine with the white, Western hero). As such, by the end of the miscegenation narratives that conclude with *Tama* (1910) and *Sunny-San* (1922), the female protagonists are completely *whitened*, and their common Asian heritage has become visually undetectable.

Tama

Tama (1910) is one of Eaton's strangest stories. It is an interracial love story but one with supernatural elements. It tells the tale of Tojin-san, a

Western professor contracted to teach at Fukui, a desolate town in Japan. Upon his arrival, he is warned of the "fox-woman." As a local officer explains:

> The fox-woman is a creature greatly to be feared. Her face and form, so said the Japanese, were of a marvelous whiteness and a beauty so dazzling that a mortal must cover his eyes to escape blindness. Her hair resembled the sunrays, so bright and glittering its color and effect. Gifted with this beauty of face and form, but devoid of soul, she had but one ruling and controlling ambition. She spent her days and nights lurking about the mountain passes, behind and within rocks and caves, luring men—aye, and women and children, too!—to destruction. (27)

The officer goes on to explain how the fox-woman is more dangerous than a regular spirit not only because of her "fiendish beauty" but also because she is "mischievous, impish, wicked, delighting as much in torturing and frightening the poor as well as the rich, little children as well as their elders" (29–30). This spirit/witch, Tojin-san discovers, is the terror of the town. She shows no fear, constantly foraging, stealing food from children and sleeping soldiers alike. The natives are also afraid of her because, as the legend warns, she can morph into any shape, like the frog in the story of Chuguro, who, being attacked by her, is "drained dry of blood" (93). Men are especially weakened by her spell, lured into her power by her irresistible beauty and ultimately destroyed. The professor, to the concern of his students, soon succumbs to the spell of the fox-woman himself, even without ever having seen her.

Beginning with this peculiar background, the story line quickly transforms from a haunting ghost story into an interracial love plot centering around vision and blindness when Tojin-san discovers that the fox-woman is seemingly a white woman: "He put back from her face the glittering veil of her hair, and as he did so his heart came up in his throat in a great, suffocating bound—for the face he uncovered was that of a white woman!" (106–7). Tojin-san learns that the fox-woman, previously thought to be an evil witch feared by all of Fukui, is, in actuality, a half-caste who became an outcast after the murder of her parents, an English sailor and a Noble Nun, by a zealous band of parishioners who sought retribution for the nun's desecration of her vows. Further, Tama, as she is named, not only looks white (she has purple/blue eyes, thin nose, and golden hair) but speaks fluent English. Most surprisingly, and perhaps most tellingly in terms of Eaton's critique of vision and detection, is that the witch woman, renowned for her quick escapes and undetectable nature, is blind.

This transformation from witch spirit who blinds anyone who gazes upon her to outcast half-caste who is herself blind is, to say the least, a strange and evocative narrative ploy. How does Eaton use this narrative to critique and/or offer new or even revolutionary ways to understand race and detection? For one, it would seem that this change strips away some of Tama's power, leaving her in a helpless, literal state of blindness. However, as noted above, she is the fear of the town. And although Tama is blind, she navigates around the wilderness with "that intuitive certainty of the blind" (179) that no full-sighted person possesses. In fact, her instincts are in a sense supernatural, being "keener than mere sight" (180–81). Although she is literally unable to see, Eaton portrays Tama as by far the most astute and visionary figure within the novel. She is so much the visionary that the people of Fukui, upon first seeing her, believe her to *be a vision*: "She seemed to their dazzled eyes a vengeful spirit, whom the Lord Buddha had uplifted. They stood as if petrified, staring at her as she swayed before them on the very lap of the god" (195).

The symbolism here is extraordinary. As a product of racial mixing who is herself visually undetectable, Tama embodies a vision of the future of the anxiety of interracial unions and race detection. However, her literal and symbolic role as blind visionary is rich with biting criticism. As a kind of racialized Teiresias figure, Tama questions the gap between seeing and knowing, knowledge and detection. More significantly, by representing Tama as sightless yet possessing an "intuitive certainty," Eaton again comments that intuition does not necessarily depend on experience (in this case, the experience of sight). Tama's intuitive clarity within her blind state is further validated during the novel's climactic ending, when Tojin-san enlists a surgeon friend to restore Tama's vision: "He would not have her this way, blind in mind and in sight. She must know the truth" (230). Tojin-san's truth, it turns out, is his own facial disfigurement. Afraid that Tama will reject him, Tojin-san avoids Tama. However, with her sight restored, Tama returns to Tojin-san, stating, "Wiz these my eyes closed . . . ad udder end those whole worl'—tha's same thing Tojin-san—I find way bag unto you!" (243). By returning to him "wiz these my eyes closed," Tama emphasizes that love as well as truth and knowledge are not gained by the mere act of seeing. In this novel, sight and vision are transitory and misleading acts, often leading to miscalculations and misinformation. Eaton not only critiques this type of "blind vision," but she also sets the stage for her last interracial plot, which elaborates the detachment between vision and knowledge.

Sunny-San

Sunny-San (1922) is Eaton's final Japanese novel, published ten years after her penultimate Japanese romance, *The Honorable Miss Moonlight*. It is also the only one of her Japanese romances to have a transnational narrative, beginning in Japan but taking place primarily in New York. Interestingly, this transnational crossing results in an ever more whitened protagonist heroine. Diana Birchall contends that *Sunny-San* is the least "Japanese" of Eaton's Japanese romances: "The language is not so stylized, the settings are less steeped in Japanese atmosphere, and the heroines grow whiter. Where Tama is a blonde fox woman, Sunny is the least Asian of all Eaton's Japanese heroines. She is blond, fair, blue-eyed, and only one-quarter Japanese, less Asian than Eaton herself" (137). According to Birchall, *Sunny-San* is a novel that minimizes Japan, making Japaneseness something to be ashamed of. As such, she reads this novel (which is set predominantly in the United States) as a transitional story that leaves behind the Japanese romances (and, for that matter, racial elements) for the more Western flair of her North American works, *Cattle* (1924) and *His Royal Nibs* (1925).

Although *Sunny-San* is very different from Eaton's other Japanese romances, I disagree with Birchall's reading. To read *Sunny-San* as erasing Japanese elements, implying an avoidance or dismissal of issues of race and difference, is to oversimplify Eaton's culminating work on race and the anxiety of detection. To the contrary, I read *Sunny-San* as illustrating a much more complex and nuanced portrayal of race, detection, and passing—this novel represents an example of how race and racial fears exist within an ever-increasing world of racially hybrid and undetectable bodies. Appropriately, it takes place in the United States at a time when racial anxieties were very much heightened and when anxiety over increased rates of interracial unions led to laws banning such unions. Publishing *Sunny-San* in 1922, Eaton was very much aware of this cultural backdrop. Even though race might no longer be visually obvious or evident, this very fact raised the political stakes. In fact, setting *Sunny-San* in the United States is quite revealing. As a biracial woman living in the United States, Eaton existed within a world that at best marginalized and at worst (socially, legally, culturally) condemned such bodies; her own life was, in fact, one of detection and undetection and all of the complexities resulting from that.[15] I read *Sunny-San* as a subtle yet innovative commentary on how race can be evoked and influential (and, perhaps, most threatening) when not easily observed in a type of "Asiatic" (to revise Toni Morrison's "Africanist" term) presence. Further, if Eaton has been promoting a rhetoric of undetection throughout her Japanese romances, it seems fitting that she ends her oeuvre by suggesting that racial distributions can be maintained even where visually absent. In other words, by demonstrating that race is everywhere, whether discernible or not, Eaton is perpetuating the anxiety of racial undetection that she herself negotiates.

Sunny-San is told in two parts. The first part occurs in Japan and tells of a young girl, Sunny, who is forced into becoming a geisha after her mother's death. A group of young American men see her being beaten and rescue her from the House of a Thousand Joys, ultimately buying her freedom. They then adopt her and form the Sunny Syndicate Limited to "care for Sunny for the rest of her days" (43). Sunny is also educated in American ways, including reading and writing, spelling, math, geography, and Christianity. The Syndicate grows very fond of Sunny but soon leaves her behind to return to America. As one of them reveals to her upon their departure, Sunny is "mainly of white blood" and, therefore, "it is possible—quite probable in fact . . . that [she] will succeed in making [herself] . . . like the people [she] desire[s] to copy" (87). Sunny declares that she will remain in Japan until she gets "civil—ise[d]" (87) enough to join them in the States. Whiteness, it seems, is what makes possible the potential for mimicry.

Before the second part of the novel begins, there is a somewhat strange narrative interruption that revisits Sunny's situation and questions her future. I quote the passage here in full:

> Consider the situation. A girl, mainly of white blood, with just a drop of oriental blood in her—enough to make her a bit different from the average female of the species, enough, say, to give a snack of that savage element attributed to the benighted heathen. Rescued by men of her father's race from slavery and abuse; provided for for the rest of her days; under the instruction of a zealous and conscientious missionary and his wife, who earnestly taught her how to save the souls of the people of Japan. Sunny's fate was surely a desirable one, and as she progressed on the one side of the water, her friends on the other side were growing in sundry directions, ever outward and upward, acquiring new responsibilities, new loves, new claims, new passions with the passing of the years. What

> freak of fate therefore should interpose at this juncture, and thrust Sunny electrically into the lives of her friends again? (100)

The "freak of fate," it turns out, is Sunny herself. As this quote not so subtly suggests, the narrative should end here. As is, it is a happy ending—Sunny is not only saved, but she has a bright, "civilized" future ahead of her saving the heathen souls of Japan. Her saviors can feel satisfied with themselves for having accomplished a charitable act. This would conclude the missionary project, and it also seems to somewhat positively revise the *Butterfly* plot (Sunny is not merely left behind but "provided for for the rest of her days"). However, what occurs for the rest of the novel changes this simplistic and almost patronizing and overly comfortable narrative and transforms it into an uncomfortable one. Sunny arrives in America and she (unconsciously? unintentionally?) wreaks emotional and intellectual chaos on everyone, disrupting not only the ease of their set ways but also upturning traditional beliefs. In this light, *Sunny-San* is no longer a conservative romance novel but one that forces us to examine how race, albeit undetectable, silently yet persistently hovers over us.

The second part of the novel begins with Sunny's sudden appearance in the States. Prior to her arrival, the Syndicate members feared for her because "she didn't belong [in the States] and she never could belong" (114). However, the person who gets off the boat is not the little, unsophisticated Japanese girl of the past but a mature young woman dressed in American fashion with Americanized ways: "But she came to their door as an American girl. . . . She simply had achieved the look of one who belonged. She was as natural in her clothes as any of their sisters or the girls they knew" (117–18). Sunny's appearance, about which the men were initially apprehensive, is an immense relief to them because she *looks* American and can pass as American. This scene is even more effective when compared to an earlier one in Japan in which Sunny, wanting to please her guardians by displaying traditional Japanese fashion and beauty, is met with laughter and condescension. While the early performance emphasizes the disparity between the two cultures (and Sunny's improbable assimilation), this new and updated Sunny demonstrates her ability to dress and look the part. In this light, as Birchall argues, Sunny's Americanization seems to imply a dismissal of her Eastern background and confirms the Syndicate's earlier premonition. However, as I describe below, Sunny's Japanese ways are not so easily discarded.

Sunny's passing into an Americanized whiteness would seem to adhere to the traditional plot of the passing narrative. But, contrary to

Birchall's claim that *Sunny-San* is a novel that dismisses Japanese elements, it actually cannot seem to escape them and develops into an antipassing tale. Sunny's emergence into the American landscape entails a complicated and charming mixture of both Japanese and Western cultures, one that seems to affect everyone who encounters her. From Sunny's initial appearance in the first part of the novel, her mixed-raced identity is a source of schizophrenic detections. Physically, she looks completely white. She has hair "almost pure gold in colour" (14) and skin as "bleached as that of the dead" (24). Upon seeing her, the Syndicate claims, "She's not a Japanese girl. . . . [S]he's as white as we are!" (18). Furthermore, upon hearing her speak, they also conclude that "a girl with hair and eyes like that wouldn't be chattering any monkey speech" (31). The discrepancy between looks and identity is reiterated later in the narrative when Sunny meets and befriends Katy Clarry, an Irish girl in New York. In a scene shortly after their meeting, Clarry reveals a moment of detective discomfort and failure in gazing upon Sunny:

> "What are you, anyway? You ain't American—at least you don't look it or talk it, though heaven knows anything and everything calls itself American to-day," said the native-born American girl with scorn. "Meaning no offence, you understand, but—well—you just don't look like the rest of us. You ain't a Dago or a Sheeny. I can see that, and you ain't a Hun neither. Are you a Frenchy? You got queer kind of eyes—meaning no offence, for personally I think them lovely, I really do. . . . ."
>
> "Katy, I are sawry thad I am not be American girl. I are born ad Japan—."
>
> "*You* ain't no Chink. You can't tell me no such thing as that. I wasn't born yesterday. What are you, anyway? Where do you come from? Are you a royal princess in disguise?" (229–30, emphasis in original)

To Clarry, Sunny is a mystery because she does not conform to the visual definition of "difference." That Clarry has a certain disdain for and awareness of foreigners is obvious. But, when Sunny reveals her Asian heritage, Clarry's pride and perhaps self-perceived sophistication are insulted. "*You* ain't no Chink," she hurriedly replies. To Clarry, "Chinkness" is obvious. Interestingly, however, she does not discern the distinction between Japanese and Chinese when she conflates both ethnicities into "Chinkness," a telling reversal in light of Eaton's own ethnic passing. What is interesting here is that Clarry questions Sunny about being in "disguise" and later even encourages Sunny to pass: "So even if you have a yellow streak in you . . . you needn't tell no one about it. No one'll be the wiser. You can trust me not to open my mouth to a living soul about it" (231). Sunny, however, rejects passing as white. Instead, she subtly yet significantly *passes along* her Japanese ways. Further, she responds to her Western observers by stating, "I are white on my face and my honourable body, but I are Japanese on my honourable insides" (34). For the men in the Syndicate as well as for Clarry, the distance between Sunny's physical appearance and her racial identification results in a category crisis. They cannot properly detect her within the traditional epistemological framework of racial science or law and, thus, they deny her Japanese traits. To detect her as really white and urge her to pass as white are easy solutions to *their own* inabilities to detect. In other words, there is a disconnect between the Syndicate's/Clarry's intuitive abilities to read/understand the racial marker upon Sunny's body versus Sunny's racial invisibility (i.e., the mark of otherness). Racial intuition here depends on the ability to detect and maintain boundaries. To be intuitive in detecting race, one must access previous stores of racial knowledges. A failure to detect these boundaries results in a certain level of discomfort to the observer whose racial knowledge is thereby called into question, not to mention the validity of the supposed racial knowledge itself. For the Syndicate and Clarry, blondness and whiteness of skin color are equated with whiteness, or, perhaps more significantly, nonwhiteness cannot include blondness and white skin. Published the same year as *Ozawa v. United States* (1922) and a year prior to *United States v. Thind* (1923), two of the most influential race cases in American immigration history, Eaton's commentary on intuiting race is especially salient here. In many ways, this novel depicts white anxiety of race detection and demonstrates the attempts to blanket that anxiety.[16]

This anxiety of detecting racial/ethnic difference foreshadows debates regarding Asian American identity formation. While some critics may question Eaton's role as "Asian American" (whether due to her seeming ethnic betrayal or her and her characters' geographical origins), Eaton's decision to situate her final Japanese romance on American soil directly addresses this concern. Eaton's transnational move is particularly revealing in light of the historical and legal circumstances of the United States in the 1920s. In addition to the race prerequisite cases mentioned earlier, the 1920s were rife with anti-immigration statutes that specifically targeted Asian Americans, including but not limited to the Cable Act (1922), which provided that "any woman who marries an alien ineligible for citizenship shall cease to be an American citizen," and the Asian Exclusion Act (1924), which barred immigration of all Asian laborers. The 1920s were also a period of heightened antimiscegenation sentiment set amid anxieties of race detection (see note 5). This is the climate within which Eaton's final Japanese romance is situated. Within this context, not only does *Sunny-San* reject shielding white detective failure, but Sunny, in *refusing* to pass for white, also *chooses* to control her own telling of her racial/ethnic identification rather than to be told upon. To echo again Amy Robinson's schematic of race passing, "to read the apparatus of passing . . . *is* to value telling over knowing" (723). For Sunny (and perhaps for Eaton as well), the ability to pass into whiteness is not always the desired option. By choosing *not* to pass, Sunny purposefully played upon white detective angst and insecurity.

In her anonymously published autobiography, *Me: A Book of Remembrance*, Eaton declared: "I would have given anything to look less foreign. My darkness marked and crushed me, I who loved blondness like the sun" (166). Statements like this force many contemporary critics to read Eaton's passing as an act of race betrayal. But I offer an alternative reading of Eaton's ideological and racial position, which is often misread in statements like this. For Eaton, "loving blondness" is not merely a statement of racist self-hatred but rather a rejection of the objectification of racial/ethnic *scrutiny*. This is evident within the full context of the quote:

> Lolly was in blue, the color of her eyes, and she looked, as always, "stunning." Beside her, I'm afraid, I appeared very insignificant, for Lolly was a real beauty. I never went anywhere with her but people—men and women, too—would stare at her, and turn around for a second look. *People stared at me, too, but in a different sort of way, as if I interested them or they were puzzled to know my nationality.* I would have given anything to look less foreign. (166, emphasis mine)

That Eaton—a biracial woman living during the height of antimiscegenation sanctions in law and culture—was often the victim of race detection is not surprising. While Lolly is described as the object of admiring looks, Eaton was a visual puzzle to be dissected, detected, and determined. The racial darkness that "marked and crushed" her is, as Frantz Fanon describes it, the "epidermal schema" that distinguished her from a normative whiteness. Eaton's sister, Edith, also reveals how she and her siblings were often scrutinized like "strange animals in a menagerie" ("Leaves" 220). Rather than racist self-hatred per se, yearning to "look less foreign," then, is a desire to escape the constant scrutiny and objectification of a persistent and forced play of racial/ethnic decoding.

To read Eaton's authorial passing as well as her Japanese romances as a type of racialized "escapist" literature is to reposition her status in (Asian) American literary history. That Asian Americans are the subject and object of visual scrutiny is not a view unique to Winnifred or Edith. From the anti-immigration and antimiscegenation legal history that desperately categorized Asians within the black-white hierarchy (as illustrated by Ian Haney-López), to the war pamphlet *How to Spot a Jap* issued by the U.S. government to help soldiers distinguish between Japanese and Chinese, to the Asians "all look alike" syndrome of the late twentieth century (as comically popularized by the Asian test on *alllooksame.com*), Asian Americans embody detective unease. It is within this context that Winnifred's "escape" into the passing game mattered in her time and still matters today.

4 / Jaundiced Eyes: The Case of Charlie Chan and the Mysterious Disappearance of a Detective Hero

In 1942, the United States Army published and distributed an "educational" pamphlet for military personnel titled *A Pocket Guide to China.* The seventy-five-page guide was distributed to the U.S. Army and Navy during their stay in China during World War II. It included translations of English phrases into Chinese (such as "Who are you?," "What do you want?," "I am an American soldier," and "I am your friend"). The guide also included a ten-page comic called "How to Spot a Jap" illustrated by Martin Caniff. The goal of the comic was to illustrate the differences between the Chinese allies and the enemy "Japs" to the American soldier, who, presumably, could not tell the difference. Differences range from physical peculiarities to behavior and speech patterns; more importantly, these differences also link natural, biological attributes (such as eyes, teeth, and height) to behavior. Their differences are compared to an "average American," who naturally embodies both physical and ethical normative standards. For instance, while the average Chinese and American men are about the same height, the average Japanese is shorter and "look as if his legs are joined directly to his chest" (66). Chinese eyes are "set like any European's or American's," but Japanese eyes have a "marked squint" and are slanted to his nose. The Chinese man has a smooth face, evenly set "choppers," and smiles easily, while the Japanese man has "buck teeth" and "usually expects to be shot" (68). Aside from physical features, another distinction is revealed in their walking pattern: the Chinese man "strides,"

Figure 2. "How to Spot a Jap" was part of an educational pocket guide distributed to U.S. soldiers during World War II. Four pages of the guide are reproduced here.

while the Japanese man "shuffles" (69). The Japanese are also very sly, experts in hiding concealed weapons in underwear and objects like pens. Their deception is particularly manipulative because they will "try to pose as natives of whatever country they're in" (75).

"How to Spot a Jap" is one of several educational "tools" distributed during World War II to help American citizens discern interethnic differences during wartime hysteria. Two weeks after the bombing of Pearl

Harbor, both *Time* magazine and *Life* magazine published "How to Tell Your Friends from the Japs" and "How to Tell Japs from the Chinese," respectively. Including images of young and middle-aged Chinese men alongside young and middle-aged Japanese men, the *Time* article forewarns of the difficulty in telling Chinese and Japanese apart: "There is no infallible way of telling them apart, because the same racial strains are mixed in both. Even an anthropologist, with calipers and plenty of time to measure heads, noses, shoulders, hips, is sometimes stumped." A few rules of thumb, however, include: (1) most Chinese avoid horn-rimmed glasses; (2) Japanese, except for wrestlers, are seldom fat. They often dry up and grow lean as they age. The Chinese often put on weight, particularly if they are prosperous (in China, with its frequent famines, being fat is equated with being a solid citizen); and (3) Japanese are hesitant, often nervous, in conversation and laugh loudly at the wrong time. On a slightly different note, the *Life* article, "How to Tell Japs from the Chinese," begins its education on ethnic differences with a caution not to injure our Chinese allies: "Innocent victims in cities all over the country are many of the 75,000 U.S. Chinese, whose homeland is our staunch ally. So serious were the consequences threatened, that the Chinese consulates last week prepared to tag their nationals with identification buttons." Beginning with a brief anthropological admission that the differences between Chinese and Japanese are measurable in "millimeters," the "typical" Chinese is "relatively tall and slenderly built" with a "parchment yellow" complexion and "delicately boned" face. The Japanese, on the other hand, "betrays aboriginal antecedents in a squat, long-torsoed build, a broader, more massively boned head and face, flat, often pug, nose, yellow-ocher skin and heavier beard." The *Life* article is also accompanied by several pictures depicting a "Chinese public servant," a "Japanese warrior," a "Chinese journalist," "tall Chinese brothers, and "short Japanese admirals," perhaps intending to evince the physically superior yet nonthreatening Chinese man versus the inferior and developmentally challenged yet callous Japanese soldier. The article notes: "Chinese wear rational calm of tolerant realists. Japs, like General Tojo, show humorless intensity of ruthless mystics."

I introduce these guides as precursors to the study of Charlie Chan to historicize the complicated and vexed relationship between Asian Americans and race detection. The epistemological question of what it is to "know" how to distinguish between Asian American ethnicities during the mid-twentieth century and beyond is one that determines life versus death, ally versus enemy. In addition to the examples above, Asian American participation in the passing act goes beyond passing for white, as Winnifred Eaton demonstrated earlier. As forced players in the "all look alike" syndrome, Asian Americans are, to a certain extent, always already passing in an American landscape heavily dependent upon racial signifiers. The inability to decipher racial borders is never more threatening and urgent than during wartime. This has been especially true for Asian Americans in both World War II and the so-called War Against Terror. For white Americans, many of whom had never seen Asian or Asian American individuals in the years preceding the attack on Pearl Harbor, race manuals were necessary primers that displayed the telling nuances of interethnic difference. For Asian Americans caught in an anti-Japanese frenzy after the bombing of Pearl Harbor, misdetection was a very real threat, one that could result in violence and/or internment. The wearing of "I am Chinese" or "I am Korean" buttons was common practice during World War II and fictionalized in Hisaye Yamamoto's "Wilshire Bus" (1950). Establishing racial distinctions could mean the difference between freedom and internment, belonging and ostracism. The 1982 beating death of Vincent Chin, often considered the impetus for the panethnic Asian American movement, illustrates the continued threat to Asian and Asian American bodies as a result of misdetections. Believed to be of Japanese descent by two white men who worked in Detroit's Chrysler automobile plant (one of whom was laid off due to the increasing Japanese auto market), Chinese American Chin was brutally beaten and killed by Robert Ebens and Michael Nitz. In the state trial, Ebens and Nitz received no jail time; during the federal trial, Nitz was acquitted and Ebens was cleared of all charges.

More recently, the need for race primers has reemerged with the 2012 shooting at a Sikh temple in Oak Creek, Wisconsin. Wade Michael Page, a forty-year-old U.S. Army veteran, killed six people, including five men and one woman, worshipping at a Sikh Temple in Wisconsin. Almost two days after the attack, Chicago's *RedEye Magazine* published a short feature titled "Who Was Temple Shooter?" with a photo of Sikh men presumably grieving at the temple. Under the picture, the caption titled "Mistaken Identity" reads: "American Sikhs say they often have been singled out for harassment, and occasionally violent assault, since the Sept. 11, 2001 attacks because they are mistaken for Muslims due to the beards and colorful turbans." Below the article and photo image is another image titled "Turban Primer," which includes five images of various men wearing turbans labeled "Sikh men," "Iranian leaders,"

"Taliban members," "Indian men," and "Muslim religious elders." Above the images, the article reads: "The turban is common headgear for men in many parts of the world. Its history stretches back thousands of years through dozens of cultures. Many of those cultures are Muslim, but turbans are not required by Islamic faith. These are some of the many variations." In short, while its title suggests that the article seeks to correctly identify the shooter, its actual agenda is to identify the bad versus the good turban-wearers. For example, "Sikh men" are described to "commonly wear a peaked turban that serves partly to cover their long hair, which is never cut out of respect for God's creation. Devout Sikhs also tuck their uncut beards up into their turbans. Sikhism originated in northern India and Pakistan in the 15th century and is one of the youngest of the world's monotheistic religions." The primer also informs us that "Taliban members wear a variety of turbans, and preferences vary. This Taliban member is wearing a very long turban—perhaps two twined together—with one end hanging loose over his shoulder." Like the *Time* and *Life* primers before it, "Turban Primer" distinguishes between those who are friendly and those we should target, almost indirectly chiding the shooter for making that mistake. As one Twitter post read, "Here's a nice Turban Primer, in case you are wondering which turban wearers are okay to shoot and which are not" (Gopal).[1]

Boiling Hard and Soft: A Crisis in Confidence

Rule #5: No Chinaman must figure in the story.—RONALD KNOX, *10 COMMANDMENTS OF DETECTIVE FICTION* (1929)

If, as some believe, the appeal of Golden Age detective fiction arises from its fundamental conservatism or, as William Stowe writes, its political, moral, and epistemological affirmation of "social structures, moral codes, and ways of knowing" (570), then the hard-boiled narrative displays the very struggle and tension with balance and order. Utilizing a psychoanalytic paradigm, for instance, Frank Krutnik argues that masculine destabilization is embedded in the very structures of the noir form, despite [its] characterization of "an overt masculinisation of both language (the aggressive and competitive 'hard-boiled' banter) and action (the predominance of violence)" (88). Krutnik also points out that these thrillers' "ostensible trajectory of 'power, omnipotence, mastery and control' . . . result in failure" (90–91) and explains the immense popularity of noir narratives as "evidence of some kind of crisis of confidence within the contemporary regimentation of male-dominated culture" (91). This crisis in confidence, claim recent critics, is intrinsically linked to a racialized concept of masculinity. In short, what is at stake in the hard-boiled narrative is the maintenance and support of white, heterosexual masculinity.

Modeling theories of whiteness via critics such as Toni Morrison, Eric Sundquist, David Roediger, Eric Lott, and bell hooks, Megan Abbott's *The Street Was Mine: White Masculinity in Hardboiled Fiction and Film* reveals the crisis of white masculinity in works by Raymond Chandler, James M. Cain, and their film noir adaptations from the 1930s through the 1950s. Through a focus on the solitary white man moving through an always evolving and developing urban space from the Great Depression era into the beginnings of the Cold War, Abbott writes that "the American construction of masculinity and femininity is linked fundamentally to racial ideology. Race and gender operate by and through each other, each using the other to seal up fissures, suture gaps, and naturalize their own performance of whiteness, blackness, masculinity, and femininity" (4). In fact, the mutually dependent construction of whiteness and masculinity within the hard-boiled tradition occurs with the very first hard-boiled detective hero, Carroll John Daly's Race Williams, who made his debut in a special issue of the *Black Mask* (1923) dedicated to a fictional debate over the Ku Klux Klan. As Sean McCann reveals, "Hard-boiled crime fiction began life directly opposed to the Klan's nativist populism" (41) *not* because its authors particularly believed in a form of racial justice. Rather, Daly's fiction and the Klan "battled for the right to possess and define the spirit of 'race,' struggling over characteristics of American inheritance and its meaning for national politics and culture" (41). For instance, Daly and Dashiell Hammett, two of the genre's early inventors, "dismissed the Klan's vision of racial community, not because they imagined a society built upon tolerance or benevolent universalism, but because they assumed that all people were driven by a self-interest that made dreams of racial obligation absurd" (85). Finally, in examining the racial codes of hard-boiled fiction, Maureen T. Reddy writes that the "dominant consciousness in hard-boiled fiction is indisputably a white consciousness, and hence the genre is substantially a 'white genre,' as Liam Kennedy notes, which 'adopt[s] a parasitic relationship to blackness'" (Reddy, *Traces* 9). As such, the detective engages in a ritual of "white bonding" that "generally takes place on a less than fully conscious level, in an exchange of glances, laughter at racist jokes, and sharing of assumptions about people of color; it can also take place in all-white gatherings, such as classrooms, and is supported by the systemic racism of most of society's institutions. . . . The ritual thus serves to strengthen the shared understanding among white people that the United States is ideologically a white society (*Traces* 10–11). In her assessment of race in American crime fiction, Reddy reminds us that extreme examples of white bonding include hate crimes against people of color. Just in the first half of 1919, during the gestation period of the hard-boiled narrative, there were twenty-five race riots across the country, and in the first year after World War I, at least seventy blacks were lynched (Reddy, "Races" 137). Further, alongside numerous race-based restrictions on immigration and citizenship (namely, the racial prerequisite cases of *Ozawa v. United States* [1922] and *United States v. Bhagat Singh Thind* [1923] mentioned earlier) and the ongoing restriction on Chinese immigration (as a result of the Chinese Exclusion Act of 1882) until the Magnuson Act, or the Chinese Exclusion Repeal Act of 1943, much of the hard-boiled detective's heroism is his "own unquestioned [maintenance of] whiteness" (Reddy, "Race" 138).

During this struggle of white masculinity, another type of racialized masculinity was beginning to emerge. Charlie Chan, often considered the antithesis to masculinity, emerged with Earl Derr Bigger's first novel, *The House without a Key*, in 1925. Throughout Biggers's six novels and the subsequent fifty-three films, Charlie Chan's legacy reveals a parallel dialogue with the hard-boiled narrative and its quest for sustained white masculinity. And the exchange occurs via a battle of "knowing." As a study of the relationship between race and detection (particularly the unease that results from failed detection), *The Arresting Eye* shows that the role of "knowing" (a.k.a. "detection") is often peculiar to specific communities where access is delimited by constraints of race, gender, sexuality, nationhood, and class. In short, knowledge is intrinsically connected to one's position within and without a particular community. As such, Reddy's reading of the hard-boiled detective's racialized ritual of "white bonding" is an effective theoretical tool for understanding the role of detection and knowing in diverse racial communities. This chapter builds upon Reddy's concept of bonding-as-knowing to illustrate how "knowing" (i.e., the white hard-boiled detective's methods as well as his larger maintenance of white ideology) is a "containment strategy" that safeguards against racial un-ease. But, as delineated in John L. Jackson's theory of "racial paranoia" (explored later in this chapter), particular ways of knowing also function as a strategic necessity for marginalized communities, which must navigate, protect against, and reject restrictive and menacing forces.

Knowing that is both restraining and liberating is exemplified in the Asian American case of Charlie Chan. While the intersection between whiteness and blackness in the negotiation of an American masculinity in hard-boiled fiction and film has been a recent focus of critical study (Abbott, McCann, James Naremore, Manthia Diawara), Charlie Chan, an iconic figure in the American detective imagination, has, nevertheless, been overlooked for the most part in critical studies of the genre.[2] Although Charlie Chan may be better labeled as a Golden Age detective reminiscent of Agatha Christie's Hercule Poirot, S. S. Van Dine's Philo Vance, or Dorothy Sayers's Lord Peter Wimsey, he is, unlike most Golden Age British detectives, American-conceived, -born, and -cultivated. Further, Charlie Chan was nurtured into a detective legend during the same historical period as the mainstays of the American hard-boiled, including Dashiell Hammett, Raymond Chandler, James M. Cain, Horace McCoy, among many others.

Generally, Charlie Chan scholarship (some of which I discuss below) has been dismissive of the novels and films as mere racist stereotype (with the exception of Charles Rzepka and Yunte Huang's recent works), focusing on the figure as caricature rather than establishing a more nuanced investigation into his contribution to the racialization and gendered production of the detective hero. This chapter intervenes in the critical disavowal by addressing a larger question: Why and how does a character like Charlie Chan become so popular and beloved during the same historical and cultural milieu that produced such archetypal expressions of white masculinity as Sam Spade, Phillip Marlowe, and Mike Hammer?

I participate in the Charlie Chan controversy not so much to take sides as to emphasize the critical need to refocus the direction of Charlie Chan scholarship. Charlie Chan reflects the very anxiety of race and detection that is the subject of this larger study; thus, to examine Charlie Chan through the theoretical framework of the anxiety of detection also engages us in a larger critical discussion, specifically in regard to the production and practice of "racial knowledges," or raced ways of knowing, as well as the rhetoric of liberal multiculturalism that pervades the critical responses to Charlie Chan (especially accusations of political correctness) that is still very relevant today. But I want to be clear. The point here is not to negate or dismiss the very real and lived experiences of Asian Americans who have endured the devastating effects of the Charlie Chan stereotype. This is a pain that clearly resonates from within the critical reception of the novels and films and one, perhaps, that produces knee-jerk reactions without leading to close examination of the source of the wound itself. Thus, my goal is to push beyond the stereotype to access the myriad of contradictions as well as the possibilities revealed within the Charlie Chan epistemological prison. As such, I read Charlie Chan as a lens through which we can understand the racial matrix of mid-twentieth-century America as it contends with the chaos, instability, and "pollution" of immigration and xenophobia, the national demoralization resulting from the Great Depression, increasing urbanization and cross-racial contact, and a developing liberalist ideal during the interwar years. To begin, I offer a brief background on the birth of Charlie Chan and his critical reception in order to contextualize his rise as well as examine the controversy behind his iconic status precariously positioned between detective hero and racist embarrassment. Then I explore Charlie Chan's legacy in fiction and film with particular attention paid to how racial masquerade (race passing's more flamboyant cousin) is utilized as a "containment strategy" that solidifies whiteness. As Michael Rogin states, racial masquerade (namely, blackface) and Americanization go hand in hand, offering new immigrants a whitening process whereby they could distance themselves from their own ethnicity by donning blackface. In this light, it is critically imperative to recast blackface performance such as "American film [which] was born from white depictions of blacks" (15) in order to highlight the relationship between racial masquerade and the maintenance of whiteness. Similarly, I explore Charlie Chan's yellowface performance as an attempt to contain the racial unease of Asians during the interwar years as well as moments when the fantasy of that masquerade is revealed. My investigation concludes with the introduction of black sidekick characters in the Monogram Pictures phase (1944–49). The black sidekick characters, particularly Mantan Moreland's Birmingham Brown, provide sites of possibility where whiteness not only encounters an epistemological struggle but also experiences banishment from an emerging Afro-Asian coalitional community.

Birth of a Legacy: The Making and Unmaking of a Chinese Detective Hero

In order to better comprehend the milieu in which Charlie Chan was born, we need to examine the historical and political climate of Hawaii, Charlie Chan's home and site of several of the literary and filmic narratives (including the first novel), during the first few decades of the twentieth century. In *Strangers from a Different Shore: A History of Asian Americans*, Ronald Takaki reveals Hawaii's unique background of ethnic diversity around the period when Hawaii became a United States territory in 1900. For instance, while Hawaiians represented 97 percent of the population in 1853, this figure drastically changed by the 1920s, with Hawaiians constituting 16.3 percent; Caucasians, 7.7 percent; Chinese, 9.2 percent; Japanese, 42.7 percent; Portuguese, 10.6 percent; Puerto Ricans, 2.2 percent; Koreans, 1.9 percent; and Filipinos, 8.2 percent (132). The major reason behind this severe increase in immigration was the growing need for cheap labor in the expanding sugar plantations, the primary source of Hawaii's economic industry. As Takaki further explains, Asians formed the majority of the population, constituting 62 percent of the Hawaiian population in 1920, while they comprised only 3.5 percent in California and 0.17 percent of the continental U.S. population, enabling them to "choose a different course than their mainland brethren" (132). It is not surprising, then, that for the Asian majority facing unfair labor practices led mostly by Caucasian employers, a "different course" included resistance and defiance such as labor strikes and rebellions. For instance, more than twenty strikes occurred throughout Hawaii in 1900, prompting numerous other strikes in the following years, including the Waipahu Plantation strike of 1906, the Japanese strike of 1909, and the Japanese/Filipino interethnic strike of 1919–20, among others.[3] These acts of rebellion not only demonstrate that Asians and Asian Americans were not the passive and docile immigrants many believed them to be but that they were able to strategically organize in order to actively struggle against and defy injustice, physical abuse, and unfair labor practices. Their refusal to remain quiet and passive helped to generate Yellow Peril fears and concerns throughout the twentieth century and resulted in such legislation as the Johnson-Reed Immigration Act of 1924, which limited the annual number of immigrants (predominantly southern and eastern Europeans, Middle Easterners, East Asians, and Indian) to 2 percent of that country's population. The year following the Johnson-Reed Immigration Act, Earl Derr Biggers published the first Charlie Chan novel, *The House without a Key*.[4]

In *Chinese American Masculinities*, Jachinson Chan offers the political and historical reasons behind the cultural need to domesticate symbols of Asian and Asian American masculinity (particularly Japanese American masculinity) during the first half of the twentieth century. These reasons (and perhaps Biggers's attraction to a *Chinese* hero rather than a Japanese one) were primarily due to the growing anti-Japanese sentiment that emerged as a result of several historical factors, including (1) Japan's victory in the Russo-Japanese War in 1904–5, which established Japan as a major world power; (2) the 1920 Japanese labor strikes in Hawaii, which exhibited the Japanese as aggressive disrupters of society; and (3) the growing threat of Japan's military powers, which ultimately led to World War II. As Chan writes, while the Japanese were continuously seen as "agitators and uncontrollable menaces" to society, the Chinese were used as "examples of how to assimilate into American culture without social disruptions. . . . By the 1940s, the Chinese became friends of America while the Japanese were officially the enemies" (52).

In 1919, Earl Derr Biggers, the author of such successful novels as *Seven Keys to Baldpate* (1913),[5] *Love Insurance* (1914), and *Agony Column* (1916), vacationed in Hawaii. According to legend, Biggers came across a newspaper article during this visit that described the fearless skills shown by the renowned Honolulu detective Chang Apana (1871–1933) in investigating an opium-smuggling ring. Inspired by what he read, Biggers stated that evil Chinese were "old stuff" in mystery stories and that an "amiable Chinese acting on the side of law and order" (Patrick Williams) had not yet been used. As a result, Biggers drew upon Apana to create the internationally recognized character Charlie Chan, one of the most beloved and popular detective figures of the twentieth century. Biggers's creation quickly rose to legendary status in six novels published between 1925 and 1932. These novels were just the beginning of the Charlie Chan industry, however. During the twentieth century, Charlie Chan became one of the most popular icons ever created, living on through more than fifty-three Hollywood films (six of which have been lost),[6] a radio series from 1932 to 1948, a play, a TV series (*The New Adventures of Charlie Chan*, 1957–58), a comic strip (1938–42), a short-lived mystery magazine in the seventies, an animated television series by Hanna-Barbera for children named *The Amazing Chan and the Chan Clan*, the release of the *Charlie Chan Chanthology* in 2004 and the *Charlie Chan Collection, Vols. 1–5* in 2006–8, Yunte Huang's publication of *Charlie Chan: The Untold Story of the Honorable Detective and His Rendezvous with American History* (2010), and, finally, the long-rumored but yet-to-be-filmed contemporary Charlie Chan movie starring Lucy Liu.

While Biggers's creation of an Asian American detective hero may have been considered somewhat radical in the 1920s and 1930s, it is believed almost a century later to be quite the opposite. By now, the attacks on the character of Charlie Chan as racist are well known but, due to critical disagreements, not necessarily well established. Although Biggers's concern in creating this character was to produce an "amiable Chinese," his intention has not prevented the critical dismissal of and outcry against Charlie Chan by ethnic studies scholars and activists in recent years. Often linked as the counterpart to Sax Rohmer's Fu Manchu character, who is described as "the yellow peril incarnate in one man" (Rohmer 13), Charlie Chan has become for many a racist symbol of Asian and Asian American masculinity in much more subtle and, thus, more disturbing ways. For instance, one of the seminal critics of Asian American literature, Elaine Kim, states that Charlie Chan's popular appeal is due to his role as a "non-threatening, non-competitive, asexual ally of the white man" (Kim 18). In other words, Charlie Chan is a "safe" hero because he represents the "model minority" stereotype. Charlie, according to the author and playwright Frank Chin, is the "good Christian Americanized Chinese American of white fantasy . . . an acceptable pervert" (17). In his short story "The Sons of Chan," Chin further critiques Biggers by calling him an "antebellum southern cracker overseer" (132). Due to his domestication, according to William Wu, Charlie is the antithesis of Yellow Peril threat. He is, on the contrary, an "example of overcompensation in an author's attempt to break away from the Yellow Peril" (174). In the introduction to her pioneering 1993 anthology titled *Charlie Chan Is Dead*, Jessica Hagedorn loudly declares: "Charlie Chan is indeed dead, never to be revived. Gone for good his yellowface asexual bulk, his fortune-cookie English, his stereotypical Orientalist version of 'the [Confucian] Chinese family'" (xiii). All the backlash against Charlie Chan has even led the detective fiction scholar Charles Rzepka to begin his recent examination of the detective hero with the declaration, "It is not for white writers to define Asian humanity in any context" (1463). Finally, and perhaps most simply and directly, in a review of Asian American literary history of the past few decades, Hua Hsu writes that while many of the key works defining the field may be combative and confusing, there is "one point of consensus: everyone hates Charlie Chan" (Hsu, review of *Recovered Legacies*).

The most public display and uproar against Charlie Chan occurred in July 2003, when Fox Movie Channel, in response to protests from various Asian American communities (including the National Asian Pacific American Legal Consortium and National Asian American Telecommunications Association), cancelled its scheduled Charlie Chan movie marathon. When the cancellation provoked numerous complaints and counterprotests, Fox rescheduled the screening, including, prior to the airing of each movie, a discussion by a panel comprised of Asian American scholars, actors, and authors addressing issues of race and representation (Morano). Revealing in the Fox debate are the criticisms from the general (white) viewing audience that the Asian American protests were overly sensitive and based on a critical blindness amplified by political correctness paranoia, a common accusation often utilized in our postracial, color-blind historical moment.[7]

The idea of a racial paranoia is implicitly established by Ken Hanke, film historian and author of *Charlie Chan at the Movies: History, Filmography, and Criticism*, when he writes that accusations that Charlie Chan's portrayal is racist are not "immediately understandable" because his entrance was a "tremendous step forward . . . [and] if anyone comes off badly in most Charlie Chan films, it is invariably Charlie's white counterparts—those dimwitted, cigar chewing Hollywoodized upholders of law and order who get nothing right until Charlie solves things for them" (xv). Further, Hanke suggests, how can Charlie Chan be so easily dismissed when he "was virtually the only positive depiction of an Oriental in film at the time?" (xv). Hanke's dismissal of Charlie Chan criticism is supported by Robert Schickel's more recent review of Yunte Huang's 2010 publication of *Charlie Chan: The Untold Story of the Honorable Detective and His Rendezvous with American History* in the *New York Times*: "There are wet, earnest commentators who think Chan should have been played by an Asian actor, conveniently forgetting that Asians were then in short supply in Hollywood, forgetting as well that the issue was not Chan's race but the respect in which he was always held. That's another reason the Chan films continue to play so agreeably today. You don't have to make allowances for any sort of casual racism in them; there is none." Huang's study, in fact, mirrors the very ambivalence aimed toward this iconic hero displayed in the above critical contradictions. Since its publication, it has been short-listed for the 2010 National Book Critics Award, the winner of the 2011 Edgar Award for Best Critical/ Biographical Book, and short-listed as a New York Times Notable Selection. Additionally, the study received praise from such scholars and literary luminaries as Gary Okihiro, Jessica Hagedorn, Stephen Greenblatt, and Annette Gordon-Reed. Charlie Chan is, indeed, not dead. Written as more of a collective biography (of Chan, Biggers, Apana, actor Warner Oland, and the author's own immigration experience), Huang's analysis begins with an anecdote about being compared to the wisecracking detective by the Harvard English department's secretary (a Caucasian woman in her late fifties). Rather than correct her, however, Huang wrote the book "in part to carry on [his] imaginary dialogue with this well-meaning lady" (xvi). The dialogue, it turns out, is addressed more to Asian American critics of Charlie Chan since Huang transforms the stereotype into an Asian American trickster figure by the book's end. Pleading for "the real Charlie Chan [to] please stand up" (the title of Huang's last chapter), Huang performs a critical rescue of Charlie Chan by arguing that like the blackface figures of Aunt Jemima, Uncle Tom, and Nigger Jim, Charlie Chan "epitomizes the creative genius of American culture and exemplifies what the critic Stanley Crouch has called 'the catalyst of the American experience'—cultural miscegenation" (283). For Huang, Charlie Chan is, in fact, a "peculiar American brand" of trickster: "It is a brand that also includes Jim Crow, the Bunker brothers, Al Jolson's Jazz Singer, and Stepin Fetchit and his numerous step-chillun. All these characters are indeed rooted in the toxic soil of racism, but racism has made their tongues only sharper, their art more lethally potent. . . . [T]he resilient artistic flower has blossomed *in spite of* as well as *because of* racism. This undeniable fact, insulting and sobering, has uniquely defined America" (287, emphasis in original).

Whether or not one agrees that the psychological damage of Biggers's Charlie Chan is in alignment with the "trickster" strategies of racist caricatures or perhaps is more reflective of another "Bigger," that of Richard Wright's tragic (anti)hero Bigger Thomas, whose story inevitably mirrors the national plot of race and crime we see today (the 2012 killing of Trayvon Martin and the subsequent acquittal of his killer, George Zimmerman, is a telling example), Huang's critical spotlight on the relationship between Asian American and African American racial formations is a necessary and timely one. This chapter concludes with long overdue elaboration upon the Afro-Asian relationship within the Charlie Chan films to further address the role of racialized detections and its subsequent revelations of a racial unease that threaten to counter the racial containment strategies of the Charlie Chan legacy. Unlike Huang's contention that blackface or yellowface figures like Uncle Tom or Charlie Chan exemplify a "creative genius" of an American "cultural miscegenation," I want to emphasize here that the story of American miscegenation is a crime narrative of rape, abduction, and the legal sanctioning of segregation. As such, in Charlie Chan's legacy where questions of cultural/racial appropriation will never cease to exist, *how* the story of Asian American detection is told and what is at stake in that telling is and always will be the central determining factor.

Will the Real Charlie Chan Please Stand Up! From Fact to Fiction to Film

Perhaps one of the first disturbing elements of Biggers's creation of Charlie Chan occurs in the very transformation of this character from fact to fiction. The transformation of the real-life Honolulu detective Chang Apana into his fictional counterpart, Charlie Chan, is an obvious containment strategy that may illuminate Biggers's authorial intent and design. Chang Apana (1871–1933) served in the Honolulu Police Department from 1889 to 1932. The official website of the Honolulu Police Department even offers a brief biographical sketch of their legendary colleague, naming him the "Real Charlie Chan" (Croom). What is telling in Biggers's literary metamorphosis, however, is the very obvious discrepancy between the real Apana and his legendary counterpart. Although little is known about Apana, he is best known for being a physical threat, hardly the "amiable Chinese" character that Biggers hoped to create. Apana was small in stature (he was barely five feet tall and weighed 130 pounds), but his authority and empowerment arose from his very physicality. As Officer Eddie Croom writes on the official website: "As an officer, Apana was fearless and energetic. He carried scars on his face and body as a result of encounters while performing his duty. Veteran officers tell stories of his daring feats, especially relating to the early days of Chinese immigration to the islands when there was much opium smuggling. The hoodlums all feared Apana, for he was the only man on the force allowed to carry a whip." This description of Apana emerges directly from the pages of hard-boiled fiction. Apana, like the tough guys of the pulp magazines and the later hard-boiled heroes such as Hammett's Sam Spade or Continental OP (whose entrance in Hammett's first novel, *Red Harvest* [1929], depicts one of the bloodiest plots in the genre) or Chandler's Philip Marlowe epitomizes what Christopher Breu describes as a "prophylactic toughness . . . organized around the rigorous suppression of affect," which was "mirrored by his detached, laconic utterances and his instrumentalized, seemingly amoral actions" (1). In addition to Apana's own version of laconic utterances (he neither read nor spoke English), his use of brute physicality in his escapades is legendary. Yunte Huang describes several of Apana's colorful exploits in which, for instance, he is thrown out of a second-floor window only to land on his feet like a cat or another incident in which he is climbing walls like a "pre-Spider-Man sleuth" (65), leaping from one rooftop to the next and arresting forty gamblers single-handedly.

But, unlike the hypermasculinized detectives of hard-boiled crime fiction who often utilize their physical prowess via their tough and gangster-like exterior, Biggers's transformation of Apana into Charlie Chan produced a comic anomaly whose physical presence generates not fear but confusion and a certain sense of feminine gentility, softening and, many would argue, emasculating the "hard" right out of the hard-boiled. This is evident in our initial introduction to Charlie Chan in the first novel, *The House without a Key* (1925):

> As they went out, the third man stepped farther into the room, and Miss Minerva gave a little gasp of astonishment as she looked at him. In those warm islands thin men were the rule, but here was a striking exception. He was very fat indeed, yet he walked with the light dainty step of a woman. His cheeks were as chubby as a baby's, his skin ivory tinted, his black hair close-cropped, his amber eyes slanting. As he passed Miss Minerva he bowed with a courtesy encountered all too rarely in a work-a-day world. . . .
>
> "Amos!" cried Miss Minerva. "That man–why he–"
>
> "Charlie Chan," Amos explained. "I'm glad they brought him. He's the best detective on the force."
>
> "But—he's Chinese!" (37)

Here, Charlie is feminized and infantilized yet oddly civilized.[8] What is interesting about Charlie's physical stature throughout the novels' portrayals is that he is, in fact, inescapable in his hyberbolic embodiment (whether via race and/or size). However, at the same time, Charlie is constantly *disembodied* throughout the novels (and, of course, he is entirely disembodied in the films due to his yellowface performance). Furthermore, his disembodiment is intimately tied to his detective skills in that while his physical body is constantly invoked, establishing his corpulence as racial excess, it is very rare to witness Charlie utilizing any physical skills to help in his detective investigations: he does not chase after criminals with gun in hand or fight with them in a demonstration of his physical strength. Not engaging in the realist practices of his contemporary hard-boiled detectives or his own real-life model, Apana, Charlie instead employs a more intuitive detective skill, one that he reveals is characteristic of his race. As Charlie announces throughout the novels, the Chinese are a psychic race. They are the "most psychic people in the world. Sensitives, like film in camera. A look, a laugh, a gesture perhaps. Something go click" (60).

It is this recourse to intuition that constitutes Charlie's potential threat; he is inscrutable and psychic, a combination that cannot be easily learned or copied.[9] Or can it? Charlie's unique detective abilities and methods, or what one character refers to as his "jaundiced eye" (*The Chinese Parrot* 186), is the source of discomfort as well as attraction for many who encounter him, including his reading and viewing audiences. However, the use of the word "jaundiced" is quite revealing and needs further examination because it captures and implies a multiplicity of meanings. First, the most obvious reference is to disease. Jaundice, typically a condition caused by the obstruction of the bile, is often physically displayed by the yellowing of the eyes, skin, fluids, and tissues. However, jaundice also means to "affect with envy or jealousy; to tinge the viewpoints or judgments of" (*OED*). Thus, while the "jaundiced eye" may point to Charlie's own diseased state of Asianness ("Chan was an Oriental, also a policeman. Such a combination was bound to look at almost any situation with a jaundiced eye" [*The Chinese Parrot* 186]), it can also refer to the envy or jealousy Charlie may induce in the people around him. In that sense, the "jaundiced eye" may not refer as much to Charlie's own subjective and "diseased" state as to the white viewers' fear of being diseased and, even worse, the realization of their inability to access, imitate, or perfect Charlie's potentially superhuman powers of detection.

But, unlike the superhuman powers of Sherlock Holmes, Charlie's powers of deduction can be mastered. In the novels (the first of which I closely examine below), Charlie's detective abilities get overshadowed by the appearance of white male amateur detectives who not only successfully detect alongside Charlie but dominate most of the plot. In fact, in the novels, Charlie functions more as a marginalized character—the Watson to the white protagonist's Sherlock—than as the main hero of the plot. Therefore, if these white amateurs can solve the crime *even without* Charlie's racially gifted intuitive skills, then Charlie's powers are not so superhuman after all; all it takes is some intelligence and common sense. Charlie Chan, then, becomes mere exotic prop. Furthermore, in addition to the display of their detective acumen, the white male amateur detectives also embark upon a parallel love plot, one that not only supersedes any suggestion and fear of Charlie's sexual threat as defined within Yellow Peril ideology (he is, in fact, the father of fourteen children!) but that also emphasizes the true hero status of the white amateur detective (he not only solves the crime but also gets the girl). It is these literary containment strategies, which I closely examine in the next section, that save white readers from any real threat Charlie may pose. In fact, because Charlie is so easily contained within all six novels, readers are able to experience the "cozy familiarity" (xv) that Hanke explains engenders our love for the Chinese detective. Charlie Chan is so loved by white audiences because he has been subdued and domesticated, reflecting a "cozy familiarity" of whiteness back onto the white viewers themselves.

THE HOUSE WITHOUT A KEY

If, as the previous chapter reveals, Winnifred Eaton's Japanese romances demonstrate a celebration of racial undetection, then Earl Derr Biggers's Charlie Chan novels (and later films) exhibit the very discomfort and fear associated with detection and race within an Asian American context during the interwar years. It is true that *The House without a Key* (1925), Biggers's first Charlie Chan novel, exposes (or detects) and criticizes white hegemony on multiple levels, including the appearance of a racialized detective figure who outwits the white police force, the threat of exposure of white imperial greed, and the ethical conflict between colonialism's gains (economic, geographic) versus its losses (greed, corruption). Ironically, this is an exposure that previous critics who have condemned Charlie Chan as "racist" have either too easily dismissed and/or completely ignored. But, while Charlie's counterhegemonic criticisms are significant and, many would argue, support the *nonracism* of Charlie Chan, this chapter contends that we must go beyond the simplistic categories of "racist" or "nonracist" in order to really understand the subtle nuances, deceptions, and, most importantly, dangers of racist discourse and ideology implicitly working throughout the Charlie Chan mysteries. As such, I argue that while *The House without a Key* (as well as other Charlie Chan novels) does incorporate a critique against white hegemony, it does so by undermining Charlie's detective authority through the appearance of a white male protagonist–turned–amateur detective hero. In other words, *House* reveals that Charlie is not really the protagonist of the plot at all; he is, in effect, overshadowed by the heroism of John Quincy Winterslip, the blueblood Bostonian whose concerns, thoughts, and actions the reader follows and identifies with throughout the narrative, resulting in Charlie Chan's marginalized, haphazard, and, therefore, ineffectual and somewhat disembodied appearance. Furthermore, while *House* may also superficially condemn imperial greed and the moral breakdown due to white expansionism, it ultimately displaces this message by making central John Quincy's love and detective plots over the larger political one of white colonialism. In this light, the initial criticisms of white hegemony ultimately get seduced and diminished by the tropical lures of island (read: colonized) temptations.

On a superficial level, *House* reads like a typical murder mystery. John Quincy Winterslip, a rich and Puritan Bostonian, is ordered by his family to travel to Hawaii in order to escort Aunt Minerva Winterslip back home (she initially went to Hawaii for a brief vacation but has remained for months with no immediate plans of returning to the mainland). But, before John Quincy's arrival, his cousin, the infamous socialite Dan Winterslip, is murdered (stabbed) in his Honolulu home. The remainder of the plot describes John Quincy aiding the local detective Charlie Chan in his investigations, which include such suspects as Jim Egan (proprietor of the Reef and Palm Hotel, who was also the last person to see Dan Winterslip alive), Arlene Compton (a.k.a. the "Widow of Waikiki," who is suspected of hungering after the Winterslip fortune and whose brooch was found by Dan's body), and Thomas Mason Brade (the son of *Maid of Shiloh*'s captain, a blackbirding ship on which Dan Winterslip was first officer). To the Winterslips' embarrassment, the majority of the mystery's unraveling entails the disclosure of Dan Winterslip's notorious and shameful past of blackbirding. In a chapter titled "The Blood of the Winterslips," we are told that Winterslip's fortune derived from the practice of "blackbirding," or slave trade in which Africans and aborigines were either recruited as contract laborers or, most likely, kidnapped into slavery and sold as indentured servants. As Reverend Mr. Upton, a former missionary, reveals to John Quincy, it was a "bloody, brutal business" (29). It is also eventually revealed that in addition to his connections with the slave trade, Dan Winterslip stole jewelry and money from his dead captain. With this money, Dan Winterslip prospered while Captain Brade's widow and son became impoverished.[10]

While it is eventually discovered that Harry Jennison, Dan Winterslip's attorney and future son-in-law, killed the victim for money, this plot is negligible in comparison to the discovery of Dan's blackbirding past as well as John Quincy's attempt to restore the integrity of his family name. It turns out that the "blood of the roaming Winterslips" (17)—a phrase initially used to describe their wanderlust, which is later revealed to be of a colonizing nature—is what is really at stake in *House*, particularly around issues of "blood" and "roaming." For parallel to the murder mystery and perhaps overshadowing it is the constant struggle and tension between West and East, civilized versus uncivilized, colonization and assimilation. Although Dan Winterslip's past centers around colonization, greed, and the enslavement of black bodies, *House* also reveals tensions and anxieties surrounding the colonization of Hawaii, or what Aunt Minerva calls the "Crossroads of the Pacific—the glamorous crossroads where, they said, in time all paths crossed again" (8). Albeit glamorous, this "crossroads" is also described as the geographical site of dangerous and foreign temptations. First, although Hawaii has been part of United States territory for decades, it is exotic enough that many still believe in its foreign status. As Aunt Minverva explains, "Only one person out of a thousand in this country knows that Hawaii is part of the United States" (22). But, whether U.S. territory or not, Hawaii is portrayed as a place that is not part of the civilized mainland; it is, in essence, an exotic "otherplace" where non-natives come to engage in excess without limitations or boundaries: "You must understand that here in the Islands a man may behave a—a bit differently than he would in the Back Bay" (6). Furthermore, it is a place that is ruled not by rationality but by emotion. As Dan's daughter, Barbara, admits to John Quincy: "This is an alien world you're entering now. Not Boston, John Quincy, nor any other old, civilized place. Not the kind of place where the mind rules. Out here it's the heart that charts our course. People you're fond of do the wildest, most unreasonable things, simply because their minds are sleeping and their hearts are beating fast. Just—just remember, please, John Quincy" (25). Here, Barbara charts the paradigmatic Manichean ideology behind colonization—civilized/uncivilized, rational/irrational, mind/heart. As such, it is *Hawaii* (not individual free will) that is at fault for every bad (white) behavior, seducing and tempting outsiders into behaving "differently" and justifying every conduct from slavery to adultery (as in the case of Dan Winterslip).

As such, John Quincy quickly realizes upon his arrival that this island lure threatens to destroy his family name; hence, the reclamation of his family's "blood" is a primary goal: "But here Winterslips had run amuck, and there was no telling what would next be dragged into the light" (92). It is, in fact, to save the Winterslip name that John Quincy initially travels to Hawaii in an attempt to bring his Aunt Minerva back to civilization. As Aunt Minerva freely admits, Hawaii has a dangerous hold upon its visitors, especially over white women: "You know what they say about white women who go to the tropics. They lose first their complexion, then their teeth, and finally their moral sense. . . . I've had to visit the dentist a good deal of late" (97). However, although Aunt Minerva was John Quincy's initial mission, his ultimate goal (and, thus, that of the novel) is to restore and safeguard white hegemonic ideals, whether through the Winterslip name, white heterosexual masculinity, or even white detective skills.

But what are some of the potential detective anxieties John Quincy is attempting to subdue? Although Hawaii may be a seductive temptress to white colonizers as well as the crossroads where "all paths cross," there are subtle yet constant references to the (white) anxiety of detection between the many divergent paths, particularly between natives and non-natives. For instance, while the detective astuteness of native Hawaiians seems almost natural and expected, they themselves escape easy detection. Our first introduction to a native occurs with Kamaikui, Dan Winterslip's servant. She is described as a "Hawaiian woman of *uncertain age* . . . a huge, high-breasted, dignified specimen of that vanishing race" (5, emphasis mine). She is so dignified, in fact, that Aunt Minerva has some trouble distinguishing her class background: "She was only a servant, but she spoke with the gracious manner of a hostess" (5). Later, John Quincy also undergoes a moment of detective hesitation when he remarks that Carlota (Jim Egan's daughter) is "Spanish *or something like that*" (12, emphasis added). On the other hand, while Kamaikui and Carlota cannot be easily deciphered, the "dapper Japanese chauffeur" (14) who meets John Quincy upon his arrival "pushed through the crowd and singling out the easterner [i.e., from the East Coast as opposed to Asia] with what seemed *uncanny perspicacity*, took complete charge of him" (14, emphasis mine). Here the Japanese chauffeur's "uncanny perspicacity" allows him to tell the difference between not only "native" versus "non-native" but "Easterner" from "Westerner" or "Midwesterner" as well. Finally, these displays of detective anxieties are emphasized by the repetitive references and allusions throughout the novel (and, for that matter, all the Charlie Chan novels) to the failures of the white police force. In *House*, even John Quincy shows himself aware of police failure when he says, "I congratulate you on your magnificent stupidity" (96).[11]

Within this Hawaiian paradise of detective anxieties, Charlie Chan is perhaps the most conflicted and potentially dangerous figure for he is at once the detective authority yet also the perpetual foreign outsider. Although Charlie describes himself as "kamaaina," or old-timer who has been an American resident for more than twenty-five years, he is consistently portrayed as an inassimilable non-American. When John Quincy meets him, ironically, at the "All-American Restaurant," he claims that he is the "only American in the place" (58), although Charlie and the Japanese American proprietor are both present. Furthermore, when John Quincy visits Charlie at his home on Punchbowl Hill, the detective is described as being completely un-American due to his dress:

> A Chinese woman—a servant, she seemed—ushered him into Chan's dimly-lighted living room. The detective was seated at a table playing chess; he rose with dignity when he saw his visitor. In this, his hour of ease, he wore a long loose robe of dark purple silk, which fitted closely at the neck and had wide sleeves. Beneath it showed white trousers of the same material, and on his feet were shoes of silk, with thick felt soles. *He was all Oriental now,* suave and ingratiating but remote, and for the first time John Quincy was really conscious of the great gulf across which he and Chan shook hands. (115, emphasis mine)

Not only Charlie's demeanor in his private habitat but also his home furnishings impress on John Quincy the gulf between the two cultures:

> John Quincy glanced about the room. On the back wall hung a scroll with felicitations, the gift of some friend of the family at New Year's. Opposite him, on another wall, was a single picture, painted on silk, representing a bird on an apple bough. . . . Beneath the picture stood a square table, flanked by straight, low-backed armchairs. On other elaborately carved teakwood stands distributed about the room were blue and white vases, porcelain wine jars, dwarfed trees. Pale golden lanterns hung from the ceiling; a soft-toned rug lay on the floor. John Quincy felt again the gulf between himself and Charlie Chan. (116)

This scene is remarkable for a number of reasons. First, it is one of the rare intrusions into Charlie's private life in either the novels or the films. In fact, apart from meeting his numerous offspring in the films and intermittent glances of the Chan family portrait, it is quite rare to glimpse any part of Charlie's private life, including his home and family life. Therefore, what is fascinating about the above scene is that John Quincy's description of Charlie's home almost reads like a chapter from an ethnographic study. It includes everything from Charlie's dress to tastes in artwork and home décor to leisure activities. Most importantly, it reveals Charlie during his "hour of ease," exposing what he is really like during his least guarded time at home. Consequently, this snapshot revelation shows that what he's really like is more Chinese than American. As such, he will never be "all American" no matter how "kamaaina" he is.[12]

Thus, if Charlie is portrayed here as a perpetual foreigner with questionable American loyalties and habits, it is not difficult to understand the dangers of his self-proclaimed, superhuman detective abilities. As

Charlie proudly announces throughout the Charlie Chan novels, he is a better detective *because* he is Chinese. While he does display Holmesian talents (such as differentiating cigarette brands in *House*), he is quick to criticize scientific methods of detection. For instance, in *House*, Charlie declares: "Finger-prints and other mechanics good in books, in real life not so much so. My experience tell me to think deep about human people. Human passions. Back of murder what, always? Hate, revenge, need to make silent the slain one. Greed for money, maybe. Study human people at all times" (59). Furthermore, Charlie also criticizes the scientific methods of his fictional predecessors by condemning the use of theoretical approaches in general. Claiming that they are too limiting, he states in *The Chinese Parrot* that "long experience has taught fatal consequence may follow if I get too addicted to a theory. Then I try and see, can I make everything fit. I can, and first think I know theory explodes in my countenance with loud bang. Much better I have found to keep mind free and open" (255). This antiscience rhetoric is reiterated in the very beginning of *Behind That Curtain* when even Sir Frederic Bruce, former head of Scotland Yard (an obvious allusion to Sherlock Holmes and his partners in detection), makes a similar claim: "The flights of genius and miracles of science which solve most of the crimes in detective stories have no real part in detective work" (299). Here, scientific theories are shown to be concepts that can be easily learned and mimicked; there is nothing extraordinary about them because they are available to and accessible by any individual with a modicum of intelligence. Charlie Chan, on the other hand, relies upon a different detective method. As he claims in *House*, the "Chinese [are the] most psychic people in the world" (60). His method, the Chinese gift of psychic abilities, cannot be learned nor copied, especially in light of Charlie's "calm, cool Oriental" (*Behind* 330) exterior, which includes the "impassive face of the Chinese" (*The Chinese Parrot* 279–80). Charlie's skills, then, are often intimidating to the people around him, resulting in such comments as. "don't be so Oriental" (*Behind* 318), and "I'm sick of you and your confounded mystery. Put your cards on the table like a white man" (*Behind* 425).

Although these psychic abilities are potentially quite threatening, the novels quickly alleviate and contain that anxiety by penetrating and devaluing Charlie's seemingly inaccessible detective skills. This is accomplished through the appearance of amateur detectives who are not only instrumental in solving the mystery of Dan's murder but who ultimately demonstrate that successful detectives are not only from China. First, Biggers's novels reveal that while Charlie may have psychic abilities, women are also portrayed as intuitive and astute detectives as well. For instance, throughout *House*, Aunt Minerva constantly impresses Charlie and others around her with her detective intelligence. Described as "no ordinary woman" (33), she is instrumental in solving the murder mystery by observing a distinguishing mark on the murderer's watch, leading even Officer Hallet to proclaim that "[she] certainly had [her] wits about [her]" (39) and that she has "a good mind" (47). Furthermore, although she doesn't get any credit, Barbara also suspects the identity of the killer alongside John Quincy and Charlie by stating that she has a certain "suspicion—a feeling—intuition" (135). The success of female intuition, in fact, appears throughout the novels. As a character in *Behind the Curtain* claims, "there are certain artifices which fool a man, but never fool a woman" (343).

But, aside from the intermittent appearances of female intuitive skills, the most damaging element to Charlie's unique psychic abilities is the intrusion of the white male amateur detective in all of the Charlie Chan novels. In *House*, John Quincy's role is to restore not only his family name but white hegemonic ideals by succeeding and overtaking Charlie's detective plot. His very name, in fact, conjures images of presidents and patriotism, everything that Charlie is not. Thus, the story centers around John Quincy almost in its entirety, describing everything from his journey from Boston to San Francisco and Hawaii to his romantic liaisons to his daily experiences in Hawaii. In other words, although *House* uses an omniscient narrator, we witness almost everything from John Quincy's point of view, including his detective journey through numerous clues and leads. His role as the story's primary detective is so central that it is he (not Charlie) who, in fact, receives threats from the murderer. In essence, then, applauding Biggers for creating the first nonwhite detective is somewhat misleading. It is, rather, John Quincy's story, one that combines a story of redemption (of the Winterslip name) with the story of restoration (of white authority). Furthermore, John Quincy's detective success parallels that of his romance quest. It is his desires for both Barbara and Carlota that is a primary motivation for John Quincy to find the murderer. As he declares: "Again he felt in his heart that flare of anger against the 'person or persons unknown' who had brought this grief upon [Barbara]. The guilty must pay—Egan or whoever. Brade or Leatherbee or the chorus girl. Pay and pay dearly—he was resolved on that" (75). By the story's conclusion, John does eventually solve the murder and, with the help of Charlie in the final climactic scene, captures Jennison and, consequently, Carlota's heart. As a result, while Charlie proudly pronounces throughout the novels that the Chinese are the "most psychic people in the world" (60), the ending reveals that the mastery of detection is not dependent upon a racial (namely, Asian) identification; in fact, the novel's end undercuts any allusion to and possible fears of that belief. If anything, *The House without a Key* demonstrates that John Quincy, the symbol of white American aristocracy, can not only deliver similar outcomes but does so in much more impressive ways, reducing Charlie's role to that of exotic assistant or sidekick. As Charlie himself announces to John, "You are number one detective yourself" (85).

Cinematic Containments and Eruptions: Sidekicks, Spectatorship, and Racial Insiderism

In "The Oppositional Gaze: Black Female Spectators," bell hooks writes about being punished as a young girl for looking because looks were seen as "confrontational, gestures of resistance, [and] challenges to authority" (115). As she reveals, "the 'gaze' has always been political in my life" (115). Hooks continues by stating that racialized power relations (particularly within the politics and economy of slavery) in denying the right to gaze had, in turn, produced an "oppositional gaze" that "opens up the possibility of agency" (116). Citing Michel Foucault, she argues that there is always a "possibility of resistance" in all relations of power and that we must search for those "margins, gaps, and locations on and through the body where agency can be found" (116):

> Spaces of agency exist for black people, wherein we can both interrogate the gaze of the Other but also look back, and at one another, naming what we see. The "gaze" has been and is a site of resistance for colonized black people globally. Subordinates in relations of power learn experientially that there is a critical gaze, one that "looks" to document, one that is oppositional. In resistance struggle, the power of the dominated to assert agency by claiming and cultivating "awareness" politicizes "looking" relations—*one learns to look a certain way in order to resist.* (116, emphasis mine)

While the rest of hooks's essay examines black "looking relations" and, in particular, black female spectatorship through a brief outline of such theorists as Stuart Hall, Frantz Fanon, Manthia Diawara, Laura Mulvey, and Mary Ann Doane, the remainder of this chapter builds upon hooks's theory through a slightly different angle. Although hooks argues for an oppositional gaze that is a type of what Manthia Diawara labels "resisting spectatorship" (128), she is also quick to emphasize that this is *inadequate* for black female spectators. Instead, hooks claims that black women create "alternative texts that are not solely reactions. As critical spectators, black women participate in a broad range of looking relations, contest, resist, revision, interrogate, and invent on multiple levels" (128).

This section examines the idea of "alternative texts" in the broader context of several Charlie Chan films by offering a reading of the Afro-Asian relationship between the racialized sidekick characters (specifically Charlie's sons and black chauffeur, Birmingham Brown) that is utilized *in opposition to* the Charlie Chan character. I find the racialized sidekick characters in these films fascinating for two main reasons. First, it is imperative that a study of race and representation within the Charlie Chan phenomenon include an examination of these sidekick characters, ironically the only "real" raced figures in the films, to witness how race can be both manipulated and controlled (yellowface) while also providing sites of eruption and unmanageability. However, just as most scholars have critically dismissed Charlie Chan, they also have generally avoided these sidekick figures, whom they identify as further examples of Stepin Fetchit's "step-chillun." Second, the sidekick characters complicate Amy Robinson's triangular theater of passing discussed earlier. Since Charlie Chan's passing act is widely acknowledged by the viewing audience (it was generally known that three white actors—Warner Oland, Sidney Tolder, and Roland Winters—played Charlie in the films), who is the duped in Robinson's triangular theater of passer/duped/in-group? Based on a close reading of four Charlie Chan films, I contend that Charlie Chan (and, as a result, the white viewing audience) is in constant struggle against being the duped and fights the fear of exclusion that arises in response to the sidekick characters' practice of racial insiderism.

In her study of the Korean American actor Philip Ahn and his use of cross-ethnic masquerade, Hye Seung Chung reveals the exclusionary process enacted via racial masquerade that creates an insider/outsider mechanism. Chung theorizes on Asian American performativity and spectatorship by building upon two scholarly lenses: (1) that of the "resistant spectator" as espoused by Stuart Hall, Manthia Diawara, bell hooks, and Peter Feng; and (2) feminist and critical race theories of masquerade and passing examined by Joan Riviere, Valerie Smith, Michael Rogin, and Judith Butler. Through her conceptualization of "Oriental masquerade" and "ethnic passing" in Hollywood's classical period of the 1930s to 1950s,

Chung asks, "Is there anything subversive about [these actors'] Oriental masquerades, anything that might restore a sense of ethnic self-esteem?" (45). Chung's response locates the site of possibility in the audible rather than the visual. For example, Philip Ahn often spoke Korean (instead of Mandarin or Cantonese) throughout his cross-ethnic performances and, subsequently, placed his generally American (white) audiences in the position of "dupe" alongside his bicultural and bilingual "ethnic clairvoyant" for whom the masquerade "is all too evident or transparent" (46). Chung gives evidence of this in *Charlie Chan in Honolulu* (1938), where Ahn plays son-in-law Wing Fu to Sidney Toler's Charlie Chan. When Wing Fu notifies Charlie in Korean that he has become a grandfather, the Korean-speaking audience becomes the in-group whereby they "derive not only subversive laughter but also establish an extratextual, cultural bonding with the diasporic actor through the mechanism of ethnic recognition" (49). Similarly, Chinese-speaking audiences "are likewise in-group clairvoyants who know that the dialogue is not Chinese and that the actor is passing" (49). Chung includes a politically charged example of Ahn's linguistic masquerade in *They Met in Bombay* (1941) starring Clark Gable and Rosalind Russell when Ahn "injected an anti-colonial message in the Korean language while playing a Japanese character in pre–Pearl Harbor Hollywood" (50). While the scene was eventually deleted, it did not prevent some Korean expatriates in Japan or what Chung refers to as "colonized members of the in-group" (50) from possibly seeing, hearing, and becoming motivated by the contentious scene that leads to the film's ban in Japan. Similar to Reddy's concept of "white bonding" discussed earlier in this chapter, these examples offer the possibility of an "Asian bonding" within the Charlie Chan films. Creating an "in-group" moment reveals a type of "knowing" that erupts *in spite of* the racial and racist restrictions placed upon the sidekick characters. No matter how psychic or intuitive Charlie Chan may be, his inability to discern between what the Asian American author and critic Frank Chin calls the "real and the fake" ultimately highlights his outsider status.

The films' struggle with racial intuition is further displayed with the entrance of black sidekick characters. But what is racialized intuition and instinct, and how does it affect detection? Is the turn to intuition and instinct always objective, without biases and preconditioning? While the act of detection as popularly applied in detective fiction is the art of solving the mystery and often relies on intuition, detection also includes acts of careful discernment that work in very nuanced ways and in very fleeting moments. A reliance on instincts and feelings is key here. For racialized subjects who are often the targets of biased beliefs, behaviors, and sanction, relying on instincts and feelings can be an act of survival. The anthropologist John L. Jackson Jr.'s study of racial paranoia offers a helpful theoretical framework here. In *Racial Paranoia: The Unintended Consequences of Political Correctness* (2008), Jackson explains that colorblindness and paranoia often go hand in hand. Because political correctness produces a subtler form of racism where racist acts may not be as obvious as separate drinking fountains, a resulting effect is racial paranoia. One definition of racial paranoia is a type of intuitive feeling where certain acts, behaviors, and conversations necessitate a particular reading and suspicion. For instance, Jackson offers the example of Congresswoman Cynthia McKinney, who accused a Capitol Hill police officer of racial profiling when he grabbed her in a congressional office building. Although McKinney never accused the police officer, Paul McKenna, of making inappropriate racist slurs, the officer's nonrecognition of the congresswoman (who had been traversing the same governmental offices for more than a decade) and subsequent grabbing of her is what Jackson calls *de cardio* racism, or a "racism [that] pivots on the subtle slight as telltale indication of hidden ill will" (101). Did the officer grab her because as a black woman she did not belong there? Or was the officer's nonrecognition of McKinney an enactment of Ellison's *Invisible Man* syndrome? Or was this occurrence not racially inflected at all? How to discern racism's "subtle slights" is where the problems of paranoia and detection become inextricably linked.

Like racial paranoia, the need to detect may occur as a result of a look, a statement, a seemingly innocent act, or even silence and the evasion of a look. A well-known example is the by now famous case of Dave Chappelle, who canceled *Chappelle's Show* in 2005 (and, subsequently, rejected $50 million) due to a discomfort experienced by a white crewmember's unnerving laughter. Hearing a white crewmember laugh "in such a way" that made him uncomfortable, Chappelle questioned the political and racial consequences of his show: "I know the difference between people laughing with me and people laughing at me," declared Chappelle (xiii). What this revelation illustrates is that racial paranoia is not an irrational knee-jerk reaction but a self-taught and experienced discernment of reading racial codes and clues. As a black comedian, Chappelle has experience receiving many different types of laughter and can discern the difference between, say, racist and nonracist laughter. What Chappelle's perceptive ear heard that day and his subsequent actions were not due to the entertainer's inability to handle fame and fortune as some critics and fans have pronounced. Rather, he cancelled the show to prevent the occurrence of continued racism. At a time when the freedom to laugh at highly racialized/racist representations is debatable within a color-blind, politically correct cultural moment, the crewmember's laughter may have been just a little too loud and a little too pointed for Chappelle's comfort. Instinct, then, is not merely a "gut feeling"; it is a learned tool. Further, Jackson emphasizes that racial paranoia is not only experienced by the disempowered; rather, it affects both blacks and whites but is experienced differently depending upon who possesses the power.

Racial intuition and paranoia are useful theoretical tools that help us better understand the struggle over what is at stake in the Charlie Chan films. As such, I pay particular attention to the Monogram Picture phase to illustrate how an Afro-Asian racial economy is employed to navigate through the anxious terrain of detection and undetection. An Afro-Asian analytical framework has been an immensely important subfield in ethnic studies in recent years via interdisciplinary scholars such as Najia Aarim-Heriot, Crystal S. Anderson, Helen Jun, Claire Jean Kim, Daniel Y. Kim, James Lee, Julia H. Lee, George Lipsitz, Bill Mullen, Gary Okihiro, Vijay Prashad, and Frank Wu. As Lipsitz writes in *The Possessive Investment in Whiteness*: "Liberal narratives about multiculturalism and cultural pluralism to the contrary, race relations in the United States have always involved more than one outcast group at a time acting in an atomized fashion against a homogeneous 'white' center. Interethnic identifications and alliances have been powerful weapons against white supremacy. All racial identities are relational; communities of color are mutually constitutive of one another, not just competitive or cooperative" (210). Claire Jean Kim builds upon the relational construction of identities via her "racial triangulation" model that proposes the simultaneous processes of "relative valorization," in which dominant group A (whites) valorizes subordinate group B in relation to subordinate group C, and "civic ostracism," in which dominant group A constructs subordinate group B as inassimilable and foreign. As such, the Monogram Pictures phase of the Charlie Chan filmography illustrates the triangular relationship between whiteness, Asianness, and blackness as they negotiate their positionality upon the racial hierarchy. But I want to emphasize that my comparative racialization here is not merely to note the counterhegemonic moments in Charlie Chan. Rather, in the words of Helen Jun: "We can read culture not merely to identify ideological shortcomings (or conversely, signs of resistance) but to understand that irrespective of intention and impulse, every text can be read for the inevitable contradictions it attempts to manage or reconcile. This more supple methodology can reveal how historically specific contradictions inherent in the institution of citizenship take shape and are negotiated in Asian American and African American cultural production" (5). Produced during the final years of World War II and into the next several postwar years, the Monogram films expose the very tensions between whites and nonwhites that the United States was experiencing internally as well as externally on the international stage. After the war, black Americans were questioning their participation in a war that fought for freedom, human rights, and democracy when they were experiencing segregation in the U.S. Army and at home. On an international scale, the United States became world leaders in the struggle against Soviet-backed communism and, thus, had to demonstrate its fight for racial justice domestically. In response, the Charlie Chan films offer an informative cultural response to the national and global struggle over freedom and justice, whites and nonwhites.

Monogram Pictures, Afro-Asian Relations, and the Displacement of Racial Anxieties

Fifty-three Charlie Chan films were made between 1929 and 1981, produced by Fox, Twentieth Century Fox, and Monogram Pictures.[13] According to the film historian Charles Mitchell, there are more Charlie Chan feature films than films about any other detective, including Sherlock Holmes. While Warner Oland (1931–38), Sidney Toler (1938–47), and Roland Winters (1947–49) are generally acknowledged to have played Charlie Chan, it is little known that the first three films featured Charlie played by Asian actors. These actors include George Kuwa in *House without a Key* (lost), Kamiyama Sojin in *The Chinese Parrot* (lost), and E. L. Park in *Behind That Curtain* (1929). The potential repercussions and possible fear of using an Asian actor to play the Chinese American detective hero is telling in these films. While the first two films are lost (metaphorically foreshadowing my argument surrounding Charlie's "disappearance" and/or disembodiment), E. L. Park's performance is limited to a mere three minutes of screen time in *Behind That Curtain*. As Mitchell declares, Chan is "virtually eliminated" (xviii) in this film, overshadowed by the central portrayal of Sir Frederic Bruce, a Scotland Yard detective who is killed early on in the novel but takes over Charlie's role in the film adaptation. When the films do feature Charlie as a central character, it is done through yellowface. Furthermore, unlike the novels where Charlie himself becomes somewhat of a marginalized sidekick character, the films routinely incorporate several racialized sidekick characters throughout the series, especially during the Monogram Pictures phase (1944–49) that starred Sidney Toler and Roland Winters as Charlie Chan.

The Monogram phase consists of seventeen films. Several of Charlie's numerous offspring appeared in all of these films and, with the exception of two (*The Red Dragon* and *Dangerous Money*), the African American actor Mantan Moreland also appeared as Charlie's chauffeur and assistant, Birmingham Brown. While Keye Luke and Sen Yung (later known as Victor Sen Yung) appeared throughout the pre-Monogram phase (playing sons Lee Chan and James Chan, respectively), I am focusing on the Monogram production phase primarily because it was during this period that the sidekick characters became much more central figures in the plot. More importantly, it was also during the Monogram phase that African Americans and Asian Americans, two very distinct communities that are often defined in opposition to each other in their quest for citizenship and national belonging, come together.

Ironically, the film historian Ken Hanke writes that it was also during the Monogram phase that the character of Charlie Chan was becoming much less "racist" because he was becoming much more "abrasive":

> The Monogram series was less concerned with the formalities of the Fox films and for the first time since the earliest Oland entries, Charlie began to be openly contemptuous of his suspects and superiors. The later Toler films featured a Charlie Chan who could, frankly, border on being downright offensive, though always in a slightly self-effacing manner. . . . Less concerned about offending sensitive viewers with a more abrasive Charlie Chan (read: a Chinese who "didn't know his place") than was Fox, Monogram actually removed a certain amount of "racist" stigma rather unfairly attached to the Fox product. (170)

Could Charlie's increasingly abrasive behavior in the Monogram pictures be a result of the more centralized role of the racialized sidekick characters? On the one hand, the presence of the sidekicks offers an easy outlet for race bashing, particularly through the castigations of Charlie himself, who, known to the audience as being white, is only "playing at" Chineseness. For instance, in one minstrel-like scene in *Shadows over Chinatown* (1946), Birmingham Brown (who is characterized as the cowardly and inept chauffeur) is seen escaping from a morgue by repeatedly running into a wall, hoping it will break into a door. Here, the audience witnesses Birmingham's incompetence—and, by extension, that of the larger African American community—but also supports the superiority of Charlie, who is seen laughing at his chauffeur's expense.

But, contrary to the films' intent, these characters also establish moments of racial critique. In his analysis of *Charlie Chan in Egypt* (1935),[14] Yunte Huang writes that the film was a "racial parable that appeared in a fraught and incendiary age in which the world seemed to be careening again toward war and cataclysm" (243). Starring a multiethnic cast of characters (Chinese, black, Jew, and Arab), the film "pitches [the] colored" against Anglo-Saxon whites "with the former united by their interest in truth and justice and the latter condemned by their insatiable hunger for material wealth" (242). By the end, Snowshoes follows the "Chinaman's path of spiritual enrichment rather than the white men's expedition that has spawned nothing but death, sadness, and destruction" (243). *Charlie Chan in Egypt*, in essence, establishes the seeds of an Afro-Asian coalition that is developed further with the introduction of Birmingham Brown.

In his filmography of the Charlie Chan films, Ken Hanke writes that the Monogram Pictures had a very strategic motive for including the character of Birmingham Brown (played by the African American actor Mantan Moreland, who is identified by Donald Bogle as one of the prominent "Stepin Fetchit step-chillun" [72])[15] in the series. According to Hanke, it was an "insurance policy" (170) through which the films would also garner an African American audience in black communities like Harlem. Whether or not the Charlie Chan films were popular within black communities is a topic too large for this project. However, similar to the theories of "white bonding" and "Asian bonding" mentioned previously, the films featuring Birmingham offer "black bonding" moments that exclude other audiences. I am less interested in the plotlines of these films than in the *function* of the racialized sidekicks working in opposition to Charlie Chan as well as in collaboration with each other. How do these sidekicks validate Charlie by ultimately aligning him with white hegemony? What are some of the potential moments of resistance in which the anxiety of detection is emphasized rather than diminished? What could have been the possible black and Asian reactions to Mantan Moreland and Charlie's numerous offspring, especially in witnessing them working together? I believe these questions are important not only to better understand the role of the Charlie Chan films in the larger framework of race relations in popular culture but also within the general politics of white, liberal multiculturalism. For to include a multiethnic cast as the films do seemingly supports Biggers's initial agenda of antiracist intent. But, as demonstrated below, rather than a welcoming of acceptance, the inclusion divulges the constant struggle over the matrix of power through which difference and its possibilities are contained and erased.

CHARLIE CHAN IN THE SECRET SERVICE

Charlie Chan in the Secret Service (1944) is the first Monogram Charlie Chan film and, unfortunately, one of the weakest. However, aside from the poor writing and slow action, there are several enlightening moments that expose some of the film's timely concerns centered around national security, patriotic pride (the plot takes place in Washington, D.C., during World War II and Charlie is now working for the American Secret Service), and the anxiety of detection (the mystery to the murder is the discovery of a master enemy, a German agent). In brief, *Charlie Chan in the Secret Service* is a mystery about the murder of George Melton, an American inventor whose plans for a powerful torpedo is hunted by the Germans. As stated by both Ken Hanke and Charles Mitchell, Charlie Chan becomes a much sharper-tongued character in this film. Furthermore, this is the first film in which we are witness to the developing Afro-Asian relations between Birmingham Brown and Charlie's offspring (in this case, Tommy Chan, #3 son, and Iris Chan, #2 daughter). As it turns out, this relationship is about much more than comic relief or marketing tactics, as Hanke would have us believe. In fact, I argue that it is because of these racialized sidekick characters that Charlie is able to empower himself, becoming a much more authoritative, courageous, and sometimes even impertinent Chinese American detective hero.

First, Charlie's talent at detection is constantly emphasized throughout the film when we are, in turn, witness to not only his children's continual failed attempts at detection but also Birmingham Brown's cowardly and constant attempts to run away from the mystery, all of which lead Charlie to declare to all three: "Always someone about to stick fly in ointment. This time I am unlucky man with three flies." Charlie's self-claimed opposition to his "three flies" is best illustrated in an early pivotal scene when he encounters all three in the basement of Melton's home. While Charlie is upstairs questioning the witnesses, Tommy and Iris contemplate breaking into the basement in a desperate attempt to aid their father. While Tommy nervously lingers at the window, Iris asks, "Are you a detective or a dud?" and pushes her brother in. Immediately after they break into the dark basement, Tommy declares that he sees someone "wearing a mask" and attacks him. When the lights are turned on, Charlie is standing on the steps, watching his son and Birmingham Brown (the one "wearing a mask") scuffling with each other. They cease and stand silently before Charlie, ashamed and nervous. Charlie takes one look at Tommy, sees his son's own face blackened with soot (it turns out Tommy is the one "wearing a mask" here), and declares, "I see double, perhaps?" Birmingham quickly replies, "If that's me, I don't look so good." When Charlie asks Tommy and Iris what they are doing there, they break out into speedy and excited Chinese. When asked by a confused Birmingham what they are saying, Charlie replies, "It's all Chinese to me!"

The symbolism of this scene is quite telling on both a literal and metaphoric level. First, it highlights the discrepancy between insider/outsider and citizen/foreigner. Charlie's declaration that "It's all Chinese to me," while meant as a joke, is ultimately not a funny matter. Rather, it is a question of belonging versus not belonging wherein Charlie, as a white actor in yellowface, is in reality not Chinese, thus emphasizing the reality of his statement. Simultaneously, however, Charlie is also aligned with Birmingham in their mutual status as linguistic outsiders. Here, their Americanness (i.e., their citizenship) is confirmed via their failure to participate in foreign-language skills. But the scene also creates another type of grouping—one that separates the "white" from the nonwhite—when Charlie, upon seeing Tommy's blackface, asks, "I see double, perhaps?" Here Charlie momentarily equates Asianness and blackness with each other. His (as well as the narrative) nervousness about this alignment (perhaps hinting at the possibility of an Afro-Asian miscegenation or coalition?) is revealed when he quickly orders Tommy to "wash face," indicating Asian Americans' temporary status as a "blackened" group that has opportunities to escape in order to become the "model minority."[16]

The anxiety of detection and passing as well as Charlie's (i.e., Sidney Toler's) own racial performance is ironically summarized at the conclusion of the movie when it is revealed that Mrs. Winters, the wealthy and dumb socialite, is actually discovered to be the sought-after German spy passing as American:

TOMMY: That Mrs. Winters wasn't so dumb at all. She was only putting on an act.
CHARLIE: I don't get it.
TOMMY (looking at Iris): Pop didn't get it.

Although Charlie is himself a passing, fictional character in a Hollywood movie, what he "doesn't get" is the awareness of the ultimate consequences of such a performance. While Charlie (a.k.a. Sidney Toler, Monogram Pictures, the white audience) may experience a sense of sly triumph with his/their in-group positioning, what he/they ultimately "do not get" is that *all* race, including whiteness, is a cultural, political, and legal construction. Here, Tommy understands that identity is about "putting on an act," a realization that his detective father fails to recognize.

CHARLIE CHAN IN THE CHINESE CAT

Released the same year as *Charlie Chan in the Secret Service*, *Charlie Chan in the Chinese Cat* (1944) further eases any fears threatening whiteness through a double displacement of the sidekick characters. If one such method of white maintenance is to ridicule his offspring in order to validate his own authority, *The Chinese Cat* illustrates an extreme example of such denigration. While Charlie is famous for his Confucius-like aphorisms throughout the novels and the films, this film reveals that what has often been believed to be peace-loving and philosophical riddles have now turned into belittling and often scornful, passive-aggressive criticisms directed toward his offspring. If one of the threats of Yellow Peril ideology includes the fear of Asian intelligence and superiority, it is not surprising that Charlie minimizes this very threat by directing constant criticisms at his children's intelligence. In this film alone, Charlie addresses almost all of his observations to his son, Tommy, highlighting his son's stupidity, ignorance, and loving albeit naïve paternal devotion:

- "Fear you are like weak limb, to which no family tree may point with pride."
- "You are smart enough to keep eyes open. Do likewise, keep mouth shut."
- "Your assistance about as welcome as water in a leaking ship."
- "You talk like rooster who thinks sun come up just to hear him crow."
- "You put two and two together and get results bigger than national debt."
- "See [statue] with no head? He remind me of you."
- "You are like turtle. After everything all over, you stick your head out and find truth right under your very nose."

I include these statements not to merely emphasize Charlie's cruel nature but to examine the purpose and intent of these harsh pronouncements. What is the function of these criticisms? As Charlie declares in *Red*

Dragon (1945), "Confucius could give answer to that. Unfortunately, Confucius not here at moment." Here, Confucius's absence is replaced by white anxiety. By attributing failure, stupidity, and cowardice to Tommy, a character who is visibly and without question an Asian American, Charlie is able to practice his growing authority as a white man passing for Chinese.[17] This is again supported later in the film when Tommy is physically rather than just verbally beaten by the suspects in order to shield his father from any harm. In fact, Charlie is standing silently and calmly while Tommy is brutally choked, beaten, and threatened with a knife. Furthermore, soon after Tommy gets beaten, Charlie directs the suspects to Birmingham Brown in order to, again, escape personal harm. The symbolism of this scene is, again, revealing in its subtle yet striking conclusion. If Charlie Chan represents white liberal celebration of difference (such as that of Biggers's authorial intent), it is often achieved at the expense of the marginalized people themselves for it is difficult to not interpret the inclusion of racialized sidekick characters in this film as the psychological, emotional, physical, and metaphoric target of white anger and vigilantism (a.k.a. liberalism).[18]

Significantly, Birmingham Brown is aware of the injustice imposed upon people of color for throughout the films, he makes several comments that are left unexamined by the rest of the plot yet importantly contribute to the films' representation of African Americans and their relationship to crime. As he declares in *Black Magic*, his connection to three murders is not a fault of his but of the law. He exclaims to the police commissioner: "It ain't my fault, Mister. It's the law. Always somebody taking me down the hall. Then, something goes 'Clang!' Then, I'm in jail again. But, by mistake." Here, while the Charlie Chan films do not directly address the legal system and its often biased and unequal treatment of people of color, Birmingham subtly expresses the inequality of the justice system for marginalized groups, especially African Americans, in the twentieth century. But, Birmingham is also aware of his position when he declares, "Free speech gonna get me in trouble yet" (*Chinese Cat*). Additionally, perhaps the filmmakers are also aware of the potential consequences of these comments when in *The Scarlet Clue*, made one year after Birmingham's statement above, the focus briefly turns to African Americans and the legal system.

THE SCARLET CLUE

In *The Scarlet Clue* (1945), the first scene in which we see Birmingham Brown occurs when he and Tommy are at the police station in order to report a black marketeer. What initially transpires as the report of a criminal activity quickly turns into Birmingham's own struggle to fight for his innocence as well as the stereotyping of black criminality in general. When Tommy declares that "[The black marketeer's] business is as dark as . . . uh . . . " and points to Birmingham, Charlie's chauffeur interjects, "It ain't exactly that dark." Here Birmingham must distinguish between the criminal behavior of this particular black marketeer who *happens to be* black from the suggestion that all blacks are potential black marketeers or criminals. What is "dark" here is the danger of darkening (i.e., race-ing) criminal behavior. While this may be an enlightening moment in which Birmingham criticizes racial stereotyping, this opportunity is quickly undermined when he reviews a book of photographs in order to point out the suspect. Looking through the book, Birmingham not only sees a picture of his Uncle Nicodemus but one of himself. As Birmingham tries to defend himself against the police officers' accusation that he is trying to trick them, the scene concludes with Birmingham literally jailing himself behind bars. Thus, what begins as a warning to not stereotype blacks with criminality concludes with the black man in jail.[19]

Although this particular scene seems to lock Birmingham behind the bars of racial limitations, there is another significant scene soon following Birmingham's pessimistic outcome that offers a moment of black resistance. As Birmingham and Tommy are trying to help Charlie solve the crime, the former encounters an old friend. Ben Carter, Mantan Moreland's frequent partner in nightclub comedy routines, enters as Birmingham's friend Ben. While this scene is in no way relevant to the plot, it is significant in that it introduces not only black camaraderie but also displays the unique skills of black intuition or racial insiderism. Here Birmingham and Ben carry on an entire conversation in which neither character completes a sentence, yet each fully understands the other's meaning:

BIRMINGHAM: Boy, it's been a long time. I haven't seen you since . . .
BEN: Longer than that. The last time I saw you, you was . . .
BIRMINGHAM: Oh, I moved from there. I moved over to . . .
BEN: How can you live in that neighborhood?
BIRMINGHAM: I don't know . . .
BEN: Now where I'm living I only pay . . .
BIRMINGHAM: It ain't that cheap, is it?
BEN: Sure it is!

BIRMINGHAM: Hey, lookee here . . . is you still married . . .
BEN: No, I divorced her.

The conversation continues, including such other topics as romance, gambling, and health. Although used primarily for comedic purposes, especially in Mantan Moreland's nightclub acts, its function here is significantly different. Placed within a film that emphasizes skills of intuition and the role of insider/outsider as defined by access to knowledge, I read this scene as resisting and critiquing Western (read: white) concepts of knowing. It is a prime example of the skills of intuition that are not available to a white audience. Birmingham and Ben are able to read each other's minds with ease and finish one another's sentences, demonstrating a sort of psychic elliptical exchange. Furthermore, they display that it is a talent unique to their community and not open for outsiders' understanding; as "racial insiderism," it is a type of community building that is a collection of shared experiences of blackness. At a time when whiteness is under assault, when whiteness is not necessarily safe from within or without, this black collective consciousness announces that communities have their own conversations (and revel in it) with or without the white gaze. In some ways, it is the *most* anxiety-producing because it demonstrates that these conversations do not have to center on whiteness; the black community, in fact, has a life beyond and exists in spite of the clasp of race and racism.

DARK ALIBI

If this exchange between Birmingham and Ben instilled a sense of discomfort in the general audience (one similar in effect to Charlie's earlier novelistic claim of Chinese psychic abilities), the filmmakers and Monogram may have later perceived such dialogue as too dangerous. *Dark Alibi* (1946) includes several other elliptical exchanges between Birmingham and Ben. But if the earlier demonstration resulted in unease and anxiety, these exchanges help to assuage those feelings quickly and effectively. Here the exchanges occur in Ben's new home—prison. While Birmingham desperately tries to keep himself out of prison and to resist the stereotyped association of blackness with inevitable criminality in *The Scarlet Clue*, Ben undermines that attempt here by returning to the Charlie Chan films as a prisoner. Furthermore, while the exchange in the film was open only to the black community (hence, demonstrating a type of black intuition others could not access), here it is appropriated and taken over by Charlie, a white man in yellowface promoting white superiority:

BEN: I've just been thinking. Do you know you owe me . . .
BIRMINGHAM: I don't owe you nothing. All I owe you is . . .
BEN: Oh no. You forgettin' the time that . . .
BIRMINGHAM: No I ain't! Do you know I had to spend . . .
BEN: You ain't never spent that much in your life. Look, my uncle wrote and told me . . .
CHARLIE: No, no, no, no, Birmingham not do that. He go see landlady and she tell him . . .
BEN: She lied. I don't owe her a cent. Listen, Mr. Chan, did you know her . . .
CHARLIE: Yeah, I met him last time, you know when . . .
BIRMINGHAM: That's right, Mr. Chan, that's the time that I took it over to . . .
Tommy: Took what over to where?
BIRMINGHAM: Oh, the check over to the tailor's.
BEN: Oh, that's what happened to that suit I never got to wear!
CHARLIE: Yeah, Birmingham go out in rain, suit shrink, tailor refuse same, so Birmingham must pay for suit!
BEN: Well, where's the suit now?
BIRMINGHAM: It's still shrinkin'. My little nephew's got it on his teddy bear.
CHARLIE: You know, that's why I like meet you boys. We understand each other so well!

Here, what occurs is not only a complete undermining but full takeover of Birmingham and Ben's previous exchanges. By participating in what I earlier term a psychic elliptical exchange, Charlie demonstrates that he can penetrate what was previously believed to be accessible only to the black community. Furthermore, while Birmingham mistakes "confusion" with "Confucius" in both *Dark Alibi* and *The Trap* by exclaiming, "Every time you open your mouth, it's *Confusion* to me," Charlie shows here that his intuitive abilities can even cross the racial border. Finally in this scene, he again emphasizes his superiority (in this case, over Tommy) by having the final say, leaving his son utterly confused:

TOMMY: Pop, I don't get it. I never get that kind of talk. How do you do it?
CHARLIE: You are familiar with pidgin English?

TOMMY: Oh, sure.
CHARLIE: Same difference.

By referring to pidgin English, or a Chinese corruption of the English language, Charlie is making a double claim. First, he equates black talk with pidgin English—both are corrupt versions of standard, proper English. Second, as the white actor in yellowface performing for a white audience and symbolizing white superiority, Charlie is also declaring that he can access, appropriate, and dominate seemingly inaccessible areas of marginalized communities, including performing racial masquerade to penetrate certain racial knowledges (in this case, blacktalk). Here Charlie not only contains the potential threat of Birmingham's and Ben's intuitive skills, but he also puts an end to any suggestion of their threat by placing Ben behind bars, literally and physically restraining the threat in jail. Overall, then, these films demonstrate that while Charlie is busy shielding white liberal anxieties by performing yellowface on one level (thereby regaining control), on another level the films are also containing the threat by utilizing the sidekick characters as objects upon which white anxiety is displaced, resulting in the re-placement of white hegemonic authority.

5 / Race Detection in a Color-Blind Era: Musings on the New Millennium

Changing direction from earlier chapters, I conclude this study by reflecting on our current state of race detection panic via multiple "texts" ranging from print media, art installations, speculative narratives, transracial adoption, and reproductive biotechnology. Some of the examples reveal this study's anxiety of detection immediately and obviously; others may not be so transparent. Some may already be the subject of several critical studies; others may have until now been overlooked. Either way, I bring them together here to emphasize that while their impact may not fully resonate if seen individually, as a collective, they expose a relevant, integrated link we otherwise may not recognize. Further, these examples reveal that our current discomfort with race extends way beyond the expected, infiltrating and even directing our behaviors in ostensibly insignificant ways. Whether obvious or not, I see these moments as reflecting our current state of racial unease, which is either a direct or indirect result of race undetection. As such, they serve to contextualize our transformational racial discomfort. Thus, I use the term "panic" above quite consciously to emphasize our ongoing national terror of and distress about racial indecipherability. In our post-9/11 historical moment, we are constantly on high alert, examining faces, behaviors, affiliations, and beliefs to determine if someone is a potential terrorist. This chapter of "musings" reveals that race detective anxiety percolates within both the obvious (such as the Homeland Security Advisory System's color-coded terror alert scale) and the not-so-apparent minutiae of our daily lives. These little details construct an American race narrative that is inseparable from our national history of detective angst; the small sampling offered here (and there are many others) reflects the ongoing and persistent terror we contend with daily. Thus, it is only by recognizing, acknowledging, and critically examining these encounters that we can begin to comprehend the full extent to which we negotiate our unease with race detection or the failure thereof. I offer these various musings from the recent past to illustrate the diverse areas in which race detective anxiety continues to maintain and sustain our insecurities and, subsequently, prescribe our behaviors.

Musing I. The Visible Unseen: Seeing and Unseeing Racial Ambiguity in Media and Art

With headlines like "The End of White America" (Hsu, Serwer) and "The Browning of America" (Hansen), we are currently witnessing a national race panic. Print media not only informs and educates, but it also speculates and envisions future scenarios. In regard to the nation's changing racial landscape, headlines also uphold our detective discomfort. As seen from "How to Tell Your Friends from the Japs," analyzed in chapter 4, *Time* magazine seems particularly sensitive to threats to the nation's racial stability.[1] One of *Time*'s most controversial covers appeared on the November 1993 special issue titled "The New Face of America," which features "New Eve," a computer-generated "morph" of the projected raced body of America's future. "Take a good look at this woman," the cover enticingly commands. "She was created by a computer from a mix of several races. What you see is a remarkable preview of . . . The New Face of America." Reflecting the racial composition of the U.S. population, "New Eve" is a mix of 15 percent Anglo Saxon, 17.5 percent Middle Eastern, 17.5 percent African, 7.5 percent Asian, 35 percent southern European, and 7.5 percent Hispanic. Much like their attempt to mitigate the racial/ethnic indecipherability of Asian ethnicities in the 1941 issue, the attractive "New Eve" with olive skin, brown hair, and hazel eyes exemplifies what Caroline Streeter refers to as a "safe hybridity" (305), a "high-tech" curiosity (305) (read: fantasy) assembled in willful ignorance of our nation's highly contested history of miscegenation. As such, Streeter contends, this elision "allow[s] for the more palatable *multicultural* to stand in for *multiracial*" (305). Or, as Donna Haraway puts it more bluntly, SimEve's cybergenesis erases the wounds and brutality of our historical past:

> All the bloody history caught by the ugly word *miscegenation* is missing in the sanitized term *morphing.* Multiculturalism and racial mixing in *Time* magazine are less achievements against the odds of so much pain than a recipe for being innocently raptured out of mundane into redeemed time. It is the resolute absence of history, of the fleshy body that bleeds, that scares me. . . . I want something messier, more dangerous, thicker, and more satisfying from the hope for multiculturalism. To get that kind of national reproductive health delivery is going to take addressing past and present sexualized racial power, privilege, exclusion, and exploitation. I suspect the nation will have to swallow the castor oil of sober accountability about such racialized sex before morphing looks like much fun to most of its citizens. (264)

For both Streeter and Haraway, morphing is a technology that effaces the critical race history of America's racist history, stripping away the realities of forced sexual exploitation and anti-immigration and antimiscegenation legislation and replacing it with a redeemed celebration of mixed-race identity. In Lauren Berlant's words, the "new face of America has the corporeality of a fetus, a body without history, an abstraction that mimes the abstraction of the American promise that retains power *because* it is unlived" (202).

In terms of the focus of this study, I would also add that morphing allows a play with and of racial difference to contain the threat of its increasing mutability. Morphing, in essence, is a new form of race passing in which racial ambiguity is contained and managed to corroborate and promote a very specific type of mixed-race body. In this way, passing still matters. As Michelle Elam argues: "Narratives of passing are significant not because they give us clues to actual extant practices but because they give us clues to extant cultural fretfulness about perceived practices whether real or imagined. It is perhaps most useful to ask then, not what does passing *look* like but what does passing *do*? What do discourses about passing culturally enable, disable, facilitate, accommodate?" (100). With New Eve, the potential threat of the ambiguously raced body that is currently looming over America's census count is contained via a morphed projection that simultaneously announces a playful warning of indecipherability (what race is she?) alongside her exact racial breakdown. In other words, in one quick click of the mouse, New Eve's racial mystery has been solved. In other words, passing is no longer a riddle to be cracked but a fetish to be marketed, contained, and appropriated

Figure 3. Time magazine's "The New Face of America" was a computer-generated "morph" of the U.S. immigrant population intended to illustrate the future look of race. (*Time*, Fall 1993 Special Issue, © 1993 Time Inc.; used under license)

to ease our current racial apprehensions. Our fears of a racial unknowing are further quenched with the proffered highly sexualized and gendered image chosen by *Time*'s programmers. Their very rendering of a technologically based (therefore seemingly "objective") imagination of the mixed-race body is telling. According to Joane Nagel, the sexualized and gendered image—"a lovely young woman, only ever-so-slightly oriental, only ever-so-slightly brown"—is essentially a "pretty, young white woman" (23). In other words, New Eve is not so dark that she is too threatening, and she is attractive (i.e., light) enough to be an object of desire (in fact, the employees at *Time* have reportedly fallen tragically in love with her).

A few years after New Eve's appearance, the American artist Nancy Burson offered another use of morphing technology to make a commentary on race in a postracial world. Debuting in 2000, the same year that an early draft of the Human Genome Project was announced, Burson's "Human Race Machine" opened at the London Millennium Dome. The "Human Race Machine" is an interactive machine that utilizes morphing technology[2] to allow viewers to observe themselves as six different races (African, Asian, white, Latino, Indian, and Middle Eastern, a category added after 9/11). Described on *nancyburson.com* as a "diversity tool," the "Human Race Machine" "gives us the opportunity to have a unique personal experience of being other than what we are, allowing us to move beyond our differences. We are all one race, the human race; one nationality called humanity. We are all the different hues of man" (Burson). Utilizing the telltale credo of color-blind ideology—that we are all of the human race—the "Human Race Machine" suggests that by seeing ourselves in the embodiment of various races, we will arrive at sameness. But Burson's progressive intentions, Jennifer González writes, are actually a "thinly veiled fantasy of *difference*" (49, emphasis in original), or what Lisa Nakamura calls "identity tourism." which offers users a "false promise of universality through the visual mechanics of race" (50). Burson's racial tourism "does not offer users any insight into the privileges or discriminations that attend racial difference" (49). Instead, the "Human Race Machine" proposes that by merely *seeing* ourselves in other racial embodiments, we will conclude that "we are all human" and live harmoniously, immediately erasing the social, political, and legal realities of everyday lives. But as Eduardo Bonilla-Silva contends in *Racism without Racists: Color-Blind Racism and Racial Inequality in Contemporary America*, the emphasis on a universal humanity is a "sincere fiction" because "it aids in the maintenance of white privilege without fanfare, without naming those who it subjects and those who it rewards . . . [where] whites can express resentment toward minorities; criticize their morality, values, and work ethic [without looking like a racist]" (3–4). As Easy Rawlins observes in Walter Mosley's *Devil in a Blue Dress*: "It was the worst kind of racism. The fact that he didn't even recognize our difference showed that he didn't care one damn about me" (126).

Shortly after Burson's art installation offered racial play as a postracial diversity tool, the *New York Times* published "Generation E.A.: Ethnically Ambiguous" (2003) to highlight our current fascination with the

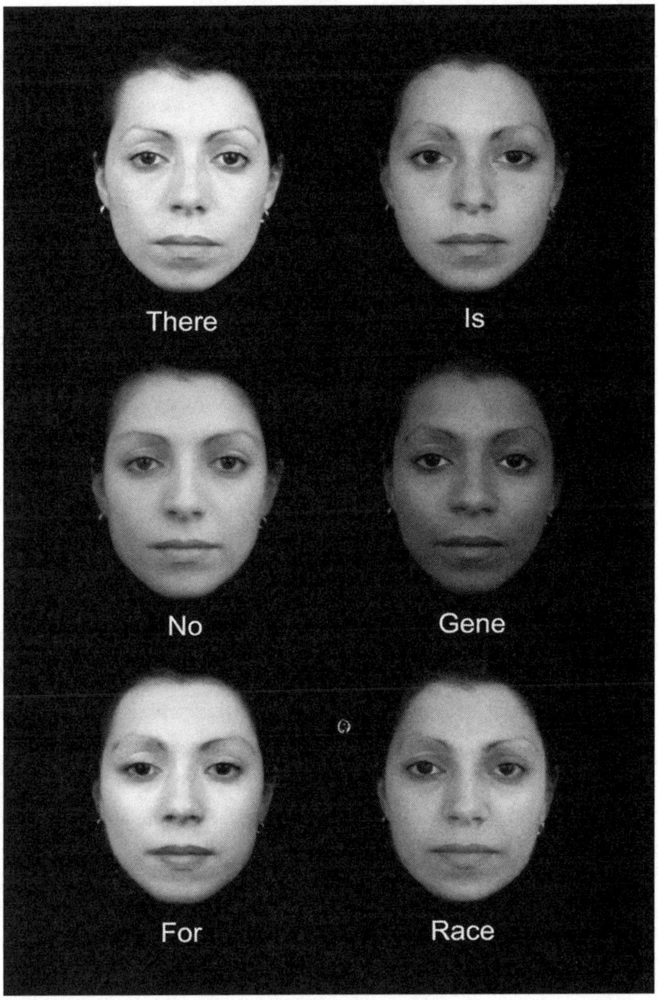

Figure 4. Nancy Burson's "Human Race Machine" (2000) is an interactive machine that allows viewers to see themselves in six different races via morphing technology. (Used by permission of the artist.)

multiracial, ethnically indecipherable body. "Ambiguity is chic," the article claims (La Ferla), becoming trendier and more marketable in the advertising and media markets. "We're seeing more of a desire for the exotic, left-of-center beauty that transcends race or class," Amy Barnett, [*Teen People*'s] managing editor, said. It "represents the new reality of America, which includes considerable mixing. . . . [I]t is changing the face of American beauty." For global marketers like H & M, models must be attractive but "neutral" (La Ferla) or racially indistinguishable. But while articles like this one on the "chic" of racial ambiguity may illustrate how far we have come since Poe's and Doyle's fictional fears of racial ambiguity, I argue that knowledge is still in high demand. As Greg Carter recently argued, while "Americans praise ambiguity [they still] prefer certainty" (193). Both the *Time* cover and Burson's art installation discussed above offer racial speculation as a possibility *only when* speculation itself is strictly contained. For *Time*, not only is New Eve a welcoming vision of America's racial future (for some, she can even pass for white), but her indecipherability is accounted for, measured to the exact percentage breakdown of her racial makeup. Similarly, the "Human Race Machine" not only offers identity tourism as a safe and temporary "holiday," but it also provides the false premise of knowing racial difference. In other words, when a participant visualizes him/herself in/as the labeled race, doesn't s/he come dangerously close to speculating his/her life upon the stereotypes (i.e., physical/biological, cultural, behavioral) of that race? Then the knowledge of being a racial other is a knowledge founded on the "safe" knowings otherwise known as racial stereotypes. But what would be the effect if, rather than disclosing the new racial identity to the participant (here is the black you, here is the Asian you), the race were undisclosed and unreadable but obviously different from the original? How would *not* knowing one's race help or hinder the ways we play at identity tourism? Or, more importantly, how would seeing oneself as racially indeterminable affect our own self-perception as well as our larger understanding of Race itself?[3] These are the possibilities that are painfully and glaringly missing from a concept like the "Human Race Machine."

Recent nonspeculative examples, such as Kip Fulbeck's *Hapa Project* (2001) and the *National Geographic*'s feature titled "The Changing Face of America" (October 2013), emphasize the need-to-know urgency quite differently from the perspective of the racially ambiguous individuals themselves. At initial glance, both the *Hapa Project* and the *National Geographic* feature seem to mirror *Time*'s New Eve in almost identical ways. They each center on an expressionless face looking directly into the camera as if to challenge the viewer's skills of racial reading. What am I?, it teasingly asks. This, of course, is the interrogation mixed-race individuals often encounter (see Pearl Fuyo Gaskins). But, unlike *Time*'s New Eve, whose identity was manufactured by her programmers and imposed upon her, the individuals in Fulbeck's *Hapa Project* and the

National Geographic feature self-identify, rejecting external labels that are inflicted upon them. In doing so, they redefine the terms of Amy Robinson's passing triad by both refusing (or not refusing) to pass and becoming the object of detections.

Kip Fulbeck's *Hapa Project* is a "multiracial identity project" that includes a book, a traveling photo exhibition, satellite community presentations, and online communities (Fulbeck). Fulbeck photographed more than 1,200 individuals of all ages, classes, and genders who self-identified as Hapas.[4] According to Fulbeck's website, "each individual was photographed in a similar minimalist style (directly head-on, unclothed from the shoulders up, and without jewelry, glasses, excess make-up, or purposeful expression)." Each photo includes a self-identified and handwritten response to the question, What are you?, because as Fulbeck describes on his *Hapa Project* website, "identity is a personal process and I'm adamant that it should be a personal decision, not one made by a community, a government or others" (Fulbeck). That identity is a "personal decision" is evidenced by the variety of responses to the question, What are you? Some give a breakdown of their various racial/ethnic backgrounds; however, many do not, as evidenced in the very first photo in the project's published book, *Part Asian, 100% Hapa*. The man with long, dark hair, light-brown eyes, and pale complexion writes, "What am I? I am exactly the same as every other person in 2500" (24). Along the same line, other responses include: "boy Eijah purple belt" (238), "I am whatever you want when you want it" (228), and "My last boyfriend told me he liked me because of my race. So I dumped him" (158). Perhaps the best responses in the collection are the scribbles and drawings from toddlers and young children (82, 138, 220) whose "gibberish," in fact, seems symbolic of the racial nonsense to which they are subjected.

But Fulbeck's desire and goal to allow participants to self-identify and, therefore, claim their own racial identity is seemingly undermined by the editorial inclusion of each participant's racial breakdown imposed above their handwritten responses. As Greg Carter notes, the individuality and humanity of the participants' unique self-identification with the official-looking typeset text creates a tension between the goal of ambiguity and the desperate need to know. Although Fulbeck states in the introduction to *Part Asian, 100% Hapa* that "what's interesting is ambiguity. What's interesting is the haziness, the blurrings, the undefinables, the space and tension between people, the area between the margins that pushes us to stop, to question" (13), the unknown is clarified in plain type. Fulbeck's explanation for the racial revelation is that he wanted to "demystify the entire phenotype question by eliminating the mystery itself—how can you keep guessing if the answer is right there?" (16). Additionally, the racial outing was a "strategy [Fulbeck] chose to purposely celebrate the fact that we *do* love finding out what each others' heritage. In many ways, we're the most interested of all" (16, emphasis in original). Here, disclosure as celebration signifies the incessant need-to-know desire we have witnessed throughout *The Arresting Eye*, but it takes on a slightly different perspective. Fulbeck, a visual artist, professor of art at U.C. Santa Barbara, and self-proclaimed Hapa, is not immune to such prevailing forces of race detective urgency. And as he writes in the introduction, the urgency is almost always embedded with dissatisfaction:

> Hapas know the question inside out. *What are you*? And we know we can't answer it any more than we can choose one body part over another. We love the question. We hate the question. And we know many times people aren't satisfied with our answers. (In my case, the only people who tell me I'm not Chinese are Chinese people—including most of my relatives.) For what it's worth, I stopped checking "Chinese" on the ethnicity question somewhere in my teens. . . . I figured if I didn't fit in a box . . . I wasn't going to lie to make myself fit it anymore. (13–14)

For Hapas, revelation is often met with suspicion and/or even animosity ("Are you sure?"), demanding more explanation and self-critique; it becomes a question that can never be answered, a detection that is endless. Thus, Fulbeck's disclosure reclaims the question for the Hapa community itself where identity is not challenged or denigrated. As Fulbeck explains: "The photo shoots themselves were electric. . . . Surrounded by others of a common thread, the what-are-you question loses its baggage, its suspicion, its various political ramifications. In this scenario, it gets used with assertion, with claim. 'Name that Asian' becomes *our* game" (16, emphasis in original). Although Fulbeck's explanation returns the outing and naming of identity onto the individuals at the heart of the guessing game, one wonders how these images (and disclosures) sustain the legacy of racial knowledge formation where knowing race is to see it. The mystery of race and race as mystery is still powerful indeed.

The *National Geographic* feature titled "The Changing Face of America" takes on a similar motivation for celebrating self-identification. The online article begins with the tagline, "We've become a country where race is no longer so black or white" under the image of two young boys, positioned side by side, one dark-skinned with brown eyes and curly,

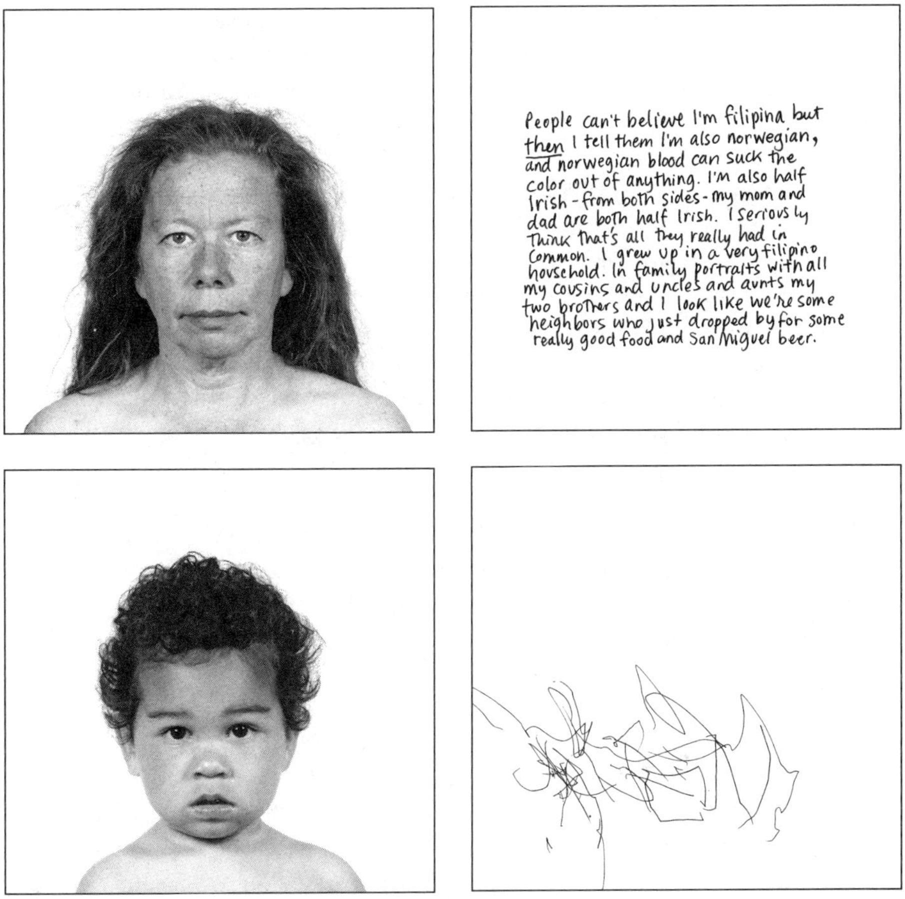

Figure 5. Kip Fulbeck's *Hapa Project*: The participant at the top is identified as "Filipina, Norwegian, Irish," and the participant at the bottom is identified as "Ghanaian, Chinese, Croatian, Scottish, Irish, German, Indian, British, Native American." (From *Part Asian, 100% Hapa* © 2006 by Kip Fulbeck; used with permission by Chronicle Books, LLC, San Francisco)

black hair and the other with very light, curly blond hair and greenish-blue eyes. Lise Funderburg, author of *Black, White, Other: Biracial Americans Talk about Race and Identity* (1994), begins "The Changing Face of America" with following query:

> What is it about the faces on these pages that we find so intriguing? Is it simply that their features disrupt our expectations, that we're

> not used to seeing those eyes with that hair, that nose above those lips? Our responses can range from the armchair anthropologist's benign desire to unravel ancestries and find common ground to active revulsion at group boundaries being violated or, in the language of racist days past, "watered down."
>
> Out in the world, the more curious (or less polite) among us might approach, asking, "Where are you from?" or "What are you?" We look and wonder because what we see—and our curiosity—speaks volumes about our country's past, its present, and the promise and peril of its future.

The article highlights the role of self-determination for mixed-race individuals elaborating on the practices of the U.S. Census Bureau (which first allowed respondents to check off more than one box in 2000) as well as revealing the variety of responses to why and how individuals self-identify. "Maximillian Sugiura, 29, says he responds with whatever ethnicity provides a situational advantage. Loyalties figure in too, especially when one's heritage doesn't show up in phenotypical facial features, hair, or skin. Yudah Holman, 29, self-identifies as half-Thai and half-black, but marks Asian on forms and always puts Thai first, "because my mother raised me, so I'm really proud of being Thai" (Funderburg). The variety of possible mixtures has resulted in new racial labels, including Blackanese, Filatino, Chicanese, Korgentinian, Juskimo, and Blaxican.

Accompanying the article is a photo gallery featuring twenty-five faces of various genders, ages, and racial mixtures. The pictures are by the renowned German photographer Martin Schoeller, who is known for his "big head" portrait technique in which individuals are photographed from a very close range against a backdrop of stark fluorescent lighting. Known for his signature style that represents "honest" portraits "showing a person for who they are and what they look like without retouching, without tricky lighting, without distortion, without crazy wide angle lenses, without any cheap tricks" (Callard), Schoeller's portraits of mixed-race identity are eerily haunting. The *National Geographic* website includes a black-and-white photo of Schoeller, who is in dreads, with the following statement: "I like building catalogs of faces that invite people to compare them. I want to challenge the way we use appearance to shape identity" ("Changing Face"). His catalogue of mixed-race faces, in fact, demands that the viewer function as a race detective in search of "clues" to connect the visible with the narrative. Like Fulbeck's inclusion of the participants' self-identification, Schoeller's subjects are also accompanied by biographical information detailing (decoding) the unreadable visage above it (name, age, city, self-identification, and census boxes checked). Thus, the viewer cannot escape participating in the race guessing game that turns into, more precisely, the race validation game ("Her green eyes or freckles must come from X," or "So that's what a mixture of X & Y would look like"), returning racial knowledge back to the biological epistemological framework.

Musing II. Racial Speculations: Imagining a Racial Future, Rewriting the Racial Past

Derrick Bell's short story "The Space Traders" (1992) asks a simple question: Would you trade all African Americans in exchange for almost unlimited wealth and resources? This is the conundrum at play when an alien ship unexpectedly lands on Earth. While Bell's speculative story ends with an unequivocal "yes," the recent 2012 outcry during President Obama's reelection condemned the story as "racist paranoia" (Schlichter) and Obama (because he had hugged Bell at a Harvard Law School rally years earlier) as a black radical. Writing for the *Atlantic*, Conor Friedersdorf responds, "Those objecting to "The Space Traders" would do well to acknowledge that for many decades of American history, including years during Professor Bell's life, a majority of Americans would have voted in favor of trading blacks for fantastic wealth, unlimited energy, and an end to pollutants." While trading blacks may not be a viable option, contemplating their fictional demise or erasure is a revealing way to critically understand how race today is both a dirty word and a "problem" that, ironically, must neither be recognized nor acknowledged in a colorblind, postracial moment.

It is telling, then, that parallel to the widespread media coverage of the "death of whiteness," we are simultaneously entertained with reports of a "death of blackness" in popular culture. This is perhaps most evident in the recent popularity of the newly reimagined *Battlestar Galactica* series (2003–9, hereinafter *BSG*). As speculative science fiction, *BSG* offers the possibilities of the "what if" scenario by speculating upon the nuances of racial mixings that continue to script our race narrative today. Mirroring the current popularity of genealogical research such as PBS's *African American Lives 1* and *2* (2006 and 2008, respectively) and *Race: The Power of an Illusion* (2003), *BSG*'s conclusion narrates the origins of humanity's heritage and genetic material. In *BSG*'s genealogical analysis, however, blackness is erased out of our evolutionary history, evidenced by the fact that all the black characters either die and/or disappear upon arrival onto the New Earth (which is strongly implied to be our current world).

The themes of genealogy and race, it turns out, are integrally connected to *BSG*'s framing anxieties of detection and passing. The premise of *BSG* involves the people of the Twelve Colonies of Kobol and the Cylons, sentient machines created by the humans for slave labor. After the Cylon War, in which the machines turned on their human masters, an armistice was declared, and the Cylons left to seek their own home. The reimagined miniseries pilot opens after a forty-year silence in which the Cylons have been completely absent until their sudden and startling reappearance and devastating attack that leaves about fifty thousand human survivors. But unlike the Cylon centurions of yesterday who were metallic automatons, the new Cylon model takes human form. In an eerie opening scene in which the humanoid Cylon confronts her human counterpart and asks him, "Are you alive?," the audience is immediately introduced to the tension between passer and soon-to-be detector. This stress is intensified when we subsequently discover that humanoid Cylons had penetrated the colonies years ago, which unsettles the humans' (and viewers') understanding of who is or is not a Cylon sleeper agent. The ultimate impact of these suspicions is revealed when Sharon "Boomer" Valerii—friend, lover, colleague, and mentee—reveals herself to be a human replicant. As a sleeper agent, Boomer has been living among humans for years, occupying their workplaces and socializing in their homes, and ultimately waiting for the signal to seek revenge on the human race. She does exactly that at the end of season 1 when she shoots her father figure, Commander Adama. Boomer's outing is, according to Eve Bennett, "the most shocking thing we ever see an individual Cylon do throughout *BSG*" (30). Boomer's act is so disturbing, Bennett continues, that it can only be understood in terms of Cylon (i.e., inhuman) programming. In other words, we can only begin to understand Boomer's cold behavior by relegating her to machine status, distancing her from "normal human terms" (30). Sharon's reduction to a calculating robot illustrates our own insecurities about Sharon's passing for human. First, only a nonhuman would cold-heartedly kill her trusted and beloved father figure. Second, and perhaps more importantly, how could we not have known Sharon was a Cylon?

Situating this larger detective unease (who is Cylon? who is human?) in the narrative background is necessary to understanding the relationship between race, racial mixing, and genealogy running throughout the show. At the end of the miniseries pilot, when the human race is threatened with extinction, President Roslin says to Commander Adama, "If we are going to survive as a species, we need to get the hell out of here and start having babies."[5] Looking at white Billy (President Roslin's assistant) and black Petty Officer Dualla/Dee, Commander Adama concurs, declaring, "They better start having babies." In each episode, the fluctuating survivor count posted on Colonial Fleet One provides a gentle reminder of this desperate need to reproduce. This call to breed, then, creates an illuminating dilemma concerning humanity's survival and the policing of procreation. While Adama's initial reaction to Billy and Dualla's blossoming romance is to call for babies, it is soon revealed that white-black unions are not the intended or desired solution.

Much has already been written (both critically and informally) about *BSG*'s problematic representation of blackness.[6] In terms of the human characters, one has only to look at Dee, Bulldog, Phelan, Elosha, and Sue-Shaun to witness the disappearance of black characters into the inevitable "black hole." Dee commits suicide; Bulldog is literally abandoned to the Cylons by Adama, only to return and be abandoned again; Phelan is a criminal (a.k.a. "felon") who is killed off by Apollo for being the immoral leader of, yes, the Black Market; the priest Elosha dies after triggering a Cylon landmine on Kobol; and Sue-Shaun begs Starbuck for death while hooked up to the Cylon fertility machine. An online commenter notes: "Every single black character was killed, murdered and mutilated in the *BSG* Universe. Adolf Hitler could not have dreamed up a more inspirational script" (Levinson). The conscious erasure of blackness is further evidenced when the Galactica fleet lands on what looks like the African continent of our historical past during the series finale. But instead of seeing dark-skinned natives, the fleet witnesses a group of pale-skinned, spear-yielding humans wandering the plains. Although our glimpse of the natives is very brief, the only recognizable codes of blackness are the paint marks covering their bodies. Dr. Cottle, Galactica's medical officer, tellingly reveals, "Their DNA is compatible with ours" ("Daybreak, Part 2"), emphasizing the culmination of their procreative mission. In other words, the light-skinned natives are genetically (and ideologically) compatible with the humans for breeding purposes. This final episode emphasizes ways in which *BSG*'s erasure of blacks and blackness reflects a form of narrative genocide in which blacks are eliminated from visions of what the Cylons foretell to be "the shape of things to come."

Perhaps *BSG*'s most telling commentary on blackness and reproduction, one that disturbingly echoes the unrelenting fear of black-white miscegenation that has been present since American slavery, occurs with the episode titled "The Farm" (season 2, episode 5). Initially created as slave labor, the Cylons are perhaps best embodied by its only black instantiation, Simon.[7] In "The Farm," Simon is a doctor attending an injured Starbuck, the Galactica fleet's blond and blue-eyed gifted Viper pilot. In this sense, Simon's blackness is signified multiple times (as Cylon slave, as visibly black, and as black sexual threat). It is under his care that Starbuck discovers she is a prisoner at a Cylon hospital, and that the Farm is a breeding ground where human women are used as "baby machines" in the Cylons' plan to create human-Cylon hybrids. Simon, who stands over a half-dressed, vulnerable Starbuck, declares:

> Gotta keep that reproductive system in great shape. It's the most valuable asset these days. . . . Finding healthy childbearing women your age is a top priority for the Resistance and you'll be happy to know that you're a very precious commodity to us. . . . You do realize that you're one of the handful of women on this planet actually capable of having children. That is your most valuable skill right now. . . . The human race is on the verge of extinction. And to be quite frank with you, potential mothers are a lot more valuable right now than a whole squadron of viper pilots.

The symbolism of this scene is clear, as Christopher Deis notes: "While Starbuck is not penetrated by Simon sexually, she is symbolically raped, penetrated surgically in her abdomen (and, likely, also penetrated medically through vaginal examinations while unconscious)" (165). The haunting of slavery reinforces the fears of black male–white female relations when Starbuck encounters Sue-Shaun, a black female resistance fighter, hooked up to machines that are harvesting her eggs. The stark image of Sue-Shaun's lifted and separated legs, with metal instruments attached to her womb, brutally echoes the subjugation of black women's bodies as enslaved reproduction delivery systems during slavery. Rather than live as a breeder, Sue-Shaun begs Starbuck to kill her, which reinforces not only the "unnaturalness" of the Cylons' dependence on reproductive technology but the horror of black women as reproducers. After Starbuck escapes, Athena tells her that the Cylons are "conducting research into human-Cylon breeding programs" because Cylons cannot reproduce biologically, and that they believe procreation is one of God's commandments. While Starbuck kills both Simon and Sue-Shaun, albeit for very different reasons, the message here is unmistakable: any suggestion of black-white procreation results in death. This is further emphasized when another variation of the Simon Cylon is literally shackled like a slave, perhaps as punishment for his role in cross-racial/species breeding, later in the season ("A Measure of Salvation"). Arguments against black-white mixing are again underscored when black female officer Dualla's relationships to two white men (Billy and Apollo) end with the death of the one who proposes to her and her own suicide in the middle of season 4.[8] *BSG*'s limited visions of black-white mixings reveal a fear of blackness that continues to prevail today.

If black-white mixing is the utterly unmentionable, Asian-white mixing is the "shape of things to come," as mixed-race Hera is often identified throughout the show. The parallel story lines of the two main Eight model clones,[9] Boomer and Athena, are significant because as visibly Asian models, they simultaneously evoke the fear of Yellow Peril paranoia within a story line already centered on Orientalized terrorism (see Hu Pegues; and Bennett). The Eight's embodiment of both fear and seduction is illustrated when multiple copies of nude Eights confront Boomer in "Kobol's Last Gleaming, Part II." This is the only time multiple clones of a Cylon model are revealed to the audience on such a large scale, implying not only the threat of the never-ending horde of Asians but also fixating Asians (especially Asian women) with their sexuality. This allusion to Asian female sexuality continues with the parallel Athena story line in which she not only seduces her victim and becomes pregnant, but her pregnancy becomes the literal and symbolic future of humanity. When Messenger Six reveals the baby to Baltar, strongly implied to be Athena and Helo's yet unborn daughter, Hera, she declares that the baby is "the guardian and protector of the new generation of God's children. The first member of our family will be with us soon, Gaius. . . . Come . . . see the face of the shape of things to come." The "face" and "shape" is mixed-raced on multiple levels: Asian-white, Cylon-human, alien-earthling. Of Greek mythological fame, Hera was the goddess of marriage, emphasizing *BSG*'s acceptable delineation of racial mixings and couplings. The racialization of this scene is significant because it outlines Baltar and Six as exemplars of the white, heteronormative couple who simultaneously welcomes and concedes the future to an Asian-white mixed-race baby. Interestingly, while Athena's name invokes the Greek goddess of wisdom and war, she is revealed to be quite the opposite when her initial Cylon threats become domesticated and contained throughout the series, transforming Athena from temptress and sleeper agent to loyal wife, soldier, and subject. It is also important to note here that the Asian-white mixing is acceptable only when the Asian partner is female, highlighting the invisibility and silencing of Asian male sexuality in *BSG*.[10]

I conclude my analysis of *BSG* with a slightly alternative reading of the show's final image of the happy, Asian-white family. If *BSG*'s ending demonstrates certain restrictions around race and racial mixing, what is actually revealed is the racial nuances—the potential of race mixing—that is unintended by *BSG* creators. The revelation that we are all part Cylon echoes the seeming antiracist message reminiscent of current color-blind ideology. As a result of the Human Genome Project's findings that we are 99.9 percent the same, common responses are "See? We're all just human! There is no such thing as race!" But discerning scholars of race will recognize that there is an anxiety of detection and undetection occurring in the final moments of *BSG*. While Athena's character is most often read as the *Butterfly* stereotype of Asian woman with white man, what is usually not noticed is that Athena's coupling is *not* an Asian-white one but a multiracial mixing for Tahmoh Penikett (the actor who plays Helo) is of mixed-race background (his mother is First Nation and his father is British). Penikett's mother, Lulla Sierra Johns, is part of the Dene Nation who was forced into a Native boarding school as a young child. She is currently an advocate for First Nation rights. In a recent interview, Penikett reveals the struggle with his mixed-race identity, especially as someone who can pass for white: "The irony is that I hated my white skin as a kid. I grew up in the Yukon. . . . I grew up in a lot of small northern communities, the majority of times with my native cousins. So I was the funny looking one, I was the minority, and oftentimes I just hated it when I was younger, I wish I grew up with darker skin. . . . I got ribbed and teased a lot because I was the 'white boy'" (Kayne). Penikett is the unintentional passer whose racial decodings are often misread. In addition to Penikett's undetectable racial background, Hera's own racial mixings problematize *BSG*'s limited possibilities of mixed-race identity. The character Hera is played by three young actresses: Lily Duong-Walton, Alexandra Thomas (older Hera), and Iliana Gomez-Martinez (older Hera). As I attempt to play detective in Hera's racial decoding, I read the actresses as mixed Asian (Vietnamese according to "Duong"), white with possible Latina background according to the Wiki photo, and Latina (also according to the surname), respectively. Of course, it is very possible that my own decoding of Hera is flawed. My point here is that this is the message *BSG* seems to have lost or ignored. In other words, in a slightly different angle from Leilani Nishime's argument in which the Athena-Helo-Hera family reflects the familiar trope of the Asian-white interracial family, this threesome actually represents the multiracial family of our present and future in which racial markers are not so easily seen or discernable.

Thus far, we have seen how speculations on race (New Eve, "Human Race Machine," *BSG*) use the rhetoric of speculation in order to limit rather than offer possibilities of the future vision of race. The creators of *BSG* may not have had the demise of blackness as an intentional story line, but this may be more revealing than not. For we must do away with the misleading assumption that racist acts are results of intent. Unintentional acts of racism and prejudice are often the more revealing of our current state of racial schizophrenia. The question of the future of blackness is a thought-provoking one. While Americans may not have the option to simply and easily rid the nation of the "race problem" as seen in Bell's "Space Traders," recent speculative narratives help to ponder potential quagmires of a futuristic America by intelligently and critically imagining possible racial scenarios. *Futurestates*, for instance, is an online series of sci-fi short films produced by the Independent Television Service (ITVS). Currently in its fourth season, *Futurestates* presents narratives created by both established and beginning filmmakers to address their visions of America's future negotations with race and difference. Stories range from illegal immigration to alternative energy to education to Internet privacy. For the sake of this study's particular focus, I will address two short films that address speculations of race in a not-so-distant U.S. landscape: "White" (season 2) and "Advantageous" (season 3). Both address the intersection of race, passing, and technology that forces us to redefine our understanding of "racial science" in the near future.

"White" (season 2) by A. Sayeeda Clarke tackles themes of race and race passing via the danger of global warming threatening human survival. The story takes place in a near-future New York City (specifically the East Village). It is "another 120 degree day," five days before Christmas. There are no cars in the streets, and Bato, the story's protagonist, is peddling his bike through the city greeting a mostly black crowd. Strewn throughout the city are flyers with images of black fists reminiscent of the Black Power movement accompanied by the phrase "not one drop" placed underneath. Bato shouts out "Not one drop!" throughout his ride through a mostly black neighborhood. When he reaches the "De Burgos Community Center," where he works, Bato tears off other flyers left on the entrance door that read, "Need extra cash? There is an easy answer: EXTRACTION."[11]

The temptation to make fast cash arises when Bato's wife, Gina, goes into premature labor. Unable to afford a clinic, Bato is desperate for cash and attempts to "borrow" from the center; when that fails, he robs someone off the street. This attempted robbery is foiled, however, when Bato realizes that his potential victim is a coworker who in an earlier scene is dark-skinned but is now bleached white. The scheme to make quick money, it is revealed, involves selling one's melanin in a sun-threatened world where darkness is a commodity needed for survival. By going to the "Melanin Extraction Center," which promises that "Together we can survive the sun," dark-skinned individuals sell their melanin to the "melanin-challenged." We are clued into the popularity of this procedure when we see Bato awaiting his extraction in front of a world map labeled "Human Skin Color Distribution." According to this map, the extraction process is a highly popular and globalized procedure (most of Africa, the map illustrates, has already been whitened). The map also shows that there is a color gradation. Bato, who is dark-brown, is currently a 35 and, as the extraction consultant reveals, will become an 11 after the procedure, otherwise known as a "blackout." While Bato initially self-identifies as Black/Puerto Rican, he must now identify as "melanin out" on future census forms.

Via its sci-fi twist, "White" is a race passing narrative in that the process of melanin extraction ultimately questions our understanding of who is or is not black. In fact, when we realize the film's extraction premise, the audience is forced to question our earlier readings of race. Was the light-skinned man in African garb who works at the center white, or is he a "blackout" volunteer? In an earlier scene, Bato declares to a young girl whose father has undergone "blackout," "You always have his inheritance right on you [pointing to her hand]." But we question Bato's claim with the film's final scene, in which his whitened arms are holding his newly born dark-skinned baby. The jarring difference between father and daughter here forces the viewer to revisit his earlier (now somewhat ambiguous) declaration about inheritance. Did Bato's previous reference to inheritance allude to skin color or something that goes deeper than pigmentation? If the former, the film asks how blackness will be understood if blacks are no longer black and whites presumably become black.[12] How do we discern now between the light-skinned whites and the "blackout" participants? As a contemporary twist to another speculative narrative published almost a century ago, George Schuyler's *Black No More* (1931), Clarke's "White" demonstrates how the tropes of passing and detection continue to play a central role in a future economy where race becomes a commodity of survival.

Writer/director Jennifer Phang's award-winning short film *Advantageous* (season 3) is another *Futurestates* creation that imagines an alternative vision of race passing. The underlying premise of the film asks how far a parent would go to secure their child's future. The year is 2041, and the world's population has soared to 10.1 billion, leading to a U.S. unemployment rate of 45 percent. The public education system has been dissolved, and students must compete for the few spots available in private magnet schools. Gwen (played by the Korean American actress Jacqueline Kim) is a single mother who works as a spokesperson for the Center for Advanced Health and Living, a cutting-edge biotech firm. The center is launching a new pilot project that offers a "pragmatic" solution to overpopulation and job saturation. As Gwen's company statement declares: "We are working to empower the average person with a pragmatic response to today's unforgiving job market. So many enter this world with disadvantages beyond our control, disadvantages which we have traditionally accepted as a part of life."

The disadvantage, as it turns out, is highly gendered. The average person most devastated by the current situation of overpopulation and unemployment is female. As Phang recently divulged in an interview for *Asia Pacific Arts*: "What makes [the film] specific to womanhood is that we're talking about a brewing backlash against women in power. As much as people talk about a "boys' club" being an issue, I've also heard men using the words 'girls' club,' and in my observation, there's this fear of men disappearing from relevance. . . . There's just a general belief system that we have to keep men safe. . . . [T]he woman is trying to use her best assets [to survive], and those assets are nested in her appearance and her age. So, it's kind of a double whammy" (Tseng). As such, the women of *Advantageous* are experiencing both the backlash against women with the societal pressure placed on female appearance. Their utter desperation and isolation is hauntingly portrayed through regular occurrences of disembodied cries coming through Gwen's apartment walls and, later, within her own bedroom walls. As Gwen's boss, Mr. Fisher, explains: "There is talk among recruiters about letting women stay unemployed. The perception is that it's safer than putting desperate men on the streets." Gender takes on a particularly vexed role when Gwen, upon the threat of losing her job to a newer (i.e., younger) spokesperson, volunteers to become the center's test subject in their new pilot project wherein souls are transferred into improved bodies. While Mr. Fisher is initially reticent, he warns Gwen that "marketing has a specific physical type in mind. They're looking at candidates that come off as a touch more universal . . . willing to give them full control over the creation of the host body." The universal body he is referencing is not only younger but racially ambiguous. After a procedure that involves the soul's transfer via multiple electrodes attached to an Asian American Gwen, we see the newer Gwen model embodying a possibly Latina, possibly Mediterranean/Middle Eastern twenty-something woman. By the end, we realize that Gwen's earlier message to her daughter—"It's good to be humble, but you need to know your value"—is one she herself ignores. In *Advantageous*, race passing involves not only adhering to a racial identity with which one does not self-identify, but it also entails the literal death—a passing—of the older self.

Musing III. Race-ing Reproduction: Reproductive Technology and New Perspectives on Racial Mixings

On November 29, 2012, the "Dear Prudence" advice column on *Slate.com* published a query from someone named "Want to Be a Dad." The father-to-be, who is white, is wondering how to broach the subject with his infertile Asian wife of his wanting all-white babies:

> Her race isn't a problem for me and I would have had no difficulty raising mixed race children, but frankly, now that I have the choice, I'd prefer my kids to be white. We live in a fairly homogeneously white area and at the end of the day I want my kids to look like me, their cousins, and the kids they'll go to school with. I don't think my wife has ever experienced racism, but I think she might understand my point of view. (Yoffe)

Via egg donation (and other fertility treatments such as sperm and embryo donation), this couple demonstrates that today we can *choose* the race of our babies. Aside from the potentially disturbing outcome in the above scenario in which the Asian woman becomes an incubator of and for whiteness, this man's query also reflects an anxiety of detection not uncommon in reproduction, particularly in today's growing field of assisted reproductive technologies, or ART. The desire for a genetic connection to one's child is a strong and powerful force, one that is desperately sought after despite the financial, emotional, and physical difficulties involved.[13] In the case of "Want to Be a Dad," the man's desire for his children to "look like me, their cousins, and the kids they'll go to school with" also reflects the parents' wish to keep secret their use of ART.[14] Whether due to the shame of infertility or for cultural and religious reasons, the need for undetection and secrecy is a central component of today's reproductive practices, and, unsurprisingly, central to the concealment is the policing of race and racial mixings.

The role of race in ART requires unpacking to situate our anxieties of race and detection within our current historical, racial, and technological climate. While the detection of yesterday relied upon the sciences to give concrete biological evidence, today's science works to further our anxieties of race detection. In many respects, ART has become the new racial science, one that foregrounds race as a determinant in the policing of reproduction, inheritance, and the future *look* of race. According to the Center for Disease Control and Prevention, the percentage of infertile women between fifteen and forty-four is 10.9 (6.7 million). Furthermore, the recent phenomenon of "designer babies" ensures everything from the embryo's sex to genetic screening (pre-implantation genetic diagnosis, or PGD) in which DNA can be scanned for certain diseases like Tay-Sachs and Down syndrome. Straight out of the science fiction film *Gattaca* (1997), advances in ART and the completion of the Human Genome Project in 2003 have now made possible techniques of genetic detection. Further, many argue that ART has created a new form of eugenics in which hair, eye, and skin color can also be selected to create the new super race. In 2009, for instance, California's Fertility Institute headed by Dr. Jeffrey Steinberg (one of the doctors who created the first test-tube babies in the 1970s) advertised the selection of physical traits such as eye, hair, and skin color. Deeming it cosmetic medicine, Dr. Steinberg's technique of unnatural selection threatens to decrease human diversity in the future. This is the outcome that may result if the reproductive desires like those of "Want to Be a Dad" are met, illuminating our current state of color-blind ideology in which one may boast of being multicultural (he is, after all, married to an Asian woman) but still have ingrained racist beliefs and desires. At a time when headlines proclaim "The End of White America,"[15] perhaps it is not too surprising that the emergence of designer babies and reproductive technologies is a growing trend. In this light, we are currently witnessing the scientific manipulation of the face of race.

I conclude this study about the anxiety of race detection by offering a very different scenario from previous chapters, but one in which the future of race and racial mixing remains a central component. As the earlier chapters reveal, much of the anxiety of detecting race centers on fears of racial mixing and its subsequent products: the mixed-race, oftentimes undetectable, body. Not only are the rates of nonwhite babies rising today,[16] but the parallel increase of biracial and multiracial birthrates has fostered an atmosphere of what the author Danzy Senna has satirically referred to as the "Mulatto Millennium." Alongside this change in demographics is our growing reliance on biotechnology and ART. Perhaps unsurprisingly, the increasing ambiguity of racial boundaries has fostered a new racial science through which you can now select your child's skin/hair/eye color but also gender, athletic abilities, weight, height, and susceptibility to certain diseases.[17] In terms of race selection, then, a white couple can have either their genetic white baby (via a white or nonwhite gestational carrier) or a nonwhite baby using an embryo adopted from a domestic or international agency. Advances in biotechnology have made it possible to birth a baby who is not of you or your partner's racial background via sperm, egg, and/or embryo donation. Without any genetic link, a white woman can birth a nonwhite baby, an Asian woman can birth a Mexican baby, and a black woman can birth a white baby. How do these new reproductive technologies then complicate our previous understandings of how race is detected and defined? Not only can we now *choose* the race of our babies, but these choices demand a new reconsideration of what we currently understand as "mixed-race" identities. Additionally, these new "mixings" also demand a reevaluation of our current climate of race detective anxieties.

Of course, it may be argued that in some ways heterosexual couples have always chosen the race of their babies through the partners they choose, often through legal, cultural, and religious prescription. But, as the above scenarios reflect, our options and choices have drastically changed via advances in science and biotechnology. Consequently, prior understandings of "mixed-race" need redefinition due to the very changing nature of what we understand as "mixing." Do the examples above, for example, illustrate "mixed-race"? Is it "mixed-race" when different races unite not genetically but biologically? For instance, if a white woman undergoes IVF treatment with a donated Asian egg and her Asian husband's sperm, is the baby considered mixed-race? Or how do we understand kinship ties in cases like Patricia Bohanon, a fifty-one-year-old white woman who gave birth to an all-Indian baby via embryo adoption in 2010? Conversely, Lisa and Brian Switzer, the white couple at the center of the documentary *Made in India* (2010), welcomed their baby girl via an Indian gestational surrogate. Or, in matters of ethnicity, how do we understand "Asianness" if an Asian couple adopts an embryo of an Asian ethnicity not their own? This is a scenario that goes way beyond but is in alignment with Winnifred Eaton's vision of Asian undetection examined earlier.

But whether or not one uses their own genetic material, the distinction between genetics and blood becomes blurred in these scenarios when it comes to understanding or identifying racial identity. The Switzers, for instance, used their own genetic embryo. Thus, their Indian gestational carrier does not share any genetic connection to the baby she carries. However, as a gestational carrier, she and the baby share blood (or the nutrients thereof), the source of nineteenth- and early-twentieth-century anxieties of race mixing.[18] The surrogate's bond with the baby she carries is illustrated in Amrita Pande's "'It May Be Her Eggs But It's My Blood': Surrogates and Everyday Forms of Kinship in India." In her study, Pande describes one surrogate's response to the need for a fetal reduction surgery, "I told Doctor Madam that I'll keep one and *didi* can keep two. After all it's my blood even if it's their genes" (384). As Pande further explains in her ethnographic study of commercial gestational surrogacy, the surrogates disrupt the traditional theories of Euro-American kinship by redefining kinship ties beyond genetics to include bodily substances such as blood and breast milk as well as the labor of gestation and giving birth. The blood bond, according to the surrogates, imparts *identity* to the child (383). Further, in writing about race and the American kinship model, Seline Szkupinski Quiroga writes that "the metaphor of blood was, and still is, code for race, with connotations regarding [quoting Amy Agigian] the 'sanctity of blood, mixing blood, white blood, black blood, and pure versus tainted blood'" (145). The American kinship model is that if you shared blood, you are family. As such, these blood ties blur the seeming nonrelation between surrogate and child.

The significance of the blood bond is perhaps most tellingly revealed in cases where racial difference trumps the genetic connection. During her ethnographic research in the San Francisco Bay area, Gillian Goslinga-Roy uncovered racist ideologies where white surrogates refused to gestate a black baby. As "Julie," a white surrogate, explains:

> It feels foreign to me, [she explained]. Different. I could carry a Japanese baby or a Chinese baby because they are white to me. Society sees them as white. But a Black child is more difficult. I'm already surrounded by controversy: I married a man thirty-two years older than me. I work in a late-term, problem-pregnancy abortion facility. And I'm a surrogate. To give birth to a Black child would add one more controversial aspect to my life and I'm not ready to be on the front page of the *National Enquirer.* (116)

Here, gestating blackness is a contamination too taboo to warrant consideration. As Goslinga-Roy points out, what is telling is "how carrying *someone else's* (white) child provoked no gut reaction in her whatsoever. . . . But the mere thought of carrying someone else's *Black* child immediately made her experience the surrogacy as a very intimate and at once very public violation of her bodily and moral boundaries" (116). The role of race is also illustrated in Charis Thompson's study of skin tone variation in egg donation practices in the United States. In one ethnographic case study, Thompson writes about a Japanese couple who had just completed an egg donation procedure at a U.S. clinic (egg donation is illegal in Japan). At their request, they were offered an Asian donor with light skin tone. But, upon learning of the donor's Korean background, the Japanese woman refused in light of Japan's colonial history with Korea. As Thompson writes: "The skin tone and other attributes no longer had the same meaning. The donor's light skin tone ceased to be attractive and desirable if it was not embedded in Japanese ancestry" (142). These cases show that while blood may not be necessarily shared between surrogate and child, there remains a strong cultural and historical fear of a racialized blood *taint* that police peoples' reproductive choices. In other words, centuries-old anxieties about racial contamination through blood or genetics remain very much alive in twenty-first-century advances in biotechnology.

The fear of racial contamination or mixing is illustrated throughout the fertility treatment process in what Foucault would call the "biopower" of ART. By managing and manipulating racial mixings, ART practitioners become fertility detectives in the policing of heredity and the future look of race. In fertility treatments, race is a central factor when matching donor egg, sperm, or embryos to the intended parents as well as in the choosing of the gestational surrogate. In her study of fertility technology, Seline Szkupinski Quiroga reveals how racial borders are policed and maintained during each step of the fertility treatment process. For example, in describing the matching process between sperm donor and recipient, she writes: "The goal of matching is threefold: (1) to increase the probability that the child's physical characteristics will be similar enough to suggest that the social parent could have contributed his own genetic material; (2) to mimic the physical attributes of what white Americans perceive as a biological family; and (3) to maintain secrecy about the use of a donor by ensuring that the child could 'pass' as a genetic child and not be mistaken as a product of the mother's sexual infidelity" (150). Quiroga explains that while the first two goals are reflective of biologism or the need to "look" like a natural family, the last goal reflects the "raced and gendered nature of the heteropatriarchal family model" (150). In other words, the child cannot harbor visual evidence of the mother's infidelity. In the ART process, this is only achieved hypothetically via a mixed-race sexual union. In order to prevent this, donor semen is "categorized racially, and sperm banks rely on donor self-identification and physiognomy to assess the validity of a donor's claim to whiteness" (150). Sperm vials are, in fact, color-coded to match the donor's racial identification (black/brown caps for African Americans, yellow caps for Asians, white caps for Caucasians, and red caps for those with "unique ancestry" such as East Indian, American Indian, Latinos, and mixed-race). Sperm banks also play race detectives through careful cataloguing of various physical characteristics in order to choose the "appropriate" donor. "This catalogue serves as a proxy for proof of a donor's racial pedigree" (150). Here, ART practitioners play race detectives by identifying and cataloguing donors' racial makeup.

The policing of certain racial mixings by ART practitioners is also illustrated in Quiroga's ethnographic study in which she interviewed several couples who chose donor sperm. In the case of Raeshell and her husband, who are both African American, for instance, the physician informed them that they didn't have any black sperm. When she offered to "take anything in [her husband's] color range . . . you know Hispanic, Puerto Rican" (155), she was told that was not "appropriate" (155). Quiroga correctly notes that while Raeshell's notions of race is fluid and the doctor's is fixed, this case also illustrates the fear of racial mixing, particularly racial lightening. For the doctor, black must remain black without any scientific intervention. Interestingly, not all instances of medical policing are negative. Charis Thompson writes about a white German couple who wished to purchase an egg from a donor of South Asian descent but was denied by the clinic director. As "new age Buddhists" who were attracted to the donor's authentic Indianness, the couple wanted a child who "looked Indian" to "simultaneously naturalize and authenticate their new religious affiliation" (143). As someone who was familiar with "U.S. racialized reproductive politics" (143), the clinic director denied the request.

These cases illustrate that new developments in science and technology, while awesome in their advancements and capabilities, also reflect long-held views about race and racial mixing. But they also reveal that our current anxieties of race detection are no longer about being able to read bodily markers. Today, understanding one's racial identity goes beyond the physical into the genetic and reproductive history of one's initial moment of conception.

Notes

Introduction

1. Early reports claimed Menezes was wearing a "bulky jacket" that may have concealed a bomb. Menezes was wearing a denim jacket and was not concealing any weapons.

2. The July 7 bombers were all identified as Muslim, including three British-born descendants of Pakistani immigrants. According to the article by Cowell and Van Natta Jr., groups linked to al-Qaeda claimed responsibility for both July attacks.

3. I realize that racial distinctions and boundaries vary in the United States, Great Britain, and Brazil that further complicate Menezes's perceived racial identity. For instance, in North America, "Asian" generally refers to East Asians while in Britain it usually refers to people from South Asia. Further, Brazil's racial distinctions are much more complicated than those of the United States (which places a much more significant role on descent) and include more than forty racial categories and hundreds of racial terms to differentiate the multiple possibilities of these categories (Marshall 119). In this light, race detection is very much a cultural and national decoding.

4. It is important to note here the dynamics of both race and gender in Wilma's giving birth to a black boy. The Stuarts' case is reminiscent of Kate Chopin's short story "Désirée's Baby" (1893), in which a foundling marries a wealthy Creole, Armand. Armand and Désirée have a baby who is noticeably black. Armand accuses Désirée of being black and scorns her. Désirée leaves with her child, never to be seen again. In the final scene, we see Armand burning all of his wife's property. He also burns a letter from his mother revealing that it is Armand who is, in fact, part black. Chopin's story reveals that while Désirée's racial identity is unknown, women carry the burden of racial reproduction; likewise, it is Wilma who is automatically assumed to be the source of black taint via infidelity rather than, say, Willem who may have black blood in his ancestry. The burden of racial reproduction placed on women, as we will see

throughout this study, is crucial to understanding the policing of female sexuality as well as the anxieties produced by reproduction.

5. It is difficult to not ask the question of how race does or does not induce anxiety in another similar case of mistaken embryo transfer. In 2009, Carolyn Savage gave birth to a baby boy in Toledo, Ohio. Soon after becoming pregnant via IVF embryo transfer, Savage learned she was carrying Paul and Shannon Morrell's biological embryo due to the fertility clinic's error. The Savages decided against termination, continued with the pregnancy, and placed the infant with the Morrells immediately after birth. Unlike the media coverage of the Fasano-Rogers case that highlighted the racial difference of the twins as a "horrible mistake," the Savage-Morrell narrative is one of generosity and bonding. Shannon accompanied the Savages on their doctor visits and was in an adjacent room during delivery. To date, the Savages and Morrells communicate regularly. Coming "full circle," as Carolyn Savage said in a *Dateline* interview, the Savages announced the birth of their twins via surrogate in 2011. How does race or the lack of a racial "intrusion" determine the dynamics of this case? Although we don't know how or if the Savages or the Morrells would have responded differently if the other couple was a different race, what is strikingly evident here is the very silence and absence of race in any discussions of the error. The intent of my observation here is not to diminish any pain both parties experienced but to highlight the anxiety of race displayed (or not) in two very similar cases. While race is *the* central focus of the Fasano-Rogers and Stuart "mistakes," the Savage-Morrell case (both couples are white) reveal very little worry about the topic because their baby could biologically pass and, thus, avoid the social stigma of infidelity and infertility.

6. Titles include "Immigrants: The Changing Face of America" (*Time*, July 8, 1985); "The New Face of America: How Immigrants are Shaping the World's First Multicultural Society" (*Time*, Fall 1993);"Our New Look: The Colors of Race" (*Newsweek*, December 31, 1999); "The Beige and the Black" (*New York Times*, August 16, 1998); "Minorities Expected to be Majority in 2050" (*CNN*, August 13, 2008); "The End of White America (*Atlantic*, January 1, 2009); and "Census: Fewer White Babies Being Born" (*CNN*, May 17, 2012).

7. Detective fiction critics will quickly point out earlier works of the genre ranging from Sophocles's *Oedipus Rex* to the Chinese Gong An stories (some of which were translated by Robert Van Gulik as the *Celebrated Cases of Judge Dee*) to Voltaire's *Zadig* (1748). Most critics, however, would agree that Poe's trilogy and his brilliant detective, C. Auguste Dupin, commenced the popularity of the detective genre as we know it today.

8. The Hottentot Venus and Chang and Eng were popular examples of racial display. Also included are the various scientific exhibitions that displayed racial scenes ranging from colonial settings to Ethiopian serenaders to the Two-Headed Nightingale (see Qureshi and Wu).

9. The reverse fear here is a white person passing for black and enslaved. The potential nightmare of this scenario occurs in reality with the case of Sally Miller (born Salomé Müller), a German immigrant and indentured servant who was accused of being part black and enslaved. In *Sally Miller v. Louis Belmonti* (1845), the Louisiana Supreme Court ruled in her favor, and Miller gained her freedom. Her identity, however, remains controversial. Miller's story was fictionalized by George Washington Cable in *Strange True Stories of Louisiana* (1890).

10. For a revealing look into Piper's experiences as a light-skinned black woman, see "Passing for White, Passing for Black." Here, Piper discusses everything from what she calls the "Suffering Test of blackness," in which she is grilled about her racial background by both blacks and whites, to historical accounts of passing and miscegenation, to relationships with whites who deny they see any racial difference.

11. In *Asian/American: Historical Crossings of a Racial Frontier*, David Palumbo-Liu discusses the role of plastic surgery and Asian American bodies. Although plastic surgery has been a popular option for Asians and Asian Americans for the past few decades, Palumbo-Liu also reveals its use immediately following World War II by white surgeons as a method of "deorientalizing" the Asian American face. As the army surgeon D. R. Millard reveals, to correct the "defect" of the Asian eye is to also induce more much credibility to a Western audience: "Due to the droop of the upper lid only the lower half of the iris is exposed. This gives the effect of an expressionless eye sneaking a peep through a slit, a characteristic [that] through fact and fiction has become associated with mystery and intrigue" (qtd. in Palumbo-Liu 100). It is important to note here that Millard emphasizes that after the surgery, the Korean was able to pass as "Mexican or Italian" (100) rather than "American."

12. According to Randall Kennedy, passing "requires that a person be self-consciously engaged in concealment" (1). Prior to this knowledge, a person is merely "mistaken" rather than "passing." My definition complicates Kennedy's explanation by including the distinction between "passing" and "(un)detection" because "mistaken" still connotes a sense of wrongdoing with conscious intent. My definition of "passing" includes both conscious and unconscious intent alongside the specificities of the passing triad. This distinction acknowledges a scenario that includes an unconscious passer and an in-group clairvoyant (to use Amy Robinson's term) who is aware of the pass.

13. It is important to note that Robert Skinner's Wesley Farrell series subverts the passer-as-criminal motif by utilizing a passer as the detective hero. While passing is oftentimes defined as an act of betrayal to the black community, here it is also shown to help the black community by fighting for civil rights and social justice concerns. For more, see Robert Skinner's *Skin Deep, Blood Red.*

14. It is interesting to note that in my multiple experiences of teaching this story to both undergraduates and graduate students, chicken legs often transform into fried chicken in students' recollections of the story, solidifying how certain foods become "raced" within cultural discourse.

15. In fact, in his study of the backgrounding of gender (including the absent husbands and the silencing of Roberta's two male friends), David Goldstein-Shirley completely erases the Chinese chauffeur from his analysis. Already erased within the cultural stereotyping of Asian men as effeminate, the Chinese chauffeur's exclusion in a study of gender is troubling.

16. The cursory yet crucial inclusion of a "Chinaman," then, begs the question of whether Morrison's experiment of racial removal would only succeed (or succeed differently) within a black-white paradigm. In other words, can an Asian character exist without racial markers and be passable enough for whiteness or would the Asian character be the "forever foreigner," too different to embody the passing white body? Rewriting Morrison's experiment with an Asian-white (or even Asian-black) matrix would make for an interesting read, indeed.

17. In fact, Rayson also makes the critique that Abel presumes Roberta's husband's blackness. Her observation that Roberta's new surname, Norton, may be attributed to the "rich white northern benefactor of a southern black college" (43) in Ralph Ellison's *Invisible Man* is a smart one. However, Rayson's suggestion of the possibility of mixed-race coupling seems color-coded and does not include Asian-white mixings.

1 / Whispers of Norbury

1. The train conductor serving as Everyman detective is also illustrated in Booker T. Washington's autobiography *Up from Slavery* (1901), published a few years after the *Plessy* decision:

> In one part of our country, where the law demands the separation of the races on the railroad trains, I saw at one time a rather amusing instance which showed how difficult it sometimes is to know where the black begins and the white ends.
>
> There was a man who was well known in his community as a Negro, but who was so white that even an expert would have hard work to classify him as a black man. This man was riding in the part of the train set aside for the coloured passengers. When the train conductor reached him, he showed at once that he was perplexed. If the man was a Negro, the conductor did not want to send him into the white people's coach; at the same time, if he was a white man, the conductor did not want to insult him by asking him if he was a Negro. The official looked him over carefully, examining his hair, eyes, nose, and hands, but still seemed puzzled. Finally, to solve the difficulty, he stooped over and peeped at the man's feet. When I saw the conductor examining the feet of the man in question, I said to myself, "That will settle it;" and so it did, for the trainman promptly decided that the passenger was a Negro, and let him remain where he was. I congratulated myself that my race was fortunate in not losing one of its members. (58–59)

Knowing where black begins and white ends may or may not be determined by physical traits (in the above, while hair, eyes, nose, and hands did not indicate blackness, flat-footedness is a sure marker for Washington and the conductor). Significant in this scene is the anxiety produced by the not knowing, ranging from the threat of black transgression (allowing a black passenger access to the white car) to the fear of white insult (questioning the potential white passenger about his racial identity). In essence, the conductor must play race detective to solve the dilemma of whether or not someone who looks white is actually white or black. Thus, the practice of race detection not only engenders anxiety in the individual being detected, but also in the detector, whose incorrect deciphering may have dire consequences indeed.

2. In more recent times, California's Proposition 187 has clear similarities with the *Plessy* case. Passed in 1994, Proposition 187 (or the "Save Our State" initiative) sought, among other things, to require health-care professionals, police, and teachers to play race detective, verifying and reporting the immigration status of all individuals, including children, as well as denying these "suspects" any social care services, health care, and education. Like the train conductors and bus drivers before them, citizens working in these fields would be required to racialize and criminalize skin color, facial features, accents, and any other indicators of "illegal" status. Passed during a time of

heightened anti-Mexican and anti-Asian immigration fears in California, Proposition 187 was approved by nearly 60 percent of the state's voters. Many organizations, including the ACLU and the California State Parent-Teacher Association, condemned the proposition as racist, and it was ultimately found unconstitutional in 1999 under Governor Gray Davis. Like *Plessy*, Proposition 187 would have placed the burden of race detection upon state and local agencies as well as individuals to ask, "What does an illegal immigrant look like?"

3. Bancroft and Motley probably refer to George Bancroft and John Lothrop Motley. Bancroft (1800–1891) was an American historian, public official, and author of the monumental work *A History of the United States*. He served as the secretary of the navy, secretary of war, and minister to Great Britain and Prussia. As an antislavery Democrat, Bancroft delivered the official memorial address on Abraham Lincoln before Congress. It is also believed that he wrote President Andrew Johnson's first message to Congress. John Lothrop Motley (1814–1877) was an American historian and diplomat. In addition to serving as the secretary of the U.S. legation at St. Petersburg and minister to Austria, Motley was appointed by President Ulysses Grant as minister to Great Britain in 1869. Both Bancroft and Motley were products of the American transcendentalist movement in Massachusetts, which centered on discussions of social reform. Thus, it would be safe to assume that the conversation between Garnet, a former abolitionist, and Doyle probably related, at least in part, to American race relations.

4. "J. Habakuk Jephson's Statement" (1884) is itself an interesting story of race and detection. Doyle's short story is based on the real unsolved mystery of the disappearance of *Mary Celeste* (in his story, Doyle confuses the name *Mary Celeste* with *Marie Celeste*, foreshadowing perhaps the flawed nature of detecting "truth"), a deserted brigantine that was found in 1872 near the coast of Portugal. What is significant in Doyle's fictional representation of a real case is his need to solve a historical mystery with criminalized blackness as the solution. According to Doyle, the *Mary Celeste* was abandoned due to a slave rebellion led by the corrupt and greedy Septimius Goring. Written about a decade before the first Sherlock Holmes tale, Doyle shows here that detecting "truth" begins (at least for Doyle) with a denigration of blackness. For the complete story, see *The Best Horror Stories of Arthur Conan Doyle*, ed. Frank D. McSherry, Martin H. Greenberg, and Charles G. Waugh (Chicago: Academy Chicago Publishers, 1989).

5. I am aware that other detective figures appeared prior to Holmes (such as Poe's Dupin trilogy, Dickens's Inspector Bucket in *Bleak House*, and Wilkie Collins's Sergeant Cuff in *The Moonstone*). While I am not denying the impact of these early figures on the genre of detective fiction, here I am concentrating on Holmes due to his sustained legacy. The center of fifty-six stories and four novels as well as numerous twentieth-century recuperations and imitations, Holmes has indisputably been the international father of detection for more than a century. My argument here is that as such, twentieth-century authors of detective fiction (specifically those writing on detection and race) write in direct response to Holmes.

6. Examples of detective fiction prior to Sherlock Holmes include William Godwin's *Caleb Williams* (1794), Charles Dickens's *Bleak House* (1853) and *The Mystery of Edwin Drood* (published posthumously and incomplete in 1870), Mary Elizabeth Braddon's *Lady Audley's Secret* (1862), Wilkie Collins's *The Moonstone* (1868), Anna Katharine

Green's *The Leavenworth Case: A Lawyer's Story* (1878), and the short detective stories by Edgar Allan Poe and Mark Twain. Examples of passing narratives include William Craft's *Running a Thousand Miles for Freedom* (1848), Harriet Beecher Stowe's *Uncle Tom's Cabin* (1852), George Washington Cable's *The Grandissimes* (1880), E. D. E. N. Southworth's *The Hidden Hand* (1888), William Dean Howells's *An Imperative Duty* (1891), Frances E. W. Harper's *Iola Leroy* (1892), among others.

7. I am aware that Metta Victor's *The Figure Eight* (1869) includes a moment of racial passing when Joe Meredith, the prime suspect in the murder of his uncle and benefactor, Dr. Meredith, blackens himself up as a mulatto waiter as part of his detection. But this passing act is more disguise (like Joe's other disguise as "Dr. Milton") than an embodiment of a racial identity. As Catherine Ross Nickerson writes, Joe's "passing" as a minstrel figure is a self-reflective one in that the "charade expresses something solemn and real about [Joe's] situation," much like Eric Lott's complex phenomenon of "love and theft" (51).

8. For example, in an investigation of Samuel George Morton, a distinguished scholar of the American school of polygeny who influenced such figures as Louis Agassiz, Gould discovered that Morton's ranking of races according to brain size was "a patchwork of fudging and finagling in the clear interest of controlling a priori convictions" (86). Perhaps more importantly, Gould found no evidence of conscious fraud, displaying the deep and entrenched workings of racist hegemony. For more information, see Gould's *The Mismeasure of Man*.

9. For more information on the blackening of the Irish and Jewish races, see Noel Ignatiev's *How the Irish Became White* (New York: Routledge, 1995); Sander Gilman's *Freud, Race, and Gender* (Princeton: Princeton University Press, 1993); and Ann Pelligrini's *Performance Anxieties: Staging Psychoanalysis, Staging Race* (New York: Routledge, 1997).

10. Gibson and Green, eds., *The Unknown Conan Doyle: Essays on Photography*, xii. According to Gibson and Green, no photographs by Doyle are known to have survived, probably due to due to chemical decomposition. Obviously, these photographs could have been an invaluable accompaniment to Doyle's writings about Africa and its natives. Unfortunately, we will have to interpret Doyle's reactions solely upon his writings.

11. *In Neither Black nor White Yet Both*, Werner Sollors explores how passing narratives, such as *The Octoroon* or *The Imitation of Life*, revealed the detection of black blood in mixed-raced subjects by the bluish tinge in the half moon of fingernails.

12. This is not the only instance where Holmes redefines legal versus ethical detection. As he declares in "The Adventure of the Blue Carbuncle," "I am not retained by the police to supply their deficiencies" (346). Therefore, many of his adventures result in the releasing of suspects, such as "The Adventure of the Blue Carbuncle and "The Boscombe Valley Mystery."

13. Many readers have presumed this to be Atlanta, Georgia. But, as I will later discuss, critics have disputed the authenticity of this detail, disagreeing as to whether John Hebron and Effie could have legally united in a marriage of miscegenation in such a racially charged state as Georgia, which illegalized black-white unions.

14. Interestingly, the passing plots are often distinguishable by gender. Female passing plots usually conclude with the death of the passer (such as Nella Larsen's *Passing*) or a return "home" to their black community (such as Charles Chesnutt's

House behind the Cedars, in which Rena Walden not only returns to her black community but also dies at the end while her brother, John, continues to pass). On the other hand, male passers, while they may continue to pass successfully, experience lifelong regret and race betrayal (such as James Weldon Johnson's passer who claims he sold his soul for a "mess of pottage").

15. The safe ending, then, demands an alternative interpretation of Holmes's final request to Watson. As Sherlock Holmes tells Watson at the end of the story, "if it should ever strike you that I am getting a little overconfident in my powers, or giving less pains to a case than it deserves, kindly whisper "Norbury" in my ear, and I shall be infinitely obliged to you" (493). At first glance, this statement reads like Holmes's call for a gentle reminder from Watson that he should show humility. But what if the gentle reminder is one that signals the *illogics* of human behavior such as amalgamation? Like Twain's ending to *Pudd'nhead,* Doyle's story of race undetectability includes safeguards to maintain a certain level of knowing (such as Lucy's blackness). But knowing is very different from understanding. Thus, I offer Holmes's request to Watson not as a request for a reminder that he may not always *know* but that there are human behaviors that exhibit themselves outside of rational thought (such as amalgamation) and that, therefore, he will never understand. For Holmes, a science-oriented man whose mental calculations depend upon empirical data, breeding across racial divides is an irrational act. In this light, cross-racial mixing according to Holmes is behavior that is odd, perplexing, and out of normal human conduct.

16. As an interesting side note, Munro also reveals that Effie "made over all her property to [him]—rather against [his] will" (482). In fact, Effie is described as being quite stubborn about it. "She would have it so, and it was done" (482). While Munro may seem like the liberal-minded husband here, what Effie's relinquishing of her financial independence does is place herself completely (again) in Munro's control. It is the need for money, in fact, that commences the mystery when Effie asks Munro for a hundred pounds. In short, then, Munro's obsession with uncovering Effie's secret is to regain his loss of patriarchal power.

2 / Intuitive Faculties and Racial Clairvoyance

1. It is important to point out here that, as Lewis and Ardizzone indicate, Davis purposely refers to Alice as "colored" rather than "black," leaving "open the meaning of race—that is, what Alice considered herself to be may have differed from what society considered her" (Lewis and Ardizzone 270n1).

2. It is telling that one of the most startling and significant aspects of this trial occurred with the questioning of Al Jolson as a witness for the defense. Due to a reference to the celebrity in one of Alice's letters to Rhinelander, Jolson was asked whether or not he knew Alice and, in essence, her character. Jolson was a well-known blackface entertainer and soon-to-be-star of *The Jazz Singer* (1927), and his participation in the trial highlighted some of the foundational questions of race: "What was race? If blackness and whiteness were such strongly divided categories, why did so many people exist between or outside of or across the social lines they drew? And what about all the new immigrants from Asia and Eastern and Southern Europe, whose physical appearances, cultural practices, and ethnic heritages did not clearly fit into American racial categories?" (Lewis and Ardizzone 102). Side-by-side photos of Jolson and Alice were also featured in several newspapers. Was Alice passing? The answer, according to the Court, was a resounding no.

3. Nonrecognition as a type of passing is different from the conscious effort to avoid recognition. In his short story "Passing," Langston Hughes writes about a son who, in the midst of passing, runs into his mother while walking with his white girlfriend. The son, Jack, writes a letter to his mother in which he apologizes for ignoring her: "That's the kind of thing that makes passing hard, having to deny your own family when you see them" (53). Here, Jack reveals one of the tragic consequences of passing for white to be the rejection of his/her black family. For the slave family separated by force, recognition is not about the denial of affiliation as much as the unawareness of it.

3 / Detecting Winnifred Eaton

1. "Eaton" refers to Winnifred throughout the chapter.

2. This chapter focuses on Eaton's Japanese romances that were published between 1899 (*Miss Numè of Japan*) and 1922 (*Sunny San*).

3. Examples include works by Amy Robinson (1994), Elaine K. Ginsberg (1996), Martha Cutter (1996, 2008), Samira Kawash (1997), Juda Bennett (1998), Gayle Wald (2000), Laura Browder (2000), Maria Sanchez and Linda Schlossberg (2001), Kathleen Pfeiffer (2003), Baz Dreisinger (2008), and Sinéad Moynihan (2011). While these works focus on black/white passing, recent works by Teresa Kay Williams (1997), Lisa Nakamura (2002), and Kenji Yoshino (2007) explore Asian American passing.

4. See Sachi Nakachi's *Mixed-Race Identity Politics in Nella Larsen and Winnifred Eaton* for an African American and Asian American comparison of race passing and mixed-race identity.

5. See Lindon Barrett's "Presence of Mind: Detection and Racialization in 'Murders in the Rue Morgue'" and Elise Lemire's "'The Murders in the Rue Morgue': Amalgamation Discourses and the Race Riots of 1838 in Poe's Philadelphia." Both are published in *Romancing the Shadow: Poe and Race*, edited by J. Gerald Kennedy and Liliane Weissberg.

6. I label Twain's narrative as a failure only in that whiteness is not preserved by the detective results. While the scientific method of detection (here, fingerprinting) works to distinguish between Tom and Chambers, it does not succeed in creating a clear racial distinction between whiteness and blackness. While Chambers is sold down the river, Tom will never be able to reaccess his white purity. In this sense, Twain's story concludes with a narrative un-ease.

7. This is narratively evidenced in Nella Larsen's *Passing*, in which the audacious tragic mulatta, Clare Kendry, suddenly dies when her passing is discovered by her white husband. The significance of Clare's death at the novel's conclusion is that the passing tale becomes a murder mystery with Clare's literal and metaphoric fall. In terms of the anxiety of undetection, whether or not Clare's death is suicide or murder (was she pushed by her part-time passing friend and rival, Irene?) takes a backseat to the realization that her death is a necessary conclusion to the legal, social, and cultural criminalization of race passing. Thus, the detection of Clare's passing is twofold: she is discovered by her duped husband *and* her passing is punished by her death.

8. A recent example of unacknowledged passing is Madeline Albright's discovery of her Jewish ancestry. Not revealed until late in life, Albright's passing as non-Jewish was not enacted with the fear of detection as a constant threat. Hence, I label her act as passing rather than undetection. Examples of undiscovered passing may include anyone who is ignorant about their own genetic history. While recent popular shows like

PBS's *African American Lives* illustrate how DNA testing can illuminate our invisible racial pedigree, there are many more people who have not undergone the test and live unaware of their own racial makeup. Some estimates claim *that* one-third of white Americans have black ancestry. As such, undiscovered passing is a much more practiced and continuing phenomenon than previously thought.

9. Kate Chopin's "Désirée's Baby" (1892), published within a year of both Doyle's and Twain's stories mentioned above, is another telling example of passing versus undetection. Désirée is discovered abandoned and subsequently adopted by the wealthy Valmondés of Louisiana. As a young woman, she marries Armand Aubigny, a wealthy scion of a Creole family. They live an idyllic life until the birth of their dark-skinned baby. Because Désirée's origins are not known, Armand accuses her of being black and rejects her and their baby. Désirée and her baby walk off into a bayou never to be seen again. The story concludes with Armand burning all memories of his wife and child as well as a letter written by his mother to his father revealing, in fact, Armand's blackness. Chopin's story is interesting because it includes both passing and undetection as the narrative's silent secret. While Armand is a passer who burns evidence of his own detection, Désirée is a passer whose race we will never know. This story illustrates how paranoia often functions within race detection, resulting in tragic endings.

10. Not all African American passing tales mirror the archetypal passing plot. For instance, Frances Harper's *Iola Leroy* (1892) is an atypical passing story whose heroine refuses to pass for white. Instead, Iola marries Dr. Latimer, another light-skinned character who also refuses to pass for white, and they work as teacher and doctor, respectively, for the racial uplift of the black community.

11. See Amy Ling, Pat Shea, Huining Ouyang, Gretchen Murphy, Carol Roh-Spaulding, Eve Oishi, Lisa Botshon, Karen Skinazi, Viet Nguyen, and Tomo Hattori.

12. Recent scholarship on Winnifred's oeuvre includes Jean Lee Cole's *The Literary Voices of Winnifred Eaton: Redefining Ethnicity and Authenticity* (2002), Dominika Ferens's *Edith and Winnifred Eaton: Chinatown Missionaries and Japanese Romances* (2002), and Diana Birchall's *Onoto Watanna: The Story of Winnifred Eaton* (2006).

13. This analysis does not include Eaton's *Heart of Hyacinth* (1903), but this story complicates and supports my reading of Eaton's commentary on race passing and the battle over identity in interesting ways. As a white woman who is raised by a Japanese woman after her mother's death, Hyacinth struggles over her white blood identity and the Japanese culture in which she was raised. Hyacinth's identity struggle eerily echoes a similar scene in Johnson's *Autobiography of an Ex-Colored Man* (1912) in which the unnamed narrator realizes his racial self by gazing in the mirror. Although the image is inconclusive for Johnson's narrator because he sees both whiteness and blackness, furthering his racial confusion, Hyacinth distinctly sees a non-Japanese reflection staring back, inducing her to declare, "That's not me. No!" (75). The story is further complicated when Hyacinth's surrogate brother, Komazawa, who is biracial (half-white, half-Japanese) is sent to England and assimilated into English ways. In this tale, Eaton further plays with the anxiety of detection when Hyacinth's "real" racial identity is unrealized by the other villagers (they assume she is biracial), leading to her breakup with Yoshida. While the following analysis of *Tama* and *Sunny-San* focuses on undetection of the mixed-race body, *Heart of Hyacinth* illustrates that Eaton was contemplating the role of undetection on multiple trajectories of the raced body (white, Japanese, mixed). For more on *Heart of Hyacinth*, see Ouyang's "Ambivalent Passages."

14. One exception is *A Japanese Blossom* (1906), which involves a Japanese man marrying an American woman.

15. *Me: A Book of Remembrance* (1915), Eaton's anonymous autobiography, reveals several struggles she undergoes as a mixed-race woman who is often detected white.

16. It is interesting to note here that although Sunny's racial identity can be made invisible, it always remains audible. Sunny's and even Katy Clarry's dialects are not only crude but disturbingly discernible. It seems that "monkey speech," as the Syndicate calls Sunny's dialect, easily outs one's race, which a visual clue may hide.

4 / Jaundiced Eyes

1. Please see www.readoz.com/publication/read?i=1051067&letter=R#page2 for the complete link to *RedEye*'s article and primer.

2. Calvin McMillin's dissertation, "The Hardboiled and the Haunted: Race, Masculinity, and the Asian American Detective" (2012), is the first and only full-length study of Asian American detection in relation to the hard-boiled. In addition to a chapter devoted to Charlie Chan, McMillin's timely study also includes chapters on Asian American noir and the contemporary Asian American authors Leonard Chang, Dale Furutani, Henry Chang, and Ed Lin.

3. For more information, see Ronald Takaki (esp. chap. 4) and Sucheng Chan (esp. chap. 3).

4. The sheer number of anti-Asian laws during Bigger's lifetime is overwhelming. Examples of such laws include the Page Law of 1875; Chinese Exclusion Law of 1882 (which was extended in 1892, 1902, and made indefinite in 1904); Scott Act of 1888; Geary Law of 1892; the San Francisco School Board's attempt to segregate Japanese schoolchildren in 1905' Executive Order 589 (1907) targeting Japanese and Korean entry to the United States; California Alien Land Law of 1913; Arizona Alien Land Law of 1917; Alien Land Laws in Washington and Louisiana in 1921; New Mexico Alien Land Law in 1922; Cable Act of 1922; the Tydings-McDuffie Act of 1934, among many others. For more information, see Sucheng Chan, Ian Haney-López, and Ronald Takaki.

5. This novel had numerous reincarnations for film and stage reincarnations, including a popular silent movie (1917) and a Broadway play (1913, 1935) by George M. Cohan, an established songwriter, singer, and actor during the first half of the twentieth century.

6. A synopsis of these lost films is available in Charles P. Mitchell's *A Guide to Charlie Chan Films.*

7. One example of a heated response from a Charlie Chan fan is a website launched soon after the Fox Movie Channel debate titled "The Truth about Charlie Chan vs. The Myths!: Is Charlie Chan Really a Harmful, Racist Stereotype?" The stated goal of this anonymously published website is to "provide you with the 'Facts' as well as show you in these photos of those individuals who played the Honorable Detective from Honolulu, that these claims are purely 'Fictional' and are in no way [an] accurate description on the films." This website provides "facts" from Asian American actors, journals, and film critics to rebuke claims of Charlie Chan's racist portrayals. As such, the writer argues that "Charlie Chan's new, real-life enemies [are] his multiculturalist critics" (http://home.thirdage.com/Movies/vaboy1960/ChanTruth, Dec. 5, 2003).

8. Celine Parreñas Shimizu's recent work on Asian American masculinity and film is a helpful theoretical tool here. Shimizu calls for an accounting and recognition of Asian American masculinity that does not, in turn, reinscribe a phallic or hegemonic masculinity, or what she calls "straitjacket masculinity." In short, Shimizu calls for an "ethical manhood" that cares for self and others (as in her reading of Bruce Lee, whose use of violence, however justified, was regretful and punished but whose aggressive behavior also displays vulnerability). The introductory description of Charlie Chan endorses a straitjacket concept of Asian American masculinity. Contrary to Shimizu's "ethical manhood" concept that warns us against reinscribing traditional notions of the masculine, however, I argue that Charlie's portrayal is a containment strategy that is precisely constructed to *ward off* the threat of an Asian military superpower during the interwar years. But Shimizu's caution against reinscribing the very foundations of heteronormativity in the critical move by Asian Americans is useful for my later reading of the black sidekick characters. If Asianness is contained and containable in the Charlie Chan films, blackness embodies a slippage that refuses strict confinement. Rather than seeing Birmingham Brown as a mere minstrel figure that embodies cowardice and the ludicrous (as evidenced literally by Birmingham's "Google" eyes, his constant jumpy and jittery responses, and his signature body quake), his character questions the immoral and unethical world of the white elite (and, thus, the institution of law) that emphasizes, seeks out, and even prioritizes greed, murder, and treachery. Thus, I read Birmingham Brown's confusion and fears thereof (read as ridicule through his minstrel-like antics) not so much as a confirmation of his uneducated or mocked status as a critique directed against the chaos, hypocrisy, and bias of white institutions of power and law that depend upon the strict confinement of (in particular, racialized) bodies. As such, Birmingham's demonstrations of fear, while initially read as unmasculine, reflect a terror of white corruption and crime that "straitjackets" certain types of masculine bodies.

9. It is important to note here that in the film *Charlie Chan in Black Magic*, Charlie also refers to his psychic abilities when he offers the police commissioner some personal information about himself that Charlie had no way to know. But Charlie quickly retracts any allusion to his psychic abilities when he admits that he received the information by calling the commissioner's wife. While the threat of psychic (and, therefore, inaccessible) powers is dismissed by the success of the white amateur detectives in the novels, Charlie himself rejects any such possibility by declaring such abilities to be a simple "trick" in the film.

10. The source of confusion behind the critical reception of Charlie Chan may be due to Biggers's seemingly harsh critique of several historical factors centering on issues of race and identity, immigration, and social justice. In *House*, he exposes the corruption and greed behind blackbirding. But Biggers also comments on other political issues such as immigration law and paper citizenship in *Fifty Candles* (1921), a novel that also centers on detection, race, and justice. *Fifty Candles* is a tale of murder and mystery that, in many ways, foreshadows many of the themes evident in the Charlie Chan stories, particularly that of passing and the anxiety of racial detection. More importantly, published two years after Biggers's vacation in Hawaii and a few years before the release of the first Charlie Chan novel, *Fifty Candles* also employs certain literary containment strategies to comment upon the threat of the inability to detect within the very real circumstances

of American legal history. It begins with a brief introduction into the immigration case of *Chang See vs. United States*. See, a Chinese man, is fighting to regain entry onto U.S. soil by declaring he is of American birth. Taken to China at the age of four, See argues that his condition precludes him from the Chinese Exclusion Act because he is, by right, an American citizen by birth. The immigration official, however, questions See's birth and accuses him of being a "paper citizen," a term that refers to a practice of switching identities that was common during the years of Chinese exclusion. The court ultimately rules that See must return to China. But, rather than seeing this occur, Henry Drew (a corrupt businessman) offers See another option: take on the identity of Hung Chin-chung, Drew's recently deceased servant, in exchange for twenty years of complete loyalty. See agrees. The mystery, then, occurs twenty years later when Drew is found murdered. As it turns out, Hung (a.k.a. See) is captured for the killing of his employer. But, while his twenty-year enslavement may have been a rightful justification for See's revenge, it turns out that the murder was due to something else entirely. Hence the narrative containment strategy. See kills Drew not because of revenge but because Drew and another man, Su Yen Hun, conspired to take away See's beloved, Mah-li. Thus, what may have initially been a commentary on the unfair practices of American legal and immigration history is quickly displaced onto vengeful murder not only of a cruel benefactor but See's own countryman. Furthermore, the guilt placed upon See is again emphasized when at his capture, See commits suicide.

11. In *The Chinese Parrot* (1926), Charlie Chan (while undercover as Ah Kim) mocks the detective skills of Constable Brackett and Office Bliss, a "big, flat-footed policeman of the usual type [with] no great intelligence . . . in his eyes" (224). Furthermore, Charlie repeatedly mocks the detective skills of Captain Flannery in *Behind That Curtain* (1928). As Charlie contemplates Flannery, he states, "How loud is the thunder, how little it rains" (345).

12. It is also important to note that in *Behind That Curtain*, Charlie again creates a large cultural gap by making a distinction between Chinese and American homes: "You mainland people—I observe what home is to you. An unprivate apartment, a pigeonhole to dive into when the dance or the automobile ride is ended. We Chinese are different. Love, marriage, home, still we cling to unfashionable things like that. Home is a sanctuary into which we retire, the father is high priest, the altar fires burn bright" (345–46). This comment is ironic for a couple of reasons. First, while Charlie emphasizes the importance of home here, we never really see him at home or even interacting with his wife and children in the novels. Furthermore, while we do witness his relationship with his children throughout the movies, he is always away from home for long periods at a time, traveling throughout the world. In fact, the final Monogram films show him at his new San Francisco residence without the presence of his wife and most of his children.

13. Unfortunately, six of the earlier films have been lost: *House without a Key* (1926), *The Chinese Parrot* (1927), *Charlie Chan Carries On* (1931), *Charlie Chan's Chance* (1932), *Charlie Chan's Greatest Case* (1933), and *Charlie Chan's Courage* (1934). Mitchell includes a synopsis of these films in *A Guide to Charlie Chan Films*.

14. While not a Monogram Picture (it was produced by Twentieth Century Fox), the film is significant due to the central role of Stepin Fetchit as "Shoeshoe" and his foreshadowing of the Birmingham Brown character later in the series.

15. According to Bogle, a "fetchit" is a "coon" character or blacks who are used as "amusement object[s] and black buffoon[s]" (7). Stepin Fetchit (a.k.a. Lincoln Perry) was also the name of the most successful black actor of the 1930s, who was also the first black actor to receive featured billing.

16. Most of the Charlie Chan films repeat certain scenes and comedic moments. In *The Trap*, Jimmy Chan's face gets blackened when he gets caught in a furnace. Here it is Birmingham who tells Jimmy that he better wash up before he sees the little "Chinese girl," again a possible reference to the dangers of Afro-Asian miscegenation.

17. It is important to note here Charlie's differing reactions according to the gender of his children. While he is extremely harsh with Tommy in *The Chinese Cat*, the next movie—*Charlie Chan in Black Magic* (1944)—exhibits his praise of Frances Chan (#1 daughter). In describing Frances, Charlie states, "Beauty of Chan family also has brains. Very fine combination." To be as directly severe to his daughters as Charlie is to his sons may be too much for audience acceptance. As such, it is not surprising, then, that the appearances of his daughters are rare in the Charlie Chan films. The film following *Black Magic* is *Jade Mask* (1945). Here Charlie returns to the usual criticisms against his son, this time Eddie Chan (#4 son), by making such comments as, "Every time you open your mouth, you put in more feet than centipede," and "You reach oversize decision with undersize brain." These criticisms against Eddie seem harsher than usual in light of Eddie's status as the "intellectual" of the Chan offspring.

18. Tommy's continued yet failed attempt to please his father is again demonstrated in *Shanghai Chest*. Here Tommy and Birmingham are walking down the street when they witness a man crawling into a house window. Believing him to be a robber, Tommy suggests they go after him in order to prove their detective skills to Charlie. As Tommy declares, "Pop will have to admit we're smart." But as it turns out, Tommy's detective intuition is mistaken (the man, who happens to be an officer of the law, is locked out of his home and thus climbs into the window). He and Birmingham end up in jail, and Charlie has to come to their rescue.

19. The theme of black male criminality is reintroduced when Birmingham encounters Willie Best in jail in *Shanghai Chest*. Best tells Birmingham that he is in jail for attempted bank robbery. In *Dark Alibi*, Birmingham also encounters Ben Carter in jail. Carter is the partner with whom Birmingham has his psychic elliptical exchanges in both *The Scarlet Clue* and *Dark Alibi*. While Carter may have performed a game of black intuition in his exchanges with Birmingham, his presence in jail demonstrates that his own intuitive skills are quite lacking when exercising criminal behavior.

5 / Race Detection in a Color-Blind Era

1. *Time*'s telling relationship to race detection occurred recently with the controversy surrounding its publication of the "Yo Decido" issue in February 2012. Alongside the title, "Yo Decido: Why Latinos Will Pick the Next President," the cover features twenty Latino-identified faces. Except one. It turns out that the man behind the "M" in "TIME" (perhaps for "mistake"?), Michael Schennum, is actually half-Chinese and half-white. "They never told me what it was for or [asked] if I was Latino," Schennum (a staff photographer for *Arizona Republic*) declared. In response, *Time* stated: "We took steps to ensure that everyone self-identified as Latino, that they are registered voters, and that they would be willing to answer our questions. If there was a misunderstanding with one of our subjects, we apologize."

The timing of this embarrassing mishap concurrent to the controversy within the Arizona legislature with SB 1070 is telling, to say the least. Arizona SB 1070 (or the Support Our Law Enforcement and Safe Neighborhoods Act) was the strictest anti-illegal immigration measure to be passed in U.S. history. The law required the police to determine the immigration status of someone arrested or detained when there is "reasonable suspicion" and was decried as an extreme form of racial profiling. In June 2012, the U.S. Supreme Court upheld the provision requiring immigration status checks but struck down three other provisions due to its violation of the U.S. Constitution. The *Time* cover mishap points to the disjuncture between a law that bases its success on the ability to read racial markers with the increased ambiguity of racial bodies, forcing us to ask, What does the Latino body look like? What does an illegal immigrant look like? What does a citizen look like?

2. Nancy Burson is best known for creating photographs using computer morphing technology, such as "The Age Machine," which gives a visual prediction of what someone will look like as they age. Utilizing this technology, Burson's work gained publicity beyond the art world when she helped find missing people, prompting both the FBI and the National Center for Missing Children to acquire her software.

3. On a side note, after the recent controversy surrounding the use of yellowface performance in *Cloud Atlas* (directed by the Wachowski siblings of *The Matrix* fame), Google received thousands of protests after launching its "Make Me Asian" app, a visual tool similar to the "Human Race Machine" that "racializes" a photographic image. Described as a "fun app" that lets you and your friends "indulge," "Make Me Asian" allows users to turn themselves "Chinese, Japanese, Korean, or any other Asians!" Particularly offensive aspects of this app are the intentional use of broken English alongside the use of slanty eyes, a Fu Manchu mustache, and rice paddy hats. Similarly, the "Design Your Dream Asian Girl" is another app that offers three ethnicities (Chinese, Taiwanese, and Korean) for whom one can choose eyes, nose, and lips. The use of technology to promote and practice racial tourism in these examples demonstrates that race is far from being *unseen*.

4. A once-derogatory Hawaiian term meaning "half," "hapa" has recently been reappropriated by mixed-race Asian Amerians, in large part through the activist commitment of Fulbeck and others.

5. The urgency to procreate is so desperate that President Roslin even declares an executive order to ban abortion. (see season 2.5, episode 7)

6. In addition to Christopher Deis, several blogs have queried *BSG*'s antiblack racism, including Uneven Steven, Uncle Sam's Cabin, and *SyFy.com*'s forum titled "Is Battlestar Galactica Racist?"

7. "They were created to make lives easier for humans," reads the miniseries' opening lines.

8. We see another version of the Simon/Four model in *The Plan* (2009), a film released after the series' finale but set during the time period of *BSG*'s miniseries to season 2. *The Plan* is told from the perspective of the Cylons, and as such we observe Simon, now married with an adopted stepdaughter, as a medic onboard *Cybele*, a cargo transport ship. This version of Simon is telling because it furthers the antiblack/white mixing of "The Farm" with a slight twist. Simon's wife, Gianna O'Neill, is played by Lymari Nadal (an American actress of Puerto Rican descent and the wife of the actor Edward James Olmos, who plays Commander Adama). In a show without racial distinction, Gianna is

obviously "othered" in that her speech is strongly accented, although visually she can pass for white. Either way, Simon's black threat is again eliminated when, after a scene of lovemaking, he releases himself out of the airlock while he declares his love for family. Out of range of any Resurrection Ship, Simon's death is permanent.

9. The humanoid Cylons comprise of two main groups: the "Significant Seven" (an Eight member—Daniel—was destroyed earlier by Cylon Number One) and the "Final Five." There are numerous copies (perhaps hundreds or thousands) of each Cylon model. Upon death, humanoid Cylons can resurrect upon the Resurrection Ship as long as the ship is in close proximity.

10. We have to only think of Gaeta's character to support the reading of Asian men being silenced. Played by the biracial (Asian-white) actor Alessandro Juliani, Gaeta is portrayed as the ultimate traitor to humanity when he sides with the Cylons. As a result, he is executed by firing squad for mutiny and treason by series' end. In the webisode revealingly titled "The Face of the Enemy," Gaeta's character is disclosed to be in a relationship with Louis Hoshi, whose Japanese-sounding surname translates to "star" in Japanese, according to *battlestarwiki.org*. Interestingly, the Asian homosexual relationship is doomed to failure, one that is further supported by Gaeta's weakness of character. For while the threat of the Asian (Cylon) woman is contained and domesticated, the Asian male is not offered the same opportunity and suffers a shameful death. As a side note, it is also important to point out that the "shape of things to come" is embodied by a containable female, rather than a perhaps more threatening male, progenitor.

11. The flyer image cleverly clues the reader into what "extraction" implies with "extrac" typed in an all-black font while "tion" uses a clear (white) font with black borders. The visual transition from the beginning to the end of the word signifies the whitening that results from the procedure.

12. The film does not address what happens to the melanin, but the strong implication is that whites undergo a medical procedure themselves in order to stain and protect their skin from the sun's damaging effects.

13. The desperate struggle for a genetic child is perhaps best illustrated in the reproductive journey of Will and Mo, two self-described health-care professionals who endured seven IVF (in-vitro fertilizations) treatments and six miscarriages before giving birth to a baby girl in 2012. Their journey can be followed on *lifeandloveinthe-petridish.blogspot.com/*.

14. It is important to note here that "Want to Be a Dad" dismisses the probability that despite the racial background of the egg donor, the child will probably look like him since his sperm is being used. The real fear here is that an Asian "taint" will automatically erase any evidence of whiteness. For this future father, tainted whiteness is not whiteness at all.

15. Hua Hsu, "The End of White America?" *Atlantic* Jan./Feb. 2009. Web. Dec. 17, 2012.

16. In May 2012, the Census Bureau announced that white births are no longer the majority in the United States. Subsequent headlines declared "Fewer White Babies Being Born" (CNN.com, May 17, 2012) and "Whites Account for under Half of U.S. Births" (*NYTimes.com*, May 17, 2012).

17. In October 2012, biologists at the Oregon Health and Science University produced early-stage human embryos from three parents (one male and two female). This new method, they argue, will someday prevent babies from inheriting rare diseases

carried by maternal genes. For more, see Dan Vergano's "Three-Parent Fertility Method Could Remove Gene Defects" in *USA Today* Oct. 24, 2012.

18. Here, I employ the anthropological premise of bodily substances deployed in the anthropology of kinship, especially the work of Janet Carsten. Although the gestational surrogate and the baby do not share blood per se, blood as substance enacts a form of kinship. Further, differing cultural responses to the question of genetics versus gestation is telling. Melissa Pashigian's study of IVF and other fertility treatments in Vietnam explains that the country's ban on surrogacy, while in itself not unusual, is noteworthy in that the government's legislation places importance on gestation rather than genetics. Through the culture's belief in a "uterine identity" where identity is conferred "through the transfer of shared nutritive and emotive substance in the womb" (44), the woman who carries the child to term is the legal mother, not the woman who contributed the genetics. This is significantly different from Western/U.S. laws on surrogacy that give genetics priority over gestation.

Bibliography

Aarim-Heriot, Najia. *Chinese Immigrants, African Americans, and Racial Anxiety in the United States, 1848–1882*. Urbana: U of Illinois P, 2003.

Abbott, Megan. *The Street Was Mine: White Masculinity in Hardboiled Fiction and Film Noir.* New York: Palgrave, 2002.

Abel, Elizabeth. "Black Writing, White Reading: Race and the Politics of Feminist Interpretation." *Female Subjects in Black and White: Race, Psychoanalysis, Feminism*. Ed. Abel, Barbara Christian, and Helene Moglen. Berkeley: U of California P, 1997. Originally published in 1993.

"Archivist of the 'Yellow Peril': Yoshio Kishi Collecting for a New America." New York University. www.apa.nyu.edu/gallery/kishi.

Bailey, Frankie Y. "African American Detection and Crime Fiction." *A Companion to Crime Fiction*. Ed. Charles J. Rzepka and Lee Horsley. Malden, MA: Blackwell, 2010.

———. *African American Mystery Writers: A Historical and Thematic Study.* Jefferson, NC: McFarland, 2008.

———. *Out of the Woodpile: Black Characters in Crime and Detective Fiction.* New York: Greenwood, 1991.

Barde, Robert, and Gustavo J. Bobonis. "Detention at Angel Island: First Empirical Evidence." *Social Science History* 30.1 (Spring 2006): 103–36.

Barrett, Lindon. "Presence of Mind: Detection and Racialization in 'The Murders in the Rue Morgue.'" *Romancing the Shadow: Poe and Race*. Ed. J. Gerald Kennedy and Liliane Weissberg. New York: Oxford UP, 2001. 157–76.

Barthes, Roland. *Camera Lucida: Reflections on Photography.* Trans. Richard Howard. New York: Hill and Wang, 1981.

Bennett, Eve. "Techno-Butterfly: Orientalism Old and New in *Battlestar Galactica*." *Science Fiction Film and Television* 5.1 (Spring 2012): 23–46.

Bennett, Juda. *The Passing Figure: Racial Confusion in Modern American Literature.* New York: Peter Lang, 1998.

Berlin, Howard M. *Charlie Chan's Words of Wisdom: A Collection of 600 Proverbs Spoken by the Cinema's Favorite Oriental Detective.* New York: Wildside, 2001.

Biggers, Earl Derr. *Agony Column.* Indianapolis: Bobbs-Merrill, 1916.

———. *Behind That Curtain in Charlie Chan: Five Complete Novels.* New York: Avenel, 1981. Originally published in 1928.

———. *The Chinese Parrot.* In *Charlie Chan: Five Complete Novels.* New York: Avenel, 1981. Originally published in 1926.

———. *Fifty Candles.* New York: Wildside, 2001. Originally published in 1921.

———. *The House without a Key.* In *Charlie Chan: Five Complete Novels.* New York: Avenel, 1981. Originally published in 1925.

———. *Love Insurance.* Indianapolis: Bobbs-Merrill, 1914.

———. *Seven Keys to Baldpate.* New York: Grosset and Dunlap, 1913.

Birchall, Diana. *Onoto Watanna: The Story of Winnifred Eaton.* Urbana: U of Illinois P, 2006.

Bogle, Donald. *Toms, Coons, Mulattoes, Mammies, and Bucks: An Interpretive History of Blacks in American Film.* New York: Continuum, 1989.

Bonilla-Silva, Eduardo. *Racism without Racists: Color-Blind Racism and Racial Inequality in Contemporary America.* Lanham, MD: Rowman and Littlefield, 2010.

Botshon, Lisa. "Winnifred Eaton (1875–1954)." *Asian American Novelists: A Bio-Bibliographical Critical Sourcebook.* Ed. Emmanuel S. Nelson. Westport, CT: Greenwood, 2000. 93–98.

Braddon, Mary Elizabeth. *Eleanor's Victory.* New York: Harper, 1863.

Breu, Christopher. *Hard-Boiled Masculinities.* Minneapolis: U of Minnesota P, 2005.

Brooks, Kristina. "Mammies, Bucks, and Wenches: Minstrelsy, Racial Pornography, and Racial Politics in Pauline Hopkins's *Hagar's Daughter.*" *The Unruly Voice: Rediscovering Pauline Elizabeth Hopkins.* Ed. John Cullen Gruesser. Urbana: U of Illinois P, 1996. 119–57.

Browder, Laura. *Slippery Characters: Ethnic Impersonators and American Identities.* Chapel Hill: U of North Carolina P, 2000.

Bruce, J. E. *The Black Sleuth.* Ed. John Cullen Gruesser. Boston: Northeastern UP, 2002. Originally published serially in 1907–9.

Burdett, John. *Bangkok 8.* New York: Knopf, 2003.

Burson, Nancy. "Human Race Machine." Web. April 29, 2014.

Butler, Judith. "Endangered/Endangering: Schematic Racism and White Paranoia." *Reading Rodney King, Reading Urban Uprising.* Ed. Robert Gooding-Williams. New York: Routledge, 1993. 15–22.

Cable, George Washington. *Strange True Stories of Louisiana.* Gretna, LA: Pelican, 1994.

Callard, Abby. "The Technique behind Martin Schoeller's Photography." *Smithsonian.com*. Web. April 30, 2014.

Carby, Hazel. Introduction. *The Magazine Novels of Pauline Hopkins*. New York: Oxford UP, 1988.

Carney, Scott. "Inside India's Rent-a-Womb Business." *Mother Jones* March/April 2010. Web. Dec. 21, 2012.

Carsten, Janet. *After Kinship*. Cambridge: Cambridge UP, 2004.

Carter, Greg. *The United States of the United Races: A Utopian History of Racial Mixing*. New York: NYUP, 2013.

Cawelti, John. *Adventure, Mystery, and Romance: Formula Stories as Art and Popular Culture*. Chicago: U of Chicago P, 1977.

Chan, Jachinson. *Chinese American Masculinities: From Fu Manchu to Bruce Lee*. New York: Routledge, 2001.

Chan, Sucheng. *Asian Americans: An Interpretive History*. New York: Twayne, 1991.

"Changing Face of America." *National Geographic*. October 2013. Web. April 30, 2014.

Chesnutt, Charles. *House behind the Cedars*. New York: Random House, 2003. Originally published in 1900.

Chin, Frank. "Come All Ye Asian American Writers of the Real and the Fake." *The Big Aiiieeeee!: An Anthology of Chinese American and Japanese American Literature*. Ed. Jeffrey Paul Chan, Chin, Lawson Fusao Inada, and Shawn Wong. New York: Meridian, 1991.

———. "The Sons of Chan." *The Chinaman Pacific and Frisco R. R. Co.* Minneapolis: Coffee House Press, 1988.

Chopin, Kate. "Désirée's Baby." *Kate Chopin: Complete Novels and Stories*. New York: Library of America, 2002. Originally published in 1893.

Chung, Hye Seung. *Hollywood Asian: Philip Ahn and the Politics of Cross-Ethnic Performance*. Philadelphia: Temple UP, 2006.

Cole, Jean Lee. *The Literary Voices of Winnifred Eaton: Redefining Ethnicity and Authenticity*. New Brunswick, NJ: Rutgers UP, 2002.

Cordell, Sigrid Anderson. "'The Case Was Very Black Against' Her: Pauline Hopkins and the Politics of Racial Ambiguity at the *Colored American Magazine*. *American Periodicals* 16.1 (2006): 52–73.

Cowell, Alan. "British Police Arrest Suspect, after Shooting Man in Subway." *New York Times* July 22, 2005.

Cowell, Alan, and Don Van Natta Jr. "Britain Says Man Killed by Police Had No Tie to Bombings." *New York Times* July 24, 2005.

Craft, William. *Running a Thousand Miles for Freedom or the Escape of William and Ellen Craft from Slavery*. In *Great Slave Narratives*. Ed. Arna Bontemps. Boston: Beacon, 1969. Originally published in 1848.

Croom, Eddie. *Chang Apana: The Real Charlie Chan*. Web. December 5, 2003.

Cuningham, Henry. "Sherlock Holmes and the Case of Race." *Journal of Popular Culture* 28.2 (Fall 1994): 113.

Curry, Ann. "The World's Least Alike Twins." *Dateline NBC*. NBC News. September 29, 2005. Web. July 17, 2013.

Cutter, Martha. "An Intricate Act of Passing: Strategies of Racial and Textual Subversion in Charles Chesnutt's 'The Passing of Grandison.'" *CEA Critic* 70.2 (Winter 2008): 20–30.

———. "Sliding Significations: 'Passing' as a Narrative and Textual Strategy in Nella Larsen's Fiction." *Passing and the Fictions of Identity*. Ed. Elaine K. Ginsberg. Durham: Duke UP, 1996. 75–100.

Décuré, Nicole. "In Search of Our Sisters' Mean Streets: The Politics of Sex, Race and Class in Black Women's Crime Fiction." *Diversity and Detective Fiction*. Ed. Kathleen Gregory Klein. Bowling Green: Bowling Green State UP, 1999. 158–85.

Deis, Christopher. "Erasing Difference: The Cylons as Racial Other." *Cylons in America: Critical Studies of Battlestar Galactica*. Ed. Tiffany Potter and C. W. Marshall. New York: Continuum, 2008. 156–66.

Diawara, Manthia. "Noir by Noirs: Towards a New Realism in Black Cinema." *African American Review* 27.4 (Winter 1993): 525–37.

Dokoupil, Tony. "What Adopting a White Girl Taught One Black Family." *The Daily Beast. Newsweek* April 22, 2009. Web. July 17, 2013.

Doyle, Arthur Conan. *The Firm of the Girdlestone: A Romance of the Unromantic*. Bloomington: Gaslight Publications, 1980.

———. "J. Habakuk Jephson's Statement." *The Best Horror Stories of Arthur Conan Doyle*. Ed. Frank D. McSherry, Martin H. Greenberg, and Charles G. Waugh. Chicago: Academy Chicago Publishers, 1989. 80–118.

———. *Memories and Adventures*. Boston: Little, Brown, 1924.

———. "The Yellow Face." *Sherlock Holmes: The Complete Novels and Stories*. New York: Bantam Dell, 2003. Originally published in 1893.

Drazen, Patrick E. "Next Stop, Norbury: Reflections on "The Yellow Face." *Baker Street Journal* 29 (1979): 16–20.

Eaton, Edith Maude. "Leaves from the Mental Portfolio of a Eurasian." *Mrs. Spring Fragrance and Other Writings*. Ed. Amy Ling and Annette White-Parks. Urbana and Chicago: U of Illinois P, 1995. 218–30.

Eaton, Winnifred. *Daughters of Nijo: A Romance of Japan*. New York: Macmillan, 1904.

———. *Heart of Hyacinth*. New York: Harper and Brothers, 1903.

———. *A Japanese Nightingale*. New York: Harper and Brothers, 1901.

———. *Me: A Book of Remembrances*. Afterword by Linda Trinh Moser. Jackson: U of Mississippi P, 1997. First published in 1915 by Century Company.

———. *Miss Numè of Japan: A Japanese-American Romance*. Chicago: Rand McNally, 1899.

———. *Sunny-San*. New York: George H. Doran, 1922.

———. *Tama*. New York: Harper and Brothers, 1910.

———. *The Honorable Miss Moonlight*. New York: Harper and Brothers, 1912.

———. *The Wooing of Wistaria*. New York and London: Harper and Brothers, 1902.

Elam, Michele. *The Souls of Mixed Folk: Race, Politics, and Aesthetics in the New Millennium*. Stanford, CA: Stanford UP, 2011.

Feng, Peter X., ed. *Screening Asian Americans*. New Brunswick, NJ: Rutgers UP, 2002.

Ferens, Dominika. *Edith and Winnifred Eaton: Chinatown Missions and Japanese Romances*. Urbana and Chicago: U of Illinois P, 2002.

Fisher, Rudolph. *The Conjure Man Dies: A Mystery Tale of Dark Harlem*. Ann Arbor: U of Michigan P, 1992. Originally published in 1932.

Foucault, Michel. *Discipline and Punish: The Birth of the Prison*. New York: Vintage, 1995.

Freud, Sigmund. "Fetishism." *Sexuality and the Psychology of Love*. New York: Collier, 1963.

———. "The Uncanny." *The Standard Edition of the Complete Psychological Works of Sigmund Freud*. Vol. 17. Trans. and ed. James Strachey. London: Hogarth, 1955. 241.

Friedersdorf, Conor. "The Ugly Campaign to Use Derrick Bell against Barack Obama." *Atlantic* Mar. 14, 2012: Web. Oct. 27, 2014.

Fulbeck, Kip. *The Hapa Project*. 2011. Web. Nov. 13, 2013.

———. *Part Asian, 100% Hapa*. San Francisco: Chronicle, 2006.

Funderburg, Lise. "The Changing Face of America." *National Geographic* Oct.2013. Web. Apr. 29, 2014.

Garber, Marjorie. *Vested Interests: Cross-Dressing and Cultural Anxiety*. New York: Routledge, 1992.

Gaskins, Pearl Fuyo. *What Are You?: Voices of Mixed-Race Young People*. New York: Henry Holt, 1999.

Gates, Henry Louis, Jr. *Figures in Black: Words, Signs, and the "Racial" Self*. New York: Oxford UP, 1987.

———. *The Signifying Monkey: A Theory of African American Literary Criticism*. New York: Oxford UP, 1988.

Gibson, John Michael, and Richard Lancelyn Green, eds. *The Unknown Conan Doyle: Essays on Photography*. London: Secker and Warburg, 1982.

Ginsberg, Elaine K. *Passing and the Fictions of Identity*. Durham, NC: Duke UP, 1996.

Goldberg, David Theo. *Racist Culture*. Oxford: Blackwell, 1993.

Goldstein-Shirley, David. "Race/[Gender]: Toni Morrison's 'Recitatif.'" *Women on the Edge: Ethnicity and Gender in Short Stories by American Women*. Ed. Corinne H. Dale and J. H. E. Paine. New York: Garland, 1999. 97–110.

Golub, Mark. "Plessy as 'Passing': Judicial Responses to Ambiguously Raced Bodies in *Plessy v. Ferguson*." *Law & Society Review* 39.3 (September 2005): 563–600.

Gopal, Anand. ""Here's a nice Turban Primer, in case you are wondering which turban wearers are okay to shoot and which are not." 13 August 2012. 8:51 AM. Tweet.

Goslinga-Roy, Gillian. "Body Boundaries, Fiction of the Female Self: An Ethnography of Power, Feminism and the Reproductive Technologies." *Feminist Studies* 26.1 (Spring): 113–40.

Gosselin, Adrienne Johnson. "Harlem Heteroglossia: The Voice of Nobody's 'Other.'" *Multicultural Detective Fiction: Murder from the "Other" Side*. Ed. Gosselin. New York: Garland, 1999. 325–49.

———, ed. *Multicultural Detective Fiction: Murder from the "Other" Side*. New York: Garland, 1998.

Gould, Stephen Jay. *The Mismeasure of Man*. New York: Norton, 1996.

Green, Anna Katherine. *The Leavenworth Case: A Lawyer's Story*. New York: Dover, 1981. Originally published in 1878.

Greenslade, William. *Degeneration, Culture and the Novel 1880–1940*. Cambridge: Cambridge UP, 1994.

Gross, Ariela. *What Blood Won't Tell: A History of Race on Trial in America*. Cambridge: Harvard UP, 2010.

Gruesser, John Cullen. *Race, Gender, and Empire in American Detective Fiction*. Jefferson, NC: McFarland, 2013.

———. "An Un-Easy Relationship: Walter Mosley's Signifyin(g) Detective and the Black Community." *Multicultural Detective Fiction*. Ed. Adrienne Johnson Gosselin. New York: Garland, 1998. 235–55.

Hagedorn, Jessica, ed. *Charlie Chan Is Dead: An Anthology of Contemporary Asian American Fiction*. New York: Penguin, 1993.

Haney-López, Ian Haney. *White by Law: The Legal Construction of Race*. New York: NYUP, 1997.

Hanke, Ken. *Charlie Chan at the Movies: History, Filmography, and Criticism*. Jefferson, NC, and London: McFarland, 1989.

Harper, Frances. *Iola Leroy, or, Shadows Uplifted*. Boston: Beacon, 1999. Originally published by Garrigues Brothers in 1892.

Harris, Trudier. "Watchers Watching Watchers: Positioning Characters and Readers in Baldwin's 'Sonny's Blues' and Morrison's 'Recitatif." *James Baldwin and Toni Morrison: Comparative Critical and Theoretical Essays*. Ed. Lovalerie King and Lynn Orilla Scott. New York: Palgrave, 2006.

Harrowitz, Nancy. "Criminality and Poe's Orangutan: The Question of Race in Detection." *Agonistics: Arenas of Creative Contest*. Ed. Janet Lungstrum and Elizabeth Sauer. Albany: State U of New York P, 1997. 177–95.

Hattori, Tomo. "Model Minority Discourse and Asian American Jouis-Sense." *differences: A Journal of Feminist Cultural Studies*. 11.2 (1999): 228–47.

Holloway, Karla. *Private Bodies, Public Texts: Race, Gender, and a Cultural Bioethics*. Durham: Duke UP, 2011.

hooks, bell. "The Oppositional Gaze: Black Female Spectators." *Black Looks: Race and Representation*. Boston: South End, 1992.

Hopkins, Pauline. *Hagar's Daughter: A Story of Southern Caste Prejudice in the Magazine Novels of Pauline Hopkins*. New York: Oxford UP, 1988. Originally published serially in 1901–2.

———. *Of One Blood Or, the Hidden Self. The Magazine Novels of Pauline Hopkins*. New York: Oxford UP, 1988. Originally published serially in 1902–3.

———. "Talma Gordon." *Spooks, Spies, and Private Eyes: Black Mystery, Crime, and Suspense Fiction of the 20th Century*. Ed. Paula L. Woods. New York: Doubleday, 1995.

———. *Winona: A Tale of Negro Life in the South and Southwest. The Magazine Novels of Pauline Hopkins*. New York: Oxford UP, 1988. Originally published serially in 1902.

"How to Tell Japs from the Chinese." *Life* Dec. 22, 1941. Cited as HTTJFC.

"How to Tell Your Friends from the Japs." *Time* Dec. 22, 1941. Cited as HTTYFFJ.

Howe, Lawrence. "Race, Genealogy, and Genre in Mark Twain's *Pudd'nhead Wilson*." *Nineteenth-Century Literature* 46.4 (March 1992): 495–516.

Hsu, Hua. "The End of White America. *Atlantic* Jan./Feb. 2009.

———. Review of *Recovered Legacies: Authority and Identity in Early Asian American Literature*. Ed. Keith Lawrence and Floyd Cheung. *Genre* 39.4 (2006): 151–54.

Huang, Betsy. *Contesting Genres in Contemporary Asian American Fiction*. New York: Palgrave, 2004.

Huang, Yunte. *Charlie Chan: The Untold Story of the Honorable Detective and His Rendezvous with American History*. New York: Norton, 2010.

Hughes, Langston. "Passing." *The Ways of White Folks*. New York: Vintage, 1990.

Hu Pegues, Juliana. "Miss Cylon: Empire and Adoption in Battlestar Galactica. *MELUS* 33.4 (Winter 2008): 189–209.

"Immigrants: The Changing Face of America." *Time* July 1985.

Irwin, John T. *The Mystery to a Solution: Poe, Borges, and the Analytic Detective Story*. Baltimore: Johns Hopkins UP, 1994.

Jackson, John L., Jr. *Racial Paranoia: The Unintended Consequences of Political Correctness*. New York: Basic Civitas, 2008.

Johnson, James Weldon. *Autobiography of an Ex-Colored Man*. New York: Penguin, 1990. Originally published in 1912.

Jun, Helen Heran. *Race for Citizenship: Black Orientalism and Asian Uplift from Pre-Emancipation to Neoliberal America*. New York: NYUP, 2011.

Kawash, Samira. *Dislocating the Color Line: Identity, Hybridity, and Singularity in African-American Narrative*. Palo Alto: Stanford UP, 1997.

Kayne, Evan. "What the Frack? Interview with Tahmoh Penikett and Aaron Douglass." *Gaycalgary.com*. May 2010. Web. Jan. 25, 2013.

Kelly, R. Gordon. *Mystery Fiction and Modern Life*. Jackson: UP of Mississippi, 1998.

Kennedy, J. Gerald, and Liliane Weissberg, eds. *Romancing the Shadow: Poe and Race*. New York: Oxford UP, 2001.

Kennedy, Randall. "Racial Passing." *Ohio State Law Journal* 62.1145 (2001).

Kim, Claire Jean. "The Racial Triangulation of Asian Americans." *Politics and Society* 27 (1998): 105–38.

Kim, Elaine. *Asian American Literature: An Introduction to their Writings and Social Context.* Philadelphia: Temple UP, 1982.

Klein, Kathleen Gregory, ed. *Diversity and Detective Fiction.* Bowling Green: Bowling Green State University Popular Press, 1999.

Knight, Stephen. *Form and Ideology in Crime Fiction.* Bloomington: Indiana UP, 1980.

Krutnik, Frank. *In A Lonely Street: Film Noir, Genre, Masculinity.* New York: Routledge, 1991.

Kumamoto Stanley, Sandra. "Maggie in Toni Morrison's 'Recitatif': The Africanist Presence and Disability Studies." *MELUS* 36.2 (Summer 2011): 71–88.

La Ferla. "Generation E.A.: Ethnically Ambiguous." *New York Times* Dec. 28, 2003. Web. Nov. 13, 2013.

Lai, Him Mark, Genny Lim, and Judy Yung. *Island: Poetry and History of Chinese Immigrants on Angel Island, 1910–1940.* Seattle: U of Washington P, 1980.

Larsen, Nella. *"Passing" & "Quicksand."* Ed. Deborah E. McDowell. New Brunswick, NJ: Rutgers UP, 1989. Originally published in 1929.

Lee, Chang Rae. *A Gesture Life.* New York: Riverhead, 1999.

Lee, Katherine Hyunmi. "The Poetics of Liminality and Misidentification: Winnifred Eaton's *Me* and Maxine Hong Kingston's *The Woman Warrior. Studies in the Literary Imagination* 37.1 (2004): 17–33.

Lehman, David. *The Perfect Murder.* New York: Macmillan, 1989.

Lemire, Elise. "'The Murders in the Rue Morgue': Amalgamation Discourses and the Race Riots of 1838 in Poe's Philadelphia." *Romancing the Shadow: Poe and Race.* Ed. J. Gerald Kennedy and Liliane Weissberg. New York: Oxford UP, 2001. 177–204.

Levinson, Paul. "*Battlestar Galactica* Series Finale: Not Goodbye but See You." *Open Levinson Blog.* March 21, 2009. Web. April 30, 2014.

Lewis, Earl, and Heidi Ardizzone. *Love on Trial: An American Scandal in Black and White.* New York: Norton, 2002.

Lind, Michael. "The Beige and the Black." *New York Times.* Aug. 16, 1998.

Ling, Amy. *Between Worlds: Women Writers of Chinese Ancestry.* New York: Pergamon, 1990.

Ling, Amy, and Annette White-Parks, eds. *Mrs. Spring Fragrance and Other Writings.* Urbana and Chicago: U of Illinois P, 1995.

Linton, Patricia. "The Detective Novel as a Resistant Text: Alter-Ideology in Linda Hogan's *Mean Spirit.*" *Multicultural Detective Fiction: Murder from the 'Other' Side.* Ed. Adrienne Johnson Gosselin. New York: Garland, 1999. 17–36.

Lipsitz, George. *The Possessive Investment in Whiteness: How White People Profit from Identity Politics.* Philadelphia: Temple UP, 1998.

Liu, Aimee. *Face*. New York: Warner, 1994.

Lombroso, Cesare. *Criminal Man*. Durham: Duke UP, 2006.

Lott, Eric. *Love and Theft: Blackface Minstrelsy and the American Working Class*. New York: Oxford UP, 1993.

Mandel, Ernest. *Delightful Murder: A Social History of the Crime Story*. Minneapolis: U of Minnesota P, 1984.

Marchetti, Gina. *Romance and the "Yellow Peril": Race, Sex, and Discursive Strategies in Hollywood Fiction*. Berkeley: U of California P, 1993.

Marshall, Gloria A. "Racial Classifications: Popular and Scientific." *The "Racial" Economy of Science: Toward a Democratic Future*. Ed. Sandra Harding. Bloomington: Indiana UP, 1993.

McCann, Sean. *Gumshoe America: Hard-Boiled Crime Fiction and the Rise and Fall of New Deal Liberalism*. Durham: Duke UP, 2000.

McDowell, Deborah. Introduction. *Quicksand and Passing*. By Nella Larsen. Ed. Deborah McDowell. New Brunswick, NJ: Rutgers University Press, 1986.

McMillin, Calvin. "The Hardboiled and the Haunted: Race, Masculinity, and the Asian American Detective." Diss. U of California, Santa Cruz. Ann Arbor: Proquest/UMI, 2012 (Publication No. 3521889).

Merivale, Patricia, and Susan Elizabeth Sweeney, eds. *Detecting Texts: The Metaphysical Detective Story from Poe to Postmodernism*. Philadelphia: U of Pennsylvania P, 1999.

Metz, Christian. "Photography and Fetish." *October* 34 (Fall 1985): 81–90.

"Minorities Expected to Be the Majority in 2050." CNN. August 13, 2008.

Mitchell, Charles P. *A Guide to Charlie Chan Films*. Westport, CT: Greenwood, 1999.

Mo and Will. *Life and Love in the Petri Dish*. Blog Her.com. Web. Dec. 15, 2012.

Moon, Krystyn R. *Yellowface: Creating the Chinese in American Popular Music and Performance, 1850s-1920s*. New Brunswick, NJ: Rutgers UP, 2005.

Morano, Marc. "Charlie Chan Ban Lifted by Fox Movie Channel." CBS News. Aug. 29, 2003. Web. May 16, 2005.

Morrison, Toni. *Playing in the Dark: Whiteness and the Literary Imagination*. New York: Vintage, 1993.

———. "Recitatif." *Confirmation: An Anthology of African American Women*. Ed. Amiri Baraka and Amina Baraka. New York: Quill, 1983. 243–61.

Mosley, Walter. *Devil in a Blue Dress*. New York: Norton, 1990.

Most, Glenn W., and William W. Stowe, eds. *The Poetics of Murder*. New York: Harcourt Brace Jovanovich, 1983.

Moynihan, Sinéad. *Passing into the Present: Contemporary American Fiction of Racial and Gender Passing*. Manchester, UK: Manchester University Press, 2011.

Mullen, Bill V. *Afro-Orientalism*. Minneapolis: U of Minnesota P, 2004.

Nagel, Joane. Race, *Ethnicity, and Sexuality: Intimate Intersections, Forbidden Frontiers*. New York: Oxford UP, 2003.

Nakachi, Sachi. "Mixed-Race Identity Politics in Nella Larsen and Winnifred Eaton." Diss., Ohio U. Dissertation Abstracts International, Section A: The Humanities and Social Sciences 62.12 (2002): 4169.

Nakamura, Lisa. *Cybertypes: Race, Ethnicity, and Identity on the Internet.* New York: Routledge UP, 2002.

"The New Face of America: How Immigrants Are Shaping the World's First Multicultural Society." *Time* Fall 1993.

Nguyen, Viet Thanh. *Race and Resistance: Literature and Politics in Asian America.* Oxford: Oxford UP, 2002.

Nickerson, Catherine Ross. *The Web of Iniquity: Early Detective Fiction by American Women.* Durham, NC: Duke UP, 1998.

O'Connor, Flannery. "The Artificial Nigger." *The Complete Stories.* New York: Farrar, Straus and Giroux, 1971. 249–70.

Oishi, Eve. Introduction. *Miss Numé of Japan: A Japanese-American Romance.* Baltimore: Johns Hopkins UP, 1998.

Omi, Michael and Howard Winant. *Racial Formation in the United States: From the 1960s to the 1990s.* Second Edition. New York: Routledge, 1994.

Onwuachi-Willig, Angela. *According to Our Hearts: "Rhinelander v. Rhinelander" and the Law of the Multiracial Family.* New Haven: Yale U P, 2013.

"Our New Look: The Colors of Race." *Newsweek* Dec. 31, 1999.

Ouyang, Huining. "Ambivalent Passages: Racial and Cultural Crossings in Onoto Watanna's *The Heart of Hyacinth.*" *MELUS* 34.1 (Spring 2009): 211–29.

Palumbo-Liu, David. *Asian/American: Historical Crossings of a Racial Frontier.* Stanford: Stanford University Press, 1999.

Pande, Amrita. "'It May Be Her Eggs But It's My Blood': Surrogates and Everyday Forms of Kinship in India." *Qualitative Sociology* 32.4 (December 2009): 379–97.

Pascoe, Peggy. *What Comes Naturally: Miscegenation Law and the Making of Race in America.* Oxford: Oxford UP, 2009.

Pederson-Krag, Geraldine. "Detective Stories and the Primal Scene." *The Poetics of Murder: Detective Fiction and Literary Theory.* Ed. Glenn W. Most and William W. Stowe. San Diego: Harcourt Brace Jovanovich, 1983. 13–20.

Penzler, Otto, ed. *Black Noir: Mystery, Crime, and Suspense Fiction by African-American Writers.* New York: Pegasus, 2009.

Pfeiffer, Kathleen. *Race Passing and American Individualism.* Amherst: U of Massachusetts P, 2003.

Piper, Adrian. "Passing for White, Passing for Black." *Transition*, no. 58 (1992): 4–32.

Pirkis, Catherine Louisa. *The Experiences of Loveday Brooke, Lady Detective.* New York: Dover, 1986. Originally published in 1894.

Poe, Edgar Allan. *Complete Tales and Poems.* New York: Vintage, 1975.

Porter, Dennis. *The Pursuit of Crime: Art and Ideology in Detective Fiction.* New Haven: Yale UP, 1981.

Prashad, Vijay. *Everybody Was Kung Fu Fighting: Afro-Asian Connections and the Myth of Cultural Purity.* Boston: Beacon, 2001.

Queen, Ellery. *The Roman Hat Mystery.* Franklin Center, PA: Franklin Mystery, 1989. Originally published in 1929.

Quiroga, Selene Szkupinski. "Blood Is Thicker Than Water: Policing Donor Insemination and the Reproduction of Whiteness." *Hypatia* 22.2 (Spring 2007): 143–61.

Qureshi, Sadiah. *Peoples on Parade: Exhibitions, Empire, and Anthropology in Nineteenth-Century Britain.* Chicago: U of Chicago P, 2011.

Rayson, Ann. "Decoding for Race: Toni Morrison's 'Recitatif' and Being White, Teaching Black." *Changing Representation of Minorities, East and West. Selected Essays. Vol. 2.* Ed. Larry E. Smith and John Reider. Honolulu: U of Hawaii P, 1996.

Reddy, Maureen T. "Race and American Crime Fiction." *The Cambridge Companion to American Crime Fiction.* Ed. Catherine Ross Nickerson. New York: Cambridge UP, 2010.

———. *Traces, Codes, and Clues: Reading Race in Crime Fiction.* New Brunswick, NJ: Rutgers UP, 2003.

Roberts, Walter Adolphe. *The Haunting Hand.* New York: Macaulay, 1926.

Robinson, Amy. "It Takes One to Know One: Passing and Communities of Common Interest." *Critical Inquiry* 20.4 (Summer 1994): 715–36.

Rohmer, Sax. *The Insidious Dr. Fu-Manchu.* New York: Dover, 1997. Originally published in 1913.

Roh-Spaulding, Carol. "Beyond Biraciality: 'Race' as Process in the Work of Edith Eaton/Sui Sin Far and Winnifred Eaton/Onoto Watanna."*Asian American Literature in the International Context: Readings on Fiction, Poetry and Performance.* Ed. Rocio Davis and Sami Ludwig. Berlin: LIT Verlag, 2002.

Rogin, Michael. *Blackface, White Noise: Jewish Immigrants in the Hollywood Melting Pot.* Berkeley: U of California P, 1998.

Rony, Fatimah Tobing. *The Third Eye: Race, Cinema, and Ethnographic Spectacle.* Durham, NC: Duke UP, 1996.

Roth, Phillip. *The Human Stain.* New York: Vintage, 2001.

Rzepka, Charles. "Race, Region, Rule: Genre and the Case of Charlie Chan." *PMLA* 122.5 (2007): 1463–81.

Sanchez, Maria Carla, and Linda Schlossberg, eds. *Passing: Identity and Interpretations in Sexuality, Race, and Religion.* New York: NYUP, 2001.

Schickel, Robert. "No. 1 Sleuth." *New York Times* Sept. 30, 2010. Web. Nov. 21, 2013.

Schiro, Anne-Marie. "Computerized Beauty." *New York Times* Aug. 9, 1994. Web. Nov. 13, 2013.

Schlichter, Kurt. "Derek Bell 'Space Traders' Review: Racist Paranoia…and George Clinton's Disembodied Head." *Breitbart.* March 8, 2012. Web. Oct. 23, 2014.

Schutz, Robert H. "Some Problems in *The Yellow Face*." *Baker Street Journal* 12 (1963): 31.

Secret Service Dime Novels. New York: Frank Tousey, 1899–1925.

Senna, Danzy. *Caucasia*. New York: Riverhead, 1999.

———. *Symptomatic*. New York: Riverhead, 2004.

Shea, Pat. "Winnifred Eaton and the Politics of Miscegenation in Popular Fiction." *MELUS* 22 (Summer 1997): 19–35.

Shimizu, Celine Parreñas. *Straitjacket Sexualities: Unbinding Asian American Manhoods in the Movies*. Stanford: Stanford UP, 2012.

Siek, Stephanie, and Joe Sterling. "Census: Fewer White Babies Being Born." *In America. CNN.com*. May 17, 2012. Web. Dec. 14, 2012.

Simons, Marlise. "Uproar over Twins, and a Dutch Couple's Anguish." *New York Times* June 28, 1995. Web. July 19, 2013.

Skinazi, Karen. "'As To Her Race, It's Secret Is Loudly Revealed': Winnifred Eaton's Revision of North American Identity." *MELUS* 32.2 (Summer 2007): 31–53.

Skinner, Robert. *Skin Deep, Blood Red*. New York: Kensington, 1997.

Smith-Pryor, Elizabeth M. *Property Rites: The Rhinelander Trial, Passing, and the Protection of Whiteness*. Chapel Hill: U of North Carolina P, 2009.

Soitos, Stephen F. *The Blues Detective: A Study of African American Detective Fiction*. Amherst: U of Massachusetts P, 1996.

———. "Queering the 'I': Black Lesbian Detective Fiction." *Multicultural Detective Fiction*. Ed. Adrienne Johnson Gosselin. New York: Garland, 1998. 105–21.

Sollors, Werner. *Neither Black nor White Yet Both: Thematic Explorations of Interracial Literature*. Cambridge: Harvard UP, 1997.

Spanos, William V. "The Detective and the Boundary: Some Notes on the Postmodern Literary Imagination." *Repetitions: The Postmodern Occasion in Literature and Culture*. Baton Rouge: Louisiana State UP, 1990. 322–42.

Stepan, Nancy. *The Idea of Race in Science: Great Britain 1800–1960*. Hamden, CT: Archon, 1982.

Stout, Rex. *Too Many Cooks*. New York: Bantam, 1995. Originally published in 1938 by Farrar and Rinehart.

Stowe, Harriet Beecher. *Uncle Tom's Cabin or, Life among the Lowly*. New York: Penguin, 1986. Originally published in 1852.

Stowe, William W. "Critical Investigations: Convention and Ideology in Detective Fiction." *Texas Studies in Literature and Language* 31.4 (Winter 1989): 570-591.

Suematsu, Dyske. "alllooksame.com." October 19, 2010.

Takaki, Ronald. *Strangers from a Different Shore: A History of Asian Americans*. New York: Penguin, 1989.

Tani, Stefano. *The Doomed Detective: The Contribution of the Detective Novel to Postmodern Italian and American Fiction*. Carbondale: Southern Illinois UP, 1984.

Tate, Claudia, ed. *Black Women Writers at Work*. Harpenden, UK: Oldcastle, 1983.

———. "Pauline Hopkins: Our Literary Foremother." *Conjuring: Black Women, Fiction, and Literary Tradition*. Ed. Marjorie Pryse and Hortense J. Spillers. Bloomington: Indiana UP, 1985. 53–66.

Tavernise, Sabrina. "Whites Account for under Half of Births in U.S." *NYTimes.com* May 17, 2012. Web. Dec. 15, 2012.

Thomas, Brook, ed. *"Plessy v. Ferguson": A Brief History with Documents*. New York: Bedford, 1997.

Thomas-Graham, Pamela. *A Darker Shade of Crimson*. New York: Pocket Star, 1998.

Thompson, Charis. "Skin Tone and the Persistence of Biological Race in Egg Donation for Assisted Reproduction." *Shades of Difference: Why Skin Color Matters*. Ed. Evelyn Nakano Glenn. Stanford: Stanford UP, 2009. 131–47.

Trenka, Jane Jeong. *The Language of Blood*. Minneapolis: Graywolf, 2005.

Trenka, Jane Jeong, Julia Chinyere Oparah, and Sun Yung Shin, eds. *Outsiders Within: Writing on Transracial Adoption*. Cambridge, MA: South End, 2006.

"The Truth about Charlie Chan vs. the Myths! Is Charlie Chan Really a Harmful, Racist Stereotype?" Web. Dec. 5, 2003.

Tseng, Ada. "Present and Future: Interview with Advantageous Director Jennifer Phang." *Asia Pacific Arts*. July 8, 2013. Web. Nov. 15, 2013.

"Turban Primer." *RedEye* Aug. 7, 2012. 3.

Twain, Mark. *Pudd'nhead Wilson and Those Extraordinary Twins*. New York: Norton, 1980. Originally published in 1894.

Vergano, Dan. "Three-Parent Fertility Method Could Remove Gene Defects." *USAToday.com*. Oct. 24, 2012. Web. Dec. 15, 2012.

Wald, Gayle. *Crossing the Line: Racial Passing in Twentieth-Century U.S. Literature and Culture*. Durham, NC: Duke UP, 2000.

Wallinger, Hanna. 2005. *Pauline E. Hopkins: A Literary Biography*. Athens: U of Georgia P, 2005.

Washington, Booker T. *Up from Slavery*. New York: Oxford UP, 1995.

Weeks, Robin, ed. *Detective Fiction: A Collection of Critical Essays*. Englewood Cliffs, NJ: Prentice Hall, 1980.

Wellman, Manly W. H. "Two Southern Exposures of Sherlock Holmes." *Baker Street Journal* 2 (1974): 422–26.

Whitehead, Colson. *The Intuitionist*. New York: Anchor, 1998.

Williams, Patrick. "Charlie Chan and the Case of the Cop Who Inspired Him." *The Charlie Chan Family Home*. Oct. 31, 2004. http://charliechanfamily.tripod.com/id78.html.

Williams, Theresa Kay. "Race-ing and Being Raced: The Critical Interrogation of 'Passing.'" *Amerasia Journal* 23.1 (1997): 61–65.

"Who Was Temple Shooter?" *RedEye* Aug. 7, 2012. 3.

Woods, Paula L. *Spooks, Spies, and Private Eyes: Black Mystery, Crime, and Suspense Fiction*. New York: Doubleday, 1995.

Wu, Cynthia. *Chang and Eng Reconnected: The Original Siamese Twins in American Culture*. Philadelphia: Temple UP, 2012.

Wu, William F. *The Yellow Peril: Chinese Americans in American Fiction, 1850–1940*. Hamden, CT: Archon, 1982.

Xiaojing, Zhou. "Introduction: Critical Theories and Methodologies in Asian American Literary Studies." *Form and Transformation in Asian American Literature*. Seattle: U of Washington P, 2005.

Yoffe, Emily. "Beyond the Pale: Should I Tell My Infertile Asian Wife That I Want All-White Babies"? In "Dear Prudence: Advice on Manners and Morals." *Slate.com*. Nov. 29, 2012. Web. Dec. 1, 2012.

Yoshino, Kenji. *Covering: The Hidden Assault on Our Civil Rights*. New York: Random House, 2007.

Films & Television Shows

"Advantageous." Dir. Jennifer Phang. *Futurestates*. Season 3, episode 1. ITVS. April 3, 2012.

African American Lives. Prod. Henry Louis Gates. PBS. 2006.

African American Lives 2. Prod. Henry Louis Gates. PBS. 2008.

Charlie Chan in Black Magic. Dir. Phil Rosen. Perf. Sidney Toler, Mantan Moreland, and Frances Chan. Monogram, 1944.

Charlie Chan in Egypt. By Robert Ellis and Helen Logan. Dir. Luis King. Perf. Warner Oland, and Stepin Fetchit. Fox, 1935.

Charlie Chan in Shanghai. Dir. James Tinling. Perf. Warner Oland and Keye Luke. Fox Film, 1935.

Charlie Chan in the Chinese Cat. Dir. Phil Rosen. Perf. Sidney Toler, Mantand Moreland, and Benson Fong. Monogram, 1944.

Charlie Chan in the Secret Service. Dir. Phil Rosen. Perf. Sidney Toler, Mantand Moreland, Marianne Quon, and Benson Fong. Monogram, 1944.

Dark Alibi. Dir. Phil Karlson. Perf. Sidney Toler, Mantan Moreland, and Benson Fong. Monogram, 1946.

"Daybreak, Part 2." Dir. Michael Rymer. *Battlestar Galactica*. Season 4, episode 20. Sci Fi Channel. Mar. 20, 2009.

"The Farm." Dir. Rod Hardy. *Battlestar Galactica*. Season 2, episode 5. Sci Fi Channel. Aug. 12, 2005.

Jade Mask. Dir. Phil Rosen. Perf. Sidney Toler, Mantan Moreland, and Edwin Luke. Monogram, 1945.

"A Measure of Salvation." By Ronald Moore, Michael Angeli, and Glen Larson. *Battlestar Galactica*. Season 3, episode 7. Sci Fi Channel. Nov. 10, 2006.

Race: The Power of an Illusion. Dir. Llewellyn Smith. PBS, 2003.

Red Dragon. Dir. Phil Rosen. Perf. Sidney Toler and Benson Fong. Monogram, 1945.

Scarlet Clue. Dir. Phil Rosen. Perf. Sidney Toler, Mantan Moreland, Benson Fong, and Ben Carter. Monogram, 1945.

Shadows over Chinatown. Dir. Terry Morse. Perf. Sidney Toler, Victor Sen Young, and Mantan Moreland. Monogram, 1946.

Shanghai Chest. Dir. William Beaudine. Perf. Roland Winters, Mantan Moreland, and Victor Sen Yung. Monogram, 1948.

Shanghai Cobra. Dir. Phil Karlson. Perf. Sidney Toler, Mantan Moreland, and Benson Fong. Monogram, 1945.

The Trap. Dir. Howard Bretherton. Perf. Sidney Toler, Victor Sen Yung, and Mantan Moreland. Monogram, 1947.

"*White*." By A. Sayeeda Clarke. Dir. Clarke. *Futurestates*. Season 2, episode 8. May 6, 2011.

Index